Castle Gap and the Pecos Frontier

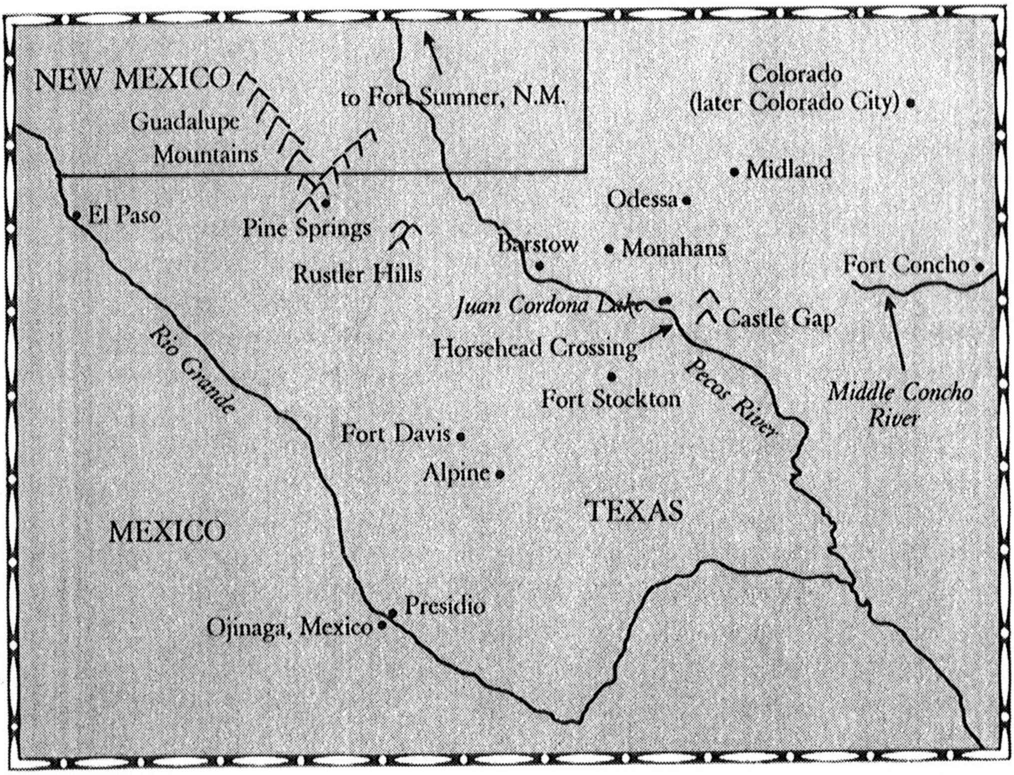

Number Six in The Chisholm Trail Series

Castle Gap
and the
Pecos Frontier

By Patrick Dearen
Foreword by Elmer Kelton

Texas Christian University Press
Fort Worth

LIBRARY OF CONGRESS
Library of Congress Cataloging-in-Publication Data

Dearen, Patrick.
Castle Gap and the Pecos frontier/by Patrick Dearen; foreword by Elmer Kelton.
p. cm.—(The Chisholm Trail series; no. 6)
Includes index.
ISBN 0-87565-030-9

1. Legends—Texas. 2. Legends—Pecos River Valley (N.M. and Tex.)
3. Texas—History. 4. Pecos River Valley (N.M. and Tex.)—History.
I. Title. II. Series.
GR110.T5D43 1988
398.2'09764'9—dc 19 88-6067
CIP

Designed by Whitehead & Whitehead
Maps by Janet Brooks

Contents

To

BOB BASS,

the nonpareil teacher who launched me into writing;

PAUL PATTERSON,

the "Pecos pilgrim" who guided me into folklore; and

MARTHA,

a real blessing in my life.

Castle Gap viewed from the east side.

Foreword

Despite the vast amount written about the history and folklore of early Texas, one region remains relatively untapped, unjustly neglected in the state's literature. That area lying between San Angelo and the Pecos River, and west to the edge of the Davis Mountains, has scarcely been scratched. Much of its history has been lost, carried to the grave by those who lived it. Some of its history, though preserved, lies forgotten in the attics and county courthouses, in browning old newspaper files and fading family photographs seldom examined by a generation who often can't

even identify the faces in the pictures. A wealth of oral folklore remains, but it has a tendency to change with every new telling, its origins now cloudy, its variations infinite.

Patrick Dearen has examined several of the legends of that region along and near the Pecos, a land forbidding but at the same time compelling, a land still half-wild into our own fathers' time. The stories are fascinating, yet frustrating. Dearen's dedicated research illustrates how difficult it is today to sort fact from fancy and find that fine line which separates history from folklore.

I grew up with much of this folklore, so the book holds a particular interest for me. As a boy on the McElroy Ranch east of Crane, I could look across our yard and clearly see the cleft that was Castle Gap, some twenty or so miles off to the southwest as the crow would fly, if he could carry a canteen that far. The land was a desert, though we would have been outraged had anyone called it that. From the awed tones with which the grownups told the stories, I became aware very early that historic significance clung to this single scallop in the range of arid mountains, blue in the distance, and to Horsehead Crossing a few miles west of it on the Pecos River. At the time I had little sense of the difference between history and folklore; the two seemed indistinguishable in the many accounts told about these places so richly endowed with both.

As a boy helping work cattle in the McElroy's south pasture, I came upon a lonely grave out amid the greasewood and the low-growing mesquite. I was told that it was the resting place of a cowboy murdered by horse thieves, who were later caught and shot or hanged, their bodies flung into a hand-dug hole we knew as Horse Well. I remember my fascination with that place, the chilly thrill of looking down that dark shaft and trying to imagine I could see the skeletons. I tried to tell myself there was nothing to it. But when we camped there with the chuckwagon a couple of times a year, I contrived to see that my father's bedroll lay between mine and that ghostly well.

Cliff Newland was the ranch's windmill man, responsible

for seeing to it that seventy-odd windmills were kept greased and properly pumping water. We Kelton brothers knew, even as small boys, that Cliff had a compelling passion, the search for buried treasure in Castle Gap. The stories were confusing to us. Sometimes it was one treasure he sought, sometimes another, and many people expressed strong doubt that any of them had ever existed. But Cliff believed in them, and the search was a constant driving force that kept him active into his nineties.

Some of the real old-timers still lived, the ones who had seen the country before it was settled, when it was still fresh and new, when a mile was a distance a man could respect and even fear. As a boy I loved to sit, quietly so I would not be sent away, listening to the cowboys and the older folks tell of the way things had been. I heard veterans speak of Horsehead Crossing in tones that made me picture an awesome landmark, perhaps haunted by the ghosts of many men and animals killed there. Even my father, still a young man at the time, had crossed horses and cattle at Horsehead, though a generation later than older riders like Dodge McGee and George and Young Lee.

I was no more than four years old when my father went over into the Monahans sandhills to work cattle and came back with a story about a long-lost wagon train, its occupants massacred by Indians. As he told it, the ghostly remains of the wagons had been found by a rancher named Joe Graham, a longtime acquaintance of Dad's. Dad had visited the site. He talked about seeing relics lying about, iron wagon tires trapped in the sand. He brought home a hand-forged claw-hammer head which had an odd squarish look, much different from the ones we knew. That old souvenir lay around our house for years, helping us conjure up images of screaming Comanche warriors and a desperate but doomed battle for life.

Patrick Dearen has devoted years to running down the facts, where they are still to be found, and much of the varied folklore which has grown up around all these places and events that played upon my imagination and enriched my young life. That he raises more questions than he can provide answers for is to be expected because of the nature of the country and its people. Many of those about whom the legends have grown were transients, simply crossing the Pecos River region on their way to somewhere else. Such was the case with those who supposedly buried their treasures in Castle Gap or near Horsehead. They had little or no continuity with those who came later as permanent settlers, those who perpetuated and built upon the legends out of their own imaginations, their own dreams.

Often these tales reveal as much or more about those who told and embellished them as about those who were figures in the stories. It is not difficult to understand why so many legends of this desolate region grew up around hidden treasures and lost mines. Contrary to the modern image of "big rich" Texas, the truth is that many Texans from the very earliest have lived, if not in poverty, at least skirting on the edge of it. Dearen's account of Will Sublett and his gold nuggets is a case in point. Though much of the story is folklore and supposition, the known facts establish that Sublett spent his life scratching hard for a dollar, his possessions scant, his lifestyle Spartan by any standard. The cold, hard truth is that most Texans of his time were in much the same condition. Is it any wonder that they were easily gripped by the dream of becoming suddenly rich, or no longer having to contend with the wolf howling at the door? Perhaps Sublett had a secret gold mine and perhaps he didn't. The people who knew him or knew of him wanted to believe he did, for he exemplified a dream they all shared. And is it any wonder that the legend grew with the telling? Subconsciously the tellers wanted the fortune to be larger, large enough that they might somehow share.

Ghost tales abound in the Pecos River region, and Dearen devotes a chapter to a persistent one in old Fort Stockton. As a boy I knew nothing of that tale, but even the McElroy Ranch had a ghost story, a very mild one about a gray mule which came up to water at Sand Camp on certain quiet nights, then disappeared.

Paul Patterson, to whom Dearen dedicates the book, told of a supposedly haunted house in which his brother John once decided to spend the night, daring the spirits. Way up after midnight, a door mysteriously opened, then closed. In a little while it did the same thing again. About the third time the door opened, John took the hint and went out through it.

Dearen's research has proven that there was a basis in fact for some of the stories I knew as a boy, though the details as I heard them were usually wildly exaggerated. The grave in the south pasture was real; the cowboy really had been murdered by horse thieves. But the thieves were not caught and killed and cast into Horse Well. One was captured, legally tried and hanged in Midland. The others got away.

Somehow the legend was more gratifying than the facts.

The lost wagon train which yielded up Dad's keepsake claw hammer was real, but Dearen shows that what actually happened to it is a total mystery and almost certainly will remain so.

Cliff Newland's lifelong search in Castle Gap was real, whether the treasures existed or not. That he never found them was of little importance, for Cliff's real treasure was the search itself. It gave his life direction and purpose; it kept him young in spirit long after his back and shoulders were bent by age. I have often wondered what the rest of his life might have been had he ever found what he sought so long. It would have been anticlimactic. Life probably would have lost much of its flavor and interest, and he might not have lived nearly so long.

And perhaps that, in a sense, is the real value of myths and legends. They stir our imaginations; they inspire in us a state of wonder that would be spoiled if all truth became known and all mysteries solved.

J. Frank Dobie was supposed to have declared of one such story that if it did not happen that way, it should have. Legends grow out of people's dreams. We cling to them because we share those dreams; we *want* to believe. That we perpetuate these old stories proves we are not that much different from those who went before us, those who created or built upon them.

Where do facts end and fancies begin in these stories? Who can say? And does it really matter all that much?

Elmer Kelton

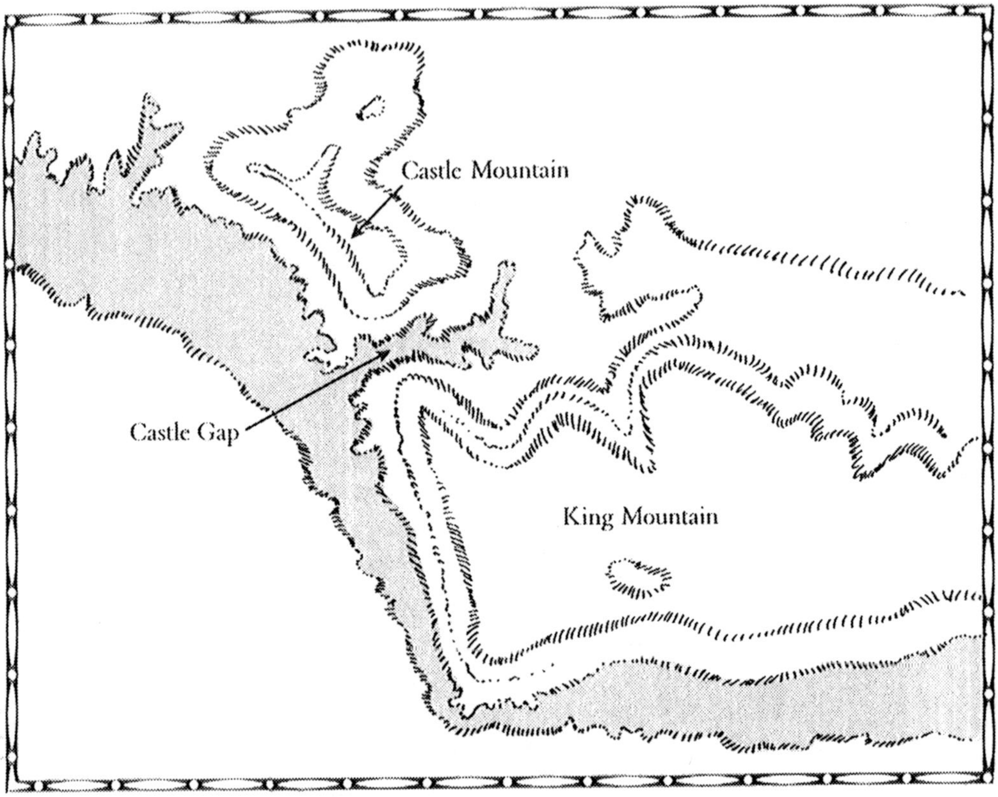
Castle Mountain
Castle Gap
King Mountain

Preface

This book was conceived the first time I stood at the cleft of Castle Gap, looked out across the greasewood plains of the Pecos, and watched the sinking sun melt into clouds of deepest indigo.

More the dawning of a new day than the dying of one, it spurred me into several years of prowling the hidden recessses of West Texas in search of its history and legends.

As a lifelong Texan, I already suspected the region's tales—the true ones and the tall ones—were as vast and varied as the land itself. But I had little idea they were capable of spawning such a sense of wonder and obsession to solve their riddles.

Like indomitable treasure hunter Cliff Newland, whom you will read about in "Castle Gap," I found my professional life revolving around the enigmas of the Pecos. What were the historical accounts behind them, the folklore versions, the reminiscences of the old-timers? Could a thread of truth bind these three? If lost riches abound in this still-frontier, why couldn't they be found? Or had they? If spirits haunt the nights of wailing winds, could they be documented on the same basis by which the judicial system subsists—eyewitness accounts?

My quest carried me thousands of miles back and forth across this sprawling region larger than most states, laid me down at night in a backpack tent or camper shell or beneath a sky studded with stars. I heard the howl of coyotes pierce the nocturnal stillness of the Pecos near Horsehead Crossing. I felt the grit of sand between my teeth as I struggled on foot through free-drifting dunes of sand which hid the secret of a lost wagon train. I hiked beneath the guarding rimrock of Castle Gap and found traces of the Comanche War Trail and fire rings of Indians and pioneers. I trudged under a searing sun across the white stretches of the salt lake Juan Cordona and tasted its brine in my throat. I explored every nook in a purported haunted structure at old Fort Stockton and slept with one eye open just outside its adobe walls. I backpacked the bastion of the Guadalupe wilderness with the secret of lost diggings as near as my next step and as distant as a century past.

And throughout, I felt myself reaching a oneness with the land, its heritage, its people. Especially its people. Without exception, landowners and tenants cooperated fully in my personal explorations, sometimes even to the point of carrying me by four-wheeler across the backcountry of their ranches. And scores of old-timers, as well as a few of lesser years, truly made this book possible by sharing with me their stories. Some of these rugged individualists since have succumbed to the ages, but they live on through dozens of hours of tapes and the pages which follow.

Of the many who fueled my quest, I wish to thank two persons for their tireless support: my wife and best friend, Mary, who shared that first Castle Gap sunset with me and helped research and edit; and Richard Galle, a fellow wanderer along those Pecos trails.

Patrick Dearen
San Angelo, Texas

Castle Gap and the Pecos Frontier

A prehistoric grinding basin at Castle Gap. Inspecting it is Gary Cutrer.

Castle Gap

At the western edge of the Edwards Plateau in Upton County, where the mesas and rimrock of the Castle Mountains yawn open to the greasewood lowlands of the Pecos River and its fabled Horsehead Crossing, lies Castle Gap. This mile-long, 421-foot-deep cut in a mesa on the Comanche War Trail long has been a focal point for westward-bound emigrants and trail bosses and, in this century, for treasure hunters seeking legendary fortunes in gold, silver, or jewels.

"There's been quite a few people that have interest in finding treasure," said Gary Cutrer, member of the family whose corporation owns portions of the gap.[1] C. C. "Smokey" Swift, who ranched beside the canyon for a half-century, was more blunt: "There's people around here that's looked a lifetime. They're just *convinced* that treasure is out there."[2]

Geologically, Castle Gap had its origins 135 million years ago as marine limestone deposits which eventually resulted in a great mesa 3,141 feet above sea level. Erosion later split the mesa to form the gap, exposing numerous marine fossils.[3]

In prehistoric times Indian nomads came seeking salt at Juan Cordona Lake, fifteen miles west of the gap, or buffalo on the Edwards Plateau.[4] The gap was a natural gateway to and from the Pecos River and Horsehead and Salt crossings westward, and springs at the site prompted Comanches to name it *Weick Pah*, or "Gap-Water."[5]

In 1535 Cabeza de Vaca and three other Spaniards may have passed through the gap en route from the Texas coast to settlements in Mexico. De Vaca's description of a north-south river with thirty leagues of plain on the west and an eastern ridge is identical with the topography of the Pecos along the Pecos-Crane county line, with desert on one side and Castle and King mountains and Castle Gap on the other.[6] More than two centuries passed before the next white men entered the break in the mesa; forty-one Spanish explorers dispatched by Captain Rabage y Teran likely passed through in the early fall of 1760 as they scouted a route from the presidio at present-day Menard to Santa Fe.[7]

Within another generation, the Spanish had settled Durango and Chihuahua south of the Rio Grande, and Indians traveled the Comanche War Trail to plunder these settlements. In parties of six to one hundred, Comanches, Kiowas, Rocky Mountain Utahs, and Plains Apaches rode by the light of the "Comanche Moon" or September full moon across the Llano Estacado, stopped to water at the spring at present-day Big Spring, and pushed on several days southwestward through arid land tenanted first by scrub mesquite and then creosote to Castle Gap.[8] The gap cleft a great mesa, which stretched from southeast to northwest and was rimmed by a ledge of limestone. The numerous individual horse paths of the War Trail converged near the mountain's base to descend alongside an arroyo which separated the mesa wall on the south from a hundred-foot-high knoll on the north. The course was crowded with creosote and lechuguilla and sentineled by yucca. Within half a mile the trail skirted on the south a side canyon with cedar-fringed spring[9] and continued on past the knoll to the gap proper. The southern wall, King Mountain, was heavy with cedars below the rimrock, while the northern slope, Castle Mountain, was covered with huge boulders. A quarter-mile further, beyond a less-pronounced hollow extending into King Mountain, the gap's walls squeezed in on the arroyo and War Trail, rendering the fossil-imbedded route only yards wide. Above, overhangs and small caves gaped as the bordering mesas rose steeply in two tiers, the first 100 feet and the second, 321 feet more. At the always windy western extremity of the pass, water seeped from the arroyo's north bluff and trickled down to form a shallow pond.[10] Numerous grinding basins and a thick layer of charcoal near the probable site of the now-disappeared west spring indicate it was a favorite camping place for Indians before they pushed on beyond a V-shaped mountain to Horsehead Crossing twelve miles west-southwest.

Dr. Henry Connelly was one of the first English-speaking men who challenged Indian supremacy through the gap. Guarded by fifty dragoons, he freighted seven wagons of bullion from Chihuahua City, Mexico, to an army post in present-day Oklahoma in 1839.[11] In the late 1840s California-bound prospectors established a wagon route from the confluence of the Conchos in what is now Tom Green County up *A-Hope Ho-Nope*, or the Middle Concho, to its head and across sixty-two miles of desert with unreliable Mustang Water Holes, Flat Rock Ponds, and Wild China Pond to Castle Gap.[12]

No place along the route west was more conducive to Indian confrontation than the pass, as John S. "Rip" Ford, Major Robert S. Neighbors, three other white men, and Comanche scout Tall Tree discovered in an April 1849 wagon route survey between Austin and El Paso del Norte. Low on supplies and having nearly lost their pack mules to a stampede caused by mustangs, the men were hit April 15 by a blizzard between the Middle Concho and the gap. They warmed before a fire of hackberry shrubs and rode on toward King-Castle mesa. Ford led as they descended into the snowy pass and came face-to-face with a Comanche warrior with lance across the withers of his horse. Ford spurred his mule up the bluff a few yards and pulled his six-shooter. The Indian stopped thirty yards distant. Ford raised a free hand and pistol to indicate peace, but the Comanche apparently thought he meant he had ten men behind him. Tall Tree rode up soon, and the Indians recognized one another, ending the potential for bloodshed. The warrior and his Indian woman, on their way back from Chihuahua with a Mexican slave and stolen livestock, slaughtered a mule for the Ford party.[13]

When Brevet First Lieutenant Francis T. Bryan's thirty-man contingent mapped a course from San Antonio to El Paso del Norte three months later, they followed the emigrant-Comanche trail and camped at dry Wild China Pond July 8. Pressing on to

Castle Gap the next day they found the road "very winding, and [descending] very deep into the mountain, the rocks rising to several hundred feet above it." The dry summer had reduced the springs to "dirty and brackish water, which sufficed to water our mules, but was unfit for any other purpose," recorded Bryan.[14]

John Russell Bartlett also found Wild China Pond dry in October 1850 when he went west as U.S.-Mexico Boundary Survey Commission chief. Continuing on through the dark, his party reached, in daylight, the Castle Mountains which, he wrote, "derive their name from the projecting cliffs of limestone, which sometimes assume the appearance of castles. The pass was exceedingly steep, and the road tortuous, frequently running between rocky walls so close together as to render it impassable for two wagons abreast. These walls were covered with immense cacti wherever the almost perpendicular surface would afford them a foothold. . . . We found among the debris of the limestone rock numerous fossil shells." The precipitous downgrade prompted the men to lock wagon wheels and force teams to go slowly, but a wagon tongue still broke at a bend. As workers effected repairs by binding it with tent poles, Bartlett wandered on foot into the reaches of the canyon, climbed the rimrock of "this wild and romantic spot," and explored the "many caverns, which, from the quantity of bones within, were evidently the habitations or resort of wild beasts."[15]

The Bartlett party emerged from the then-dry pass to reach Horsehead Crossing and water without falling prey to their thirst, but a westward-bound group Bartlett met when he returned from California in 1852 was less fortunate. The emigrants had counted on finding springs at Flat Rock Ponds, Wild China Pond, and Castle Gap, but when these proved dry they struggled on toward the Pecos seventy-two hours without water. They almost died of thirst and did lose many of their cattle and mules.[16]

James B. Leach also expected water to be available in the gap when he and a road-improvement party traveled west from Tennessee to reroute and improve the southern wagon road from El Paso to Yuma, Arizona, in 1857. The men watered at Mustang

The greasewood plains of the Pecos as viewed from a cave at Castle Gap.

Water Holes and continued toward the gap through the night of September 28. With the mesa near, a scouting party reported water holes in the pass could not be reached safely in the dark. Pressing on an hour before daylight the next morning, they followed the road into the gap half a mile to "the pools of water which are the sole dependence of the traveller westward between Mustang Ponds and the Pecos River, and this water is by no means permanent or reliable," according to the official journal.

There, while the men cooked breakfast and the animals drank and grazed the scant herbage of the bluffs, the writer did what few persons passing through this domain of the Comanche ever did—he paused long enough to reflect on the wilderness crags about him: "There is something of the romantic in the general appearance of this gap or chasm.... Rocky walls, some hundreds of feet in height, hem in and overhang the traveller [and] the shrill war whoop of the 'Camanche' has so often echoed through the mazes of the pass.... This sterile spot afford[s] nourishment to some twelve or fifteen different varieties of the Cactus family. A number of varieties of flowers were also in bloom, some of them quite pretty.... It is a noticeable fact that almost every shrub tree and bush and indeed every growth of whatever description in this section is armed at all points with innumerable thorns."[17]

From 1858 to 1861 Butterfield Overland Mail stages passed through the gap two times a week on their 2,795-mile, twenty-five-day trips between Tipton, Missouri, and San Francisco.[18] The first westbound stage went through on the night of September 25, 1858, en route to fresh mules at Horsehead Crossing. The only through passenger, Waterman L. Ormsby, slept as the stage navigated the pass, but earlier along the arid expanse between the Middle Concho and Castle Gap he had observed nature's dominion: "Far as the eye could reach along the plain—decayed and decaying animals, the bones of cattle and sometimes of men (the hide drying on the skin in the arid atmosphere), all told a fearful story of anguish and terrific death from the pangs of thirst."[19]

Soon after that monumental journey Butterfield constructed

a two-story stage station of native rock at the gap's west end, where a spring supplied the needs of attendants and stage teams.[20] Tradition dictates that a man by the name of Valentine and his wife served as overseers of the lonely outpost,[21] which Colonel Thomas B. Hunt delineated in an 1869 sketch as consisting of two structures (one possibly a barn) lying immediately south of the road.[22] This site is across the arroyo from the present historical marker on the north bank, where jumbled rocks suggest another one-time building.

The Civil War ended Butterfield's government contract, but stages bearing the imprint of another company followed; Ben Ficklin used the gap as a route to El Paso from San Antonio beginning in the fall of 1867.[23]

More than mail sacks entered the pass in the 1860s, however, as cattle drovers came seeking markets to the southwest or on the upper Pecos. In 1864 William A. Peril drove the first herd of any size through the gap en route from the Texas Hill Country to Chihuahua,[24] but the most noteworthy cattle drive occurred in the spring of 1866, when Charles Goodnight, Oliver Loving, and eighteen men trailed two thousand Longhorn steers and breeding cows to Fort Sumner, New Mexico, from the Brazos in North Texas by way of the Middle Concho and Castle Gap. The seventy-five-mile stretch from the headwaters of the Middle Concho to the Pecos proved demanding for cattle accustomed to watering daily; the two water sources lay five to seven days apart at the ordinary pace of a drive. By the morning of the third day on the arid plain, Goodnight realized that the beeves would have to be driven unceasingly. When they reached Castle Gap in the middle of the following night, the herd smelled dampness in the air and stampeded through the pass. Goodnight made a daring and reckless ride through the dark to halt the leaders and save the herd. At daybreak he rode to the Pecos on a fresh horse and returned with full canteens. By then, the hands had gone three days without sleep and the cattle three days without water, forcing Goodnight and four men to drive the stronger two-thirds of the herd on to Horsehead Crossing. After a near-disaster when the beeves plunged wildly into the river, Goodnight returned to the gap and helped drive the drags. Thirty-year-old Goodnight, who already had been awake three days, rode seventy-two miles that day, evidence of the perseverance that led him to drive 250,000 more beeves through the gap the next decade.[25]

The initial cattle drive by Goodnight and Loving opened up the Goodnight-Loving Trail for hundreds of succeeding drovers, who used the route as a springboard to push cattle as far north as Montana. Indians who long had ridden the War Trail to plunder northern Mexico now saw in those herds enough meat to supply their rancherias a long while, as well as important barter for dealing with *comancheros* (traders) of New Mexico.[26] The canyon, especially, offered little defense against ambush, and in early 1867 Comanches swooped down from the overhanging bluffs and drove away cattle boss Lew Soyer's entire herd. Left without livelihood in the midst of the arduous Goodnight-Loving Trail, some of the cowboys pushed on for Fort Sumner while others retreated.[27]

Goodnight possessed a native intelligence shared by few trail bosses. Returning the seven hundred miles from Fort Sumner to the Brazos in 1867, he and a dozen hands were attacked by Indians along the Pecos above Horsehead. They successfully defended themselves and reached the crossing by dusk. There Goodnight feigned setting up camp and continued on, avoiding possible confrontation with the same war party by navigating Castle Gap at night. The next day he encountered a westbound herd stretched out a mile and a half and warned the trail boss to tighten up his herd. "Let 'em come," said the other man. "I'd like to sample those damned Comanches." In Castle Gap, the trail boss got his wish. Comanches torched his wagons and drove away every steer.[28]

In 1869 three cowhands from the Middle Concho's Tankersly Ranch safely trailed a herd through the gap to Fort Sumner, but when they rode into the pass on the return trip, Indians attacked and killed two of the men.[29] Such incidents prompted numerous U.S. Army scouting patrols in a region guarded only by Fort Stockton forty-six miles southwest. In 1868 Company G, 41st Infantry, set up a fifteen-man picket in the gap, but on June 4 the soldiers were ordered twelve miles eastward to Wild China Pond.[30] On a scout in August 1869, Colonel Thomas B. Hunt noted the effect of the Goodnight-Loving Trail: "Castle Mountain Cañon is about two miles long, very rough and rugged with a few alkaline waterholes and full of dead cattle. The water is totally unfit to drink for man or beast. . . . Road from Canyon to river, heavy sandy plain, full of dead cattle."[31]

In 1872 a thousand cattle went mad with thirst in the gap as a drizzle fell. For two days cowhands tried to drive the steers through to the Pecos, but the herd would only bawl and mill about. Finally, the men, desperate for water themselves, abandoned them to die.[32]

As late as 1879 Apache war parties made occasional raids into the area, prompting the continued attention of the U.S. Army. That year, Troop B, Tenth Cavalry, received orders to camp in Castle Gap if water was available and to pinpoint all water sources in the Castle Mountains.[33]

Such actions helped secure the region once and for all against Indian depredations, and in the summer of 1887, C.C. Childress, then three, and his grandparents passed peacefully through the gap en route to Fort Davis from Brown County. Not having watered since Wild China Pond, they stopped at the west seep near the ruins of the Butterfield stage stand. "The water came off the north side of the hill and ran down into a big old cedar water trough" hewn from a single tree, said Childress. "We watered our horses there at the stand. There was a house standing there and [someone] was using it. It was made out of dirt and little chunk rocks."[34]

Though the days of the Comanche War Trail had passed, travelers still had to protect themselves from Mexican *bandidos*. In 1890, according to a folktale in the region, Sam Murray and his partner returned to their line camp on a Pecos country ranch near present-day Iraan to find Mexican bandits had stolen their horses and saddles. They trailed the gang through the lower Pecos badlands and into Castle Gap. But there the raiding party rendezvoused with another gang, and the two cowboys knew they were hopelessly outnumbered. Retreating toward the McElroy Ranch eleven miles northeast, the pursuers became the pursued, and they faced even greater desperation when the horse of Murray's friend dropped. Rather than trying to outrun the bandits by riding double, the men divided, with Murray galloping on and his partner hiding. As Murray escaped, one of the bandits spotted the man afoot, roped him, and dragged him to death.

When Murray reached the McElroy Ranch headquarters, a small posse quickly formed. Tracking down the Mexicans, Murray and the ranchhands administered "frontier justice" inside Castle Gap: they hanged the *bandidos* from a big hackberry tree. They buried his friend in the south pasture of the McElroy Ranch, but similar respect was not paid the *bandidos*; returning to the gap sometime later, Murray found the bodies still swinging from the tree.[35]

Contemporary newspaper accounts give a somewhat different version of the incident. On July 21, 1890, according to one article, Murray noted the theft of saddles and his quirt from Stiles Ranch near Centralia Draw, well east of the gap. Taking up the trail, Murray recruited Will Landrum from Bartlett's spread, and together they tracked the bandits westward to Hurd's Ranch. There, the two men secured fresh horses and assurance from ranch owner Hurd and a cowhand, McGruder, that they would follow close behind to render support. Pushing onward approximately twenty-five miles, Murray and Landrum overtook their quarry and, from a distance, identified the Mexicans' saddles as the stolen items. Leaving Landrum to watch the *bandidos*, Murray retreated to expedite the promised aid from Hurd and obtain additional troops from the nearby TX Ranch. Unsuccessful, he galloped his horse back to Landrum and the outgunned cowboys continued the pursuit westward.

At 4:00 p.m., as the cowhands came upon Murray's quirt in the road in or near Castle Gap, the Mexicans attacked from behind, sending the two men fleeing. In the ensuing chase the two men separated, with half the *bandidos* following Murray and the other half Landrum. Murray later said he last saw Landrum two miles distant and holding a two-hundred-yard lead on two pursuing riders. Reaching the TX Ranch, Murray returned with aid and found Landrum's hat and saddled horse, then a pool of blood ten to fifteen feet off the road. At the end of a drag trail through bordering brush they discovered Landrum's body, two knife wounds piercing the chest. Three of the Mexicans ultimately were captured and tried for the crime, and twenty-year-old Lorenza Perrez died on the gallows in Midland after having confessed to wielding the murder weapon.[36]

For centuries the thirteen miles from Castle Gap's east rift to Horsehead Crossing had been a stretch in which only the wicked tarried. As the nineteenth century waned, however, hardy ranchers moved herds out into the creosote sands and kept them there. Samuel Toliver Dawson, who as a four-year-old had endured Indian attack while trekking the gap with his parents in 1864, brought his cattle and horses to this vast open range in 1897 and was among the many who staked claims along the Pecos in 1903.[37] Not until 1910 did anyone homestead to within three miles of the canyon.[38]

The pass continued to be used as a route west through the first decade of the twentieth century. Ranchhands for T. R. Long and the Curries of Glasscock County trailed sheep through in 1904,[39] and Joe Conger (later Upton County commissioner) camped in the gap's dry streambed while headed for Balmorhea that same year.[40]

Ever since a wagon route first had been cleared through the gap in 1839, water from infrequent rains had drained down the arroyo on the road's north side and a shallow depression on the other. But sometime after 1910 a fresno crew working for treasure hunter Billy Pool shoveled thousands of cubic feet of dirt across the ditch and altered the flow of the runoff onto the road bed. The water began to gouge out great chunks of the trail and eventually closed the gap as a practical route.[41]

In its long history, Castle Gap was more than a passageway

for cattle drovers and emigrants; it also comprised a viable route for transporting bullion, army payroll, strongboxes of gold and silver coins, and outlaw booty. But its bluffs provided a perfect site for ambush and the numerous caves ideal locations for caches, and by the time wagons first headed west en masse in 1849, the gap was already the supposed site for lost treasure.

Some tale-tellers believe gold was cached in the gap back in the days of Coronado, who in 1540 rode north from Mexico's west coast in search of the fabled seven cities of gold. He crossed southern Arizona and central New Mexico, then pushed eastward thirty-three days across the Llano Estacado, dropping into a canyon and then a ravine before turning back. Some historians think these landmarks were Palo Duro Canyon and the North Concho valley, respectively, but others believe he reached Castle Gap. There, legend asserts, he buried gold he had acquired on the march, left markings in the rocks to point the way, and slew a man so his ghost would guard the Head Spaniard's Treasure.[42]

Two and a half centuries later a second treasure, the so-called Catholic Cross Cache, supposedly found its way to the gap area. In 1780, according to the best-known version of the tale, priests fled Mexico or California with diamonds, gold bullion, and gold vases. At the foot of V Mountain and its twin three miles west-northwest of Castle Gap, they camped and considered the wealth, enough to make twenty-five families rich for life. Indians may have killed two members of the group prior to the priests loading the booty from carts to fifteen burros; a variant account even maintains that outlaws later killed everyone. The versions generally agree, however, that the priests buried the treasure on V Mountain. They supposedly made the grotto appear to be the grave of an Indian chief and carved markings throughout the Castle Mountains, some of them underground and others false; even a pseudo grave was included. Their task finished, they swore never to disturb the treasure and, according to most accounts, pushed on to the northeast, where at modern-day Big Spring they etched a hint into a rock. The inscription, "Look for huge cross, 77, then look for V-shaped mountains,"

V Mountain as seen from the summit of Castle Mountain.

reportedly surfaced years later and was considered a sure clue. Someone realized Castle Gap lay about seventy-seven miles from Big Spring and saw in the twin V mountains the required topographical feature. The treasure hunters who embraced the marking failed to reckon, however, with the probability that Spanish priests would have measured distances in leagues.

By hack and burro team in the 1800s came a one-hundred-year-old El Paso woman who supposedly had been with the priests' party. Leaving her two grandchildren, including ten-year-old Susie, to make camp at the base of V Mountain, she climbed to the summit but never disappeared beyond. When she returned she assured the youngsters the treasure never had been disturbed. In 1927 the woman's granddaughter, known as "Cot

House Susie," returned to operate a flophouse six miles north in Crane and tell the story to her oilfield patrons.

An elderly woman encountered by Smokey Swift may have been a factual basis for the garbled folklore account. "Back in 1929 Swede Anderson brought an old Mexican woman, eighty, ninety years old, out from El Paso," Swift related. "Paid her expenses and everything. She was supposed to be a survivor of that ambush. When she got here she looked things over and told him, 'It's on that round mountain around the Point [V Mountain] between Crane and McCamey,' but to leave it alone, that the spirits would get 'em if they bothered it."

Castle Gap, however, is not the only site mentioned for the Catholic Cross Cache. Another version claims that in the 1846–1848 Mexican-American War, priests who realized the inevitable defeat of Mexico fled the upper Rio Grande with Catholic church wealth in order to deprive the United States of it. Somewhere in the Pecos country of Texas they stepped off four hundred paces along a spring's south and west flow, buried silver in a flour barrel and gold in a horseshoe keg, and marked the site with a small cross.[43]

By the midpoint of the nineteenth century, Castle Gap supposedly gained its third lost treasure. "I talked to one man who went through Castle Gap in the '49 gold rush," said Billy Rankin, who rode the gap horseback in 1926. "He was too young to remember when his parents took him out, but he remembered when he came back through. They were supposed to have had horseshoe kegs full of gold, and one of them got lost. He came back in '29 or '30—he was an old man then—looking for the place where the horses may have watered, thinking they may have kicked it overboard." He left empty-handed, however.[44]

It was 1860, if legend is to be believed, when a westbound Butterfield coach entered the pass with a cargo that included a strongbox of gold and silver—either U.S. Army payroll intended for West Texas forts or private money bent for Chihuahuan mines where silver bullion could be had at below-market prices. But outlaws lying in wait on overhanging ledges had their own plans for the strongbox and opened fire, sending the stage plummeting into the arroyo. Descending and killing the occupants, gang members directed a male slave who had not been a partner to the murders to gather loose coins from the burst strongbox as they pillaged the bodies. From King Mountain above, a lookout noted dragoons approaching from Horsehead Crossing and rode down to tell his comrades. Realizing they could not outdistance the patrol with the burden of the booty, they shoved it inside a cave on King Mountain and had the slave help them seal the entrance with mud, rocks, and brush. Riding west out of the gap, they turned northward to dodge the patrol. When the soldiers discovered the crime they pursued and overtook the men at a spring in the sands. In the ensuing fight, only the slave survived as he crawled away through the shinnery. The next day, however, he too was captured and taken to Fort Stockton to face murder and robbery charges. When the Civil War broke out he was taken to a prison in Ohio, where he stayed seven years, persistently denying any part in the murders. Finally he agreed to reveal the cache in exchange for freedom. Reaching Castle Gap in 1868, the negro uncovered a few gold and silver coins from the gully but was unable to relocate the cache. Believing him a liar, his captors returned him to prison.[45]

Other tales of buried stage booty abound. Supposedly, when Old Bill Castle and Little Bill Castle came to Castle Gap as stage station attendants in the 1860s, they watched so many coaches pass through with gold that they finally plotted a robbery. On the day an eastbound stage was expected, Little Bill hid on the rimrock and waited for the older man's signal. When the stage arrived and Old Bill learned it carried gold, he waved a flag from the roof and the younger Castle scurried down for the holdup. Authorities finally decided the Castles were the bandits and dispatched troops from Fort Stockton. Old Bill headed for the rimrock and was fatally shot, but Little Bill was pursued to Castle Bluff on the Trinity River, where he fell. In his last breaths he spoke of $100,000 in gold he had cached at Castle Gap.[46]

A similar tale holds that outlaws used the gap as a base from

The rimrock and boulder-strewn slope of Castle Mountain within Castle Gap.

which to hold up numerous wagons and stages; reportedly, they left $40,000 stashed in the side canyon on the gap's east end.[47]

In the late 1860s, say legend-tellers, a U.S. Army wagon train—en route from El Paso to San Antonio with gold and rifles—was attacked by Comanches in the gap. The soldiers were besieged for days, and the last few survivors realized they had to keep the rifles out of the hands of war chief Grey Wolf, a half-breed also known as Jim Caldwell. The doomed soldiers climbed the slope at night and stashed firearms and gold beneath a ledge charged with gunpowder, then set it off to bury all. Only one soldier escaped, but when he came back years later he could not remember the cache's location.[48]

The most famous of Castle Gap's treasure stories had its origin in 1867, when Maximilian, the Austrian archduke who ruled as emperor of Mexico from 1864 to 1867,[49] supposedly sent

a wagon train northward with his inheritance after his reign began to crumble in March 1867. Eventually sent before a firing squad, he purportedly gave each of his executioners a gold coin.[50] But the vast part of his wealth, according to legend, was lost in the vicinity of Castle Gap.

Long before the tale became further garbled in the mid-1920s oil boom, line camps carried an oral tradition: Six or eight Missourians and former raiders with William C. Quantrill and Frank James met Maximilian's subordinates at Presidio del Norte and hired on as guards for a supposed cargo of flour bound for a ship in Galveston. At Horsehead Crossing, a Missourian secretly checked beneath the tarps and found the fortune, prompting the one-time guerrillas to plot a mass murder. In Castle Gap the next night they carried out their plans, burned bodies and wagons, and cached the booty. Planning to return, they rode east. One man became ill and stayed behind at Fort Concho in present-day San Angelo. Following his companions' course when he was better, he found them slain by Indians, outlaws, or Texas Rangers on the San Saba River near Fort McKavett. He wandered northeastward, intending to gain the assistance of Frank and Jesse James in reclaiming the treasure. But in North Texas or southern Oklahoma he camped by happenstance with horse thieves and was imprisoned until he succumbed to illness. On his deathbed he told of the Castle Gap murders and drew a map detailing Maximilian's treasure.[51]

Though the numerous versions of the tale are enough to confound any student of history, common threads bind the oral traditions prior to the mid-1920s and the earliest written accounts: Between Presidio del Norte and the Pecos, ex-Confederate soldiers were hired as guards by a northeast-bound wagon train. At a camp near the Pecos they learned the cargo was treasure rather than agricultural products. Between Horsehead Crossing and the plain east of Castle Gap, the ex-soldiers killed caravan members and cached the booty with plans to return for it. Pushing eastward, they battled with enemies, and a single survivor rode to North Texas or Oklahoma and ended up in an asylum or jail. On his deathbed he told the story and detailed the treasure's location. The name Black generally surfaces in these accounts as one of the outlaws, the captain of the rangers that killed the gang, the doctor who tended the dying man, or an early seeker of the treasure.

Variants sometimes associate Maximilian's treasure with the Gulf of Mexico or a mountain range in southern New Mexico. In one account, some members of Maximilian's party survived the massacre and later returned to transport the wealth from the gap to the Texas Gulf Coast. Shuttling it by small boat toward an awaiting ship, they saw it sink to the bottom of the sea when a tropical storm struck.[52] In another version, unidentified persons relocated Maximilian's inheritance to the San Andres Mountains on present-day White Sands Missile Range in New Mexico. In 1937 Earnest "Doc" Noss reportedly found gold bars in a cave at that site, only to watch a landslide seal the cache; Noss was later shot to death by his partner in the venture to reclaim the ingots.[53]

With such wealth supposedly lying in or near Castle Gap, treasure hunters inevitably came; frequently, Maximilian's inheritance was the object of their search. In 1885 five Austrians reportedly dug at the gap two months,[54] and a few years later a judge named Black and Eastland County lawyer Truman H. Conner came with a map supposedly drawn by the dying man and handed either to Black's brother or a friend of Conner's. It contained vague landmarks which did not coincide with the topography, however, and though Conner would look again in the 1920s after Black died, they found only burned wagon irons to suggest that treasure was near.[55]

Wagon irons should not have been considered unusual along this "Interstate 20" of the Old West, but the fact that some had been burned intrigued treasure seekers. "My husband made lots of money from people coming there and wanting to know where those old wagon irons were left," said Cora Dawson Smith, who lived near Horsehead Crossing in 1910. "We'd seen them lots of times, but we didn't pay much attention to them—they were just old wagon irons left where wagons were burned. But he'd go up there and show it to them and they'd pay him five or ten dollars."[56] In 1911, C. C. Childress and three companions likely came across the same relics just west of the canyon, as well as the remains of a stagecoach to the north,[57] and E. N. Beane found blackened wagon irons on the summit of King Mountain above the gap in 1927.[58]

Such physical evidence, though shaky, prodded successive generations of seekers to continue the hunt for Maximilian's treasure. In 1908 several Oregon men looked unsuccessfully despite the strong pull on their mineral rod.[59] In 1928 a treasure hunter encountered "fifty or sixty" fellow seekers at a single time in the gap.[60] It was not uncommon for searchers in the first three decades of the twentieth century to claim they had direct knowledge, as Cody Bell learned when he began ranching the gap in 1925.

"People would come by real often and take him out behind the barn and show him a map," said his son Cody Bell, Jr., of Rankin. "It was always somebody on their deathbed that gave them the map. Supposedly there had been a spring there and the outlaws had walked around a triangular rock which had fallen from above, dipped up water for their horses, stepped off so many paces west, and buried the treasure. They took him down there one time and found a triangular rock, and a crack in the face like it could have been a wet weather spring."[61]

Billy Rankin, who lived in the flats only a few miles west of the gap, remembered a man who came in 1929. "He and these other people supposedly had a map about where the treasure was buried," he said. "This fellow at my place was supposed to be a son of one of the outlaws that had killed Maximilian's troops. [The treasure] was supposed to have been buried at the south side of the gap at a spring, but there wasn't a spring there when I was first through there in '26. But they'd had a stage stand there and were supposed to have gotten water from a spring. The man looked and looked, but if he ever found any more than pig tracks I don't know what it was. Some people thought for a long time that a wagon train burned there, but this old fellow said it was a corn train. I never did see any ruins of that wagon train."[62]

In 1930 or 1931, said Smokey Swift, the supposed actual pair of men who had received the deathbed map came looking. "They spent three years digging for that stuff out here," said Swift, who remembered one of the Illinois men was named Whitey. "They had twenty- to thirty-foot-deep holes. One of 'em died here; the other one finally left."

Although in 1935 Swift found homemade wagon wheel irons where wagons or ox carts evidently had been destroyed a half-mile south of the stage station ruins, he never became a victim of gold fever like so many others. "I'll bet you there's been a thousand or two over the last forty years looking," he said. "They dig more on my place [adjoining the pass on the west] than they do at the gap itself. Most of the digging takes place within a mile or two of the gap. We've had all types, every type in the world, digging out there. There's not a month of the year go by without somebody coming down here digging."[63]

It is not always Maximilian's inheritance that draws attention. A boy named Sublett who heard a false tomb had been left by priests as a clue to the Catholic Cross Cache supposedly came upon a crude headstone while helping his father cut cedars for fence posts near Castle Gap. Sighting along its edge he saw a distant cave and begged his father to dig below the stone. The man decided not to disturb the grave, however, and the marker disappeared into legend.[64] In 1935, meanwhile, three Catholic priests from Mexico came to the Cody Bell Ranch ostensibly in search of the Catholic Cross Cache. A chart they displayed pinpointed a three-cornered rock on a bluff as the site of the treasure. A ranchhand escorted them to the location and then undertook chores elsewhere; when he returned he found a deep hole at the spot and the priests and possible contents of the pit gone.[65]

Two years later in 1937, said Swift, an old treasure hunter dug throughout the twelve-mile stretch between the Pecos and the gap for whatever bonanza he might find and unearthed nothing but sand.[66]

The most ambitious quest came in 1968. Two Amarillo brothers gained permission from officials to dig at then-Castle Gap Park, a hundred-acre parcel at the gap's west end, leased to Upton County in May 1968 by Jacobs Livestock Company and reclaimed in 1985.[67] They used a backhoe to carve a modest hole, then bulldozed out a gully forty feet deep, eighty feet wide, and one hundred eighty feet long, to find nothing. The massive excavation, left unfilled, bears mute testimony to the extent to which man will go in search of a legend.[68]

Jacobs Livestock Company owed its beginnings to Caton Jacobs, who purchased the land in 1936. "The family members still think that maybe there's some treasure out here," said his grandson, Gary Cutrer. "My grandfather had the attitude that he was going to work for a living and not bother for the treasure, and that's kind of the way I am. But my uncle [Jacobs's firstborn son] and his cousin used to look for it in all the overhangs and caves. He said one time his cousin dropped him down and held him by his feet in this hole and he raised up inside a cave with a flashlight and there were rattlesnakes all over, lying there looking at him."

An old-model Studebaker served as a physical illustration to the Jacobs family of lives lost among legends. "My granddad had a worker who, with his buddy, had a new Studebaker, and they came out here to the ranch to work sheep and live," recounted Cutrer. "They put their Studebaker up on blocks of flat rocks to save the tires. And he became obsessed with finding the treasure; he said one night he was riding his horse out and a light started dancing around him and so he started following it. He stayed out here till he had to go to an old folks home, and that Studebaker just rusted, rotted on those flat rocks."

Seekers at the gap resort to both folkloric and "scientific" methods. Cutrer, whose study of engineering left him leery of dowsing, recalled "a man from Lamesa that wanted to look for treasure in 1982, and he had a scientific version of the witching stick. He told me he had invented something that would pick up electromagnetic frequencies given off by gold, silver, diamonds, and he could dial diamonds or he could dial gold or silver. I didn't want to have anything to do with that. But he stood out on the corner of Castle Mountain section and did his witching rod deal and said there's two treasures—one with large quantities of gold and silver and one with large quantities of silver and diamonds and a small amount of gold." The two parties could not come to terms on contractual details, however, and no search was undertaken.[69]

Cutrer recalled others whose quests were even more bizarre. Encouraged by a supposed eyewitness report that a man had parked along an Upton County road, inspected an eastern pocket of King Mountain, and returned from a cave "marked by a four-by-four" with a burlap bag full of silver bars, relatives came seeking. "Their theory was, they could go on the west side—the prevailing winds are from the west—and open up a crack in the rimrock, burn some old tires, and watch the black smoke blow through and blow out this cave," said Cutrer. "So that's what they did; they spent about five or six weekends out here chinking away at a crevice in the rimrock."

In the mid-1980s an Odessa man and two others simply grasped pick and bailing bucket to seek the Catholic Cross Cache at the west end of the gap. "These men got out there and they dug every Sunday for six or eight weeks, and they got down twenty-five feet hand-digging with a pick," related Cutrer. "And they'd find a piece of limestone rock and say, 'Look! This is a church!' 'Yeah! That's a church!' Or horse, or arrowhead pointing that way. And it would be four inches long, so they'd move over four feet and dig down four feet."

Other hunters have been less gullible and have tried to base their excavations on documentation. One who searched for Maximilian's treasure seemed privy both to burned wagon irons and the deathbed map supposedly received by a Doctor Black. "This man worked in the oilfields in the thirties and forties out here, and he used to come down and find big areas of burned wagon parts," said Cutrer. "They got picked up during the second world war for scrap. He'd also done research on the Black family. He had found some descendants of Doctor Black in Arizona, and he talked to the oldest family member and they said, yeah, they remembered seeing the map, but that it had been destroyed."[70]

The name of one treasure seeker stands above all others in the Castle Gap area—Cliff Newland. "He spent a lifetime digging for that out there," said Smokey Swift. "It kept him alive until he was almost ninety-four. I had to take him out there once a week when he got feeble. He always had markers to go by. He'd say, 'You see that arrow out there on that mountain?' And he'd point it out and I couldn't see a thing."

Newland was born February 15, 1886, in Ennis, Texas. When he was two, his parents carried him to Cummins in Sterling County, where they lived in a tent and later in a two-room house. But the town vanished after Sterling City was selected as county seat in 1891; temporarily relocating to that site, the Newlands eventually moved to a ranch twenty miles south of Garden

City. In early adulthood Newland worked on Glasscock County ranches and trailed sheep through Castle Gap for T. R. Long and the Curries. In 1928 he assumed duties as windmill mechanic for the McElroy Ranch north of Castle Mountain and took up treasure hunting. He first looked for Maximilian's gold, then the Head Spaniard's and Catholic Cross caches. He dowsed with a bamboo cane split into a "V," a metal bolt or bottle of quicksilver dangling on a string, or a pair of copper welding rods bent at ninety-degree angles. When seeking silver, he would place a dollar coin in the bolt or fork of the cane, while gold demanded a twenty-dollar gold piece.

Four hundred years after Coronado's push into Texas, Cliff Newland and Crane pool hall operator Swede Anderson found a half-mile stretch of burned rocks on the first shelf of a mountain five miles north of McCamey and south of Castle Gap. On the ledge they discovered three apparently hand-carved steps leading up to a rock cairn on a ten-foot-wide point, where rested a stone eight feet long, five feet wide, and seven inches thick. Spurred by nearby markings, they moved the stone with jack and crowbar and found a skeleton which a Crane doctor told them was human; further, they learned that this method of burial was not typical of Southwestern Indians.

The find set Newland seeking the Head Spaniard's, or Coronado's, treasure, which he believed he would locate if he solved the mystery of the markings that pointed either to treasure or other signs. Ninety varas north of the grave he found a cairn covering a stone which had been rubbed smooth. Half a mile north he found a carving of the Little Dipper on a long-dead cedar, and in Castle Gap he found rock markings of a moccasin track and bear paw which continued on the same course. But there the trail ran dry; many of the signs seemed intended to lure would-be looters astray.

Others, meanwhile, exhumed a human skeleton near the gap, and Newland and Anderson decided to dig deeper at the site with the aid of a black man whose grandfather once had sketched the location of treasure for him. A yard down they found horse bones and teeth which they concluded were from the dead man's mount, but the grave only confused Newland until a fellow treasure hunter became wedged in a shallow cave in the canyon and discovered nine triangular lead bars. On the ledge above the cave, Newland noted several holes that everyone had incorrectly assumed to be Indian corn grinding bins; they formed a triangle with two sides fifty-eight inches long and a base twice that. Placing a stake in the middle of the base and sighting through the vertex, he saw the grave of the horse and rider in one direction and the original tomb with the large stone in the opposite.

Another seeker, relying on a tradition passed down to an old Indian from his forefathers, searched for markers hidden underground. Seeing the treasure hunter unearth apparent clues, Newland used his witching stick to follow the concealed signs more than a mile. They ended at a surface marker pointing to previously discovered etchings of a pigpen and an Indian climbing a wall. Now certain Spanish treasure was near, Newland remembered gaining a strong pull for gold and silver at the pigpen and exhuming two plates. At the time he had assumed they were from a chuckwagon; now he concluded they must have been left by Spaniards. But the surface marker also pointed out the two V-shaped hills, three miles west-northwest of the gap, where the Catholic Cross Cache supposedly lay.

The mingling of trails led Newland to confer with Lod Calahan, an early-day cattle inspector for the Texas and Southwestern Cattle Raisers Association; Calahan said an old Mexican had claimed the original route through King-Castle mesa was not by way of Castle Gap. A friend of Newland proceeded to track a wagon road from Horsehead Crossing south to Soda Lake and east to King Mountain, and together they found traces of wagon wheel ruts angling up to the summit. Convinced now that V Mountain would have been well off course for the priests who purportedly planted the Catholic Cross Cache, Newland considered the variant account which held that the bonanza was buried in a barrel and a keg along a spring's south and west stream bed. It prompted him to witch Rustler Spring twenty-three miles southwest of Orla in Culberson County. But this spring flowed north, a discrepancy which bothered Newland until he learned from the son of an old-time trail driver that a fresno crew had altered the flow from its true south and west course. Still, Newland found nothing at the site, so he again turned to Castle Gap.

There, he decided to dowse for the $40,000 outlaws supposedly cached in a grotto of the side canyon extending into King Mountain. Scouring the gulch, he found a hand-cut rock fifteen inches square and six inches thick. He was certain it once had sealed the entrance to the cache but never could determine the booty's location.[71]

The confusing search, in and near the gap, for multiple treasures often sharing common markers carried Newland through five decades, and sometimes others joined him. "I knew him and respected him and learned to love him," I. C. "Tiny" Earp of Crane said. "He and I would get up lots of times at four o'clock in the morning and we'd be draining oil out of those windmills before you could see the top, in order to have enough time for us to go dig for treasure at Castle Gap. He was the technical end of the thing and I was the pick-and-shovel man."

Newland did his best to teach Earp how to read the all-important treasure markers. "I must have been a poor student," said Earp, "because he could show me a sign and I couldn't see it whenever he was showing it to me. Anyway, it meant something to Cliff, and he was always after me, knowing that I cowboyed around all over the country, to be very well aware. He said he needed one or two more clues and he could go right to that Maximilian's treasure."

On horseback northwest of the gap one day, Earp came upon a partly buried wagon tongue thirty feet from a depression which bore evidence of a one-time excavation. He soon returned with Newland and Swede Anderson. "After we arrived on location, we looked around and right due north about one hundred varas was a dwarf mesquite tree on the point of the mountain," said Earp. "It was about six feet tall and probably had a trunk on it four or five inches in diameter. There was a big section, prob-

Castle Gap seen from the west side, with sign announcing now-defunct Castle Gap Park.

ably the width of the diameter of the tree and maybe five inches across, that had been cut out with an ax and a big 'X' chopped in. It lined up with a big cave across the canyon."

They were excited at the prospects, but winter cold forced them back to their pickup.

> On the way back to town, we all agreed that neither one of the three would go out unless the other two were

> present. For the first time I felt like, well, there's treasure. Being a poor man and having a family, I had to work and it was about three months before I so happened to work that country horseback again. And where I'd found this thing, they'd had a bulldozer out there and scraped that whole hill down.
>
> So our pact not to go back out didn't hold true. I don't mean that Cliff wouldn't have given me my third of it, because I guarantee he would have if he'd've found it. The next time I saw Cliff we laughed about it. He never did say that he had done it, but he never did say that he hadn't. But since he never did want to go back out anymore to that location, I felt sure maybe he had been through there.[72]

Most persons calmly accepted Newland's treasure-hunting exploits as an interesting quirk of his personality, but Earp once made the mistake of disdaining his efforts to his face.

> He'd worked me pretty hard digging for that treasure up there, and we never did find a blamed thing, but we spent a lot of hours over there on McElroy payroll looking for it. One day we were out on the McElroy Ranch pulling a windmill. We were eating our lunch and I told ol' Cliff, "Cliff, you can't find *anything*. Hell, you're just fooling yourself. You never have found any treasure and you're not going to." Made him mad. But I was about half-serious about the thing because I knew we were going to finish that windmill and go dig another hole in the ground.
>
> He said, "All right, you take these coins out there and you hide 'em anywhere you want to. Don't spread 'em out over a very big area and I'll find every one of 'em." I said, "Boy, that's a good test."

Newland turned away and Earp buried the coins, then the older man produced his witching stick. "That rascal found every doggoned coin," said Earp. "He'd walk over one of those coins and that thing would drop right down to it, then he'd reach down, brush the sand away, and pick up the coin."[73]

Encouraged by such successes, Newland scoured Castle Gap's rimrock thoroughly. "One time Cliff found a cave closed in by rocks and just *knew* he'd found it," said Smokey Swift.[74] But Newland's only "success" was to add to the canyon's treasures—he lost a twenty-dollar gold piece from his dowsing rod; borrowing a similar coin to search for it, he lost that one as well.[75] He never became discouraged, however. "They call you a fool for looking and smart if you find it," he said.[76]

"You know, ol' Cliff was always just one step away from it—the next day was always gonna be *it*," said Paul Patterson of Crane. "That kept him going forty years."[77] Newland's daughter-in-law, Bonnell Newland of Crane, concurred: "He had enthusiasm; he expected to find it. He never really found anything of value, but I really think that was his life. And that was a gold mine within itself: it kept him going."[78]

Others not nearly so persevering as Newland, however, supposedly found material treasure. A stranger named Alexander once related to Newland that when he was fifteen, an old San Antonio woman told him that three Mexican men from San Antonio dug for Maximilian's gold at the gap's west side; after an eight-week stay they returned to San Antonio and displayed wealth.

Newland became convinced a small sinkhole near the gap was the site of their find. Ten feet across and twelve feet deep, it was situated beside a playa near the wagon road and adjacent to the spot where Jim Meek of McCamey found a Mexican coin die.[79] That and a European-style dagger, however, were the only artifacts Meek unearthed in a search that began about 1910 and lasted half a lifetime.[80]

Others were reportedly luckier. A surveyor named John Calvert supposedly came across a wagon train with gold buried in the sands near the gap early in the twentieth century and returned periodically to replenish his finances.[81] Folklore also holds that a German engineer named Wallenstein prospered in California after leaving an empty hole just east of the gap.[82]

A tradition passed along to successive generations of Castle Gap ranchers tells of the good fortune of one twentieth-century cowboy. "Supposedly, a hand of my grandfather's found a saddle-bag full of gold coin," related Gary Cutrer, who himself found only a wagon axle and Indian artifacts.[83] Whether that unidentified ranchhand was an active seeker is not known, but in legend fate generally smiles on those who do not search.

"On the TX Ranch there was a Mexican boy, a horse wrangler, and his horses got out from ranch headquarters eight or ten miles away from Castle Gap and he went looking for them," related Billy Rankin. "This wrangler supposedly found a gold brick four or five miles northwest of the gap, in a cave at the Point [V Mountain]."

The boy did not recognize the brick as gold but kept it to use as a doorstop when he moved to Uvalde long afterward. A young man delivering groceries to his home realized its worth and purchased it from the old Mexican. The money the young man obtained from the bar "got him his first start," said Rankin. Later, he was known as Vice President John Nance Garner.[84]

Other glimpses of the Catholic Cross Cache at V Mountain occasionally have been cited. "A youth, who is said to have a map of the exact location of the cache, came here only to find that it had been removed, with indications that the removal had been made a short time previously," a West Texas newspaper reported on November 11, 1927.[85]

Additional undocumented finds supposedly made in or near the gap include a silver bar, six hundred to eight hundred dollars in gold coins, four or five English coins, and eight or ten gold coins buried in a can.[86] Smokey Swift once encountered "an ol' boy who'd just found a Mexican coin about the size of a dime and dated 1850-something," and witnessed a man and his wife unearthing a cap and ball pistol in a holster ten to twelve feet below ground level.[87] Unquestioned riches finally surfaced in the 1950s when uranium deposits and oil were found on King Mountain,[88]

Site of an extensive treasure dig in 1968 at Castle Gap's west end.

but lost treasure still is what attracts most persons to Castle Gap in search of legend and truth.

The old-timers who have watched many come and go have their own reflections. "We're sure it's out there, but we're all waiting for somebody else to find it," said Ann Clark, longtime gap-area resident and archivist at Rankin Museum in Rankin.[89]

"Well, I kinda believe there must've been something there at one time," said Paul Patterson. "But I'm kinda like Cliff—I think somebody must've got it. I don't believe there's anything now. With all this modern equipment they surely must've found it."[90]

"I'm satisfied that if wages had been paid for all the hours spent looking, it'd be a durn sight more than any treasure buried there," said Billy Rankin. "There's been more time lost hunting it than it was worth if they'd found it. I haven't kicked a rock over looking for it. Now, if I was riding a horse through and he kicked over a rock and there it was, well, I'd stop and reach down and get it—but I'm not going to help him kick any over."[91]

"According to history it's supposed to be there—if somebody hasn't got it," said Smokey Swift. "I wouldn't say it's *not* there, but I wouldn't spend ten minutes looking for it. I've never turned a shovel looking for it and I'm not going to either. It's something people want to believe—they're fanatics. When I'm dead and gone, they'll still be hunting—I'm sure they will."[92]

And the believers will still flock to the gap, to look and wonder and dig in these hills of legend.

Horsehead Crossing

Its shores have known bloodshed for centuries, from the time of Indians afoot to *conquistadores* to westbound wagoners and cattle drovers.

The very name "Horsehead Crossing" suggests the violent history of this ford on the Pecos River, southwest of Crane and twelve miles west-southwest of Castle Gap.

The land in which it lay was even identified with hell by early venturers. "When a bad man dies he goes either to hell or the Pecos," said buffalo hunters of the sandy desert around the moat-like river.[1] These barrens seemed no kinder to a Spanish man of God who, it is said, once rode like the devil to get across this part of hell.[2]

Nothing ever tarried at Horsehead's shores except the coyote and vulture, for Indians, outlaws, rattlers, and the broiling sun turned the crossing into a graveyard. Once, Charles Goodnight counted thirteen graves at the site, with all but one the result of gun battles. Goodnight wrote, "I shall never forget the impression made upon me by those lonely graves, where rested cowboys killed in battle with one another after having fallen out while crossing the long stretch without water."[3]

But crossings were rare throughout the six hundred miles of the Pecos, which heads near Santa Fe, New Mexico, to cross arid land to the Rio Grande in Texas. Void of trees and valley, the river appears suddenly and its banks drop steeply. "If our driver had not been on the lookout we might have been wallowing in its muddy depth," said Waterman L. Ormsby, the only through passenger on the first Butterfield stage in 1858.[4]

Ormsby echoed the observations of other early travelers. "As we approached, we looked in vain for the usual indications of a stream; for, owing to the want of trees or bushes, it was not seen until we were within a few yards of it," said John Russell Bartlett of his 1850 crossing. "The Pecos resembles a great canal rather than a river. . . . [It] has not a single tree or shrub along its banks, nor has it any valley or bottom land near. It runs with a dark rapid current between high perpendicular banks, cut through various strata of clay and sand. On both sides is a vast open prairie, entirely destitute of trees, though scantily covered with mezquit, and other plants of the desert."[5]

Few rivers are more crooked than the Pecos, a fact which confounded some venturers. In the dark of September 26, 1858, as Ormsby and the first Butterfield stage reached Horsehead, the driver cried out and blew a bugle to rouse the stage stand attendant. "We obtained an answer, as we supposed, from the other side of the river, telling us to drive up stream, which advice we followed, when to our astonishment we found ourselves in a camp on the same side of the river," said Ormsby.[6]

Another pioneer awoke one morning in his camp on the Pecos to see his hobbled team half a mile away and across the river. Swimming across six times, he finally reached his horses to find them on the same side as his camp.[7] But cattle drover Sam McGlothing found an advantage in the crooks of the river. Trailing herds up the Pecos to New Mexico, he gained valuable sleep for his hands by bedding the cattle in pronounced river bends that required but a single night rider. Cattle packed the ground so hard that the sites remained grassless for decades.[8]

Because of the channel's moat-like nature, the Pecos proved a natural barrier to man and beast alike. Buffalo were common east of the river, yet virtually nonexistent on the opposite shore.[9] Lured by the sustenance these animals provided, nomadic Indians of the Trans-Pecos may have been the first ever to ford what was to become known as Horsehead Crossing. That tribes situated west of the Pecos hunted buffalo beyond the river is documented: the Jumanos of the Presidio area traveled the Salt Trail to cross the Pecos at Salt Crossing, ten miles above Horsehead,[10] and they gave buffalo hides to a party of early Spanish explorers.[11]

Castle Gap as seen from the probable location of Horsehead Crossing (photo by author, assisted by Richard Posey and Richard Galle).

At least three parties of Spanish explorers passed Horsehead in the sixteenth century. Cabeza de Vaca may have crossed the Pecos at Horsehead in his 1535 trip from the Texas Gulf Coast to Sonora, Mexico, and Antonio de Espejo certainly passed by it in 1583 in following the *Rio de las Vacas*, or Pecos, in a search-and-rescue mission for the Fray Augustin Rodriguez party. The inclusion of 115 horses and mules in Espejo's expedition also would prove significant, for the Indians had begun to acquire mounts through straying, capture, or theft.[12] In 1590 Gaspar Castano de Sosa and 170 persons, spurred by dreams of colonization and riches, followed the Pecos past Horsehead before he was arrested as the leader of an unauthorized expedition.[13]

The next important expedition came almost a century later, when Captain Juan Dominguez de Mendoza, a detachment of soldiers, two missionaries, and several Indian guides and servants reached the Pecos in 1684. Naming it the *Salado* for its briny qualities, they forded the river "at the foot of a great rock" eleven miles downstream of present-day Girvin.[14] In his diary Mendoza described two topographical features that indicate he passed Horsehead. On January 14 he found "a great saline," possibly Juan Cordona Lake, a salt basin ten miles above Horsehead which long had been important to Indians. The next day he camped at a spot on the river from which Castle Gap was greatly evident: "On the other side of the river towards the east, about four leagues [10.5 miles] apparently, there is a little range of mountains; from it extends a small mesa; above this rises another little mesa, which commands a wide prospect."[15]

Downstream two days later, Mendoza recorded an event that presaged Horsehead's future. Passing countryside charred by fire, Mendoza's party halted a league from an Indian rancheria and was greeted by a contingent of Jediondos Indians on foot and horseback.[16] Already the horse had become vital to the Indians of the Southwest, and Mendoza's friendly encounter would be eclipsed by other, more ominous meetings along the Pecos.

By the beginning of the nineteenth century, Comanches were savaging *haciendas* in Mexico by the light of autumn's "Comanche Moon," when rains brought the wasteland grasses alive and left pockets of water. Warriors, their families, horses, and dogs passed over the Comanche War Trail—actually "twenty-five deep, worn, and much used trails [which] made a great road," as Captain William Henry Chase Whiting wrote in 1849[17]—and converged on the Pecos at the narrow Horsehead Crossing. Horsehead became not only the gateway for stolen livestock and other loot but also the "Place of Tears" where captive Mexican children were separated from their mothers and taken in different directions beyond the Pecos.[18]

For a very few, Horsehead meant freedom. In 1855 a supply wagon train rescued two malnourished Mexican boys from the creosote desert. Enslaved by Comanches marauding in Mexico, the youths, ages eight and ten, had escaped at Horsehead by slipping off their mounts as a horse herd was driven across.[19]

Such a crossing may have provided Horsehead with its name, although there are conflicting accounts. When John Salmon "Rip" Ford reached Horsehead in 1849 while surveying the region for a possible wagon route from San Antonio to El Paso, he noted the "large number of skeletons of horse heads lying on both sides of the river." His Comanche guide Guadalupe, a "captain of one of the upper bands," explained their origin: "The crossing, being on the main trail to and from Chihuahua, was a favorite camping place, both going and coming. The first water hole southwest of the crossing was sixty miles distant. Indians returning from Mexico, with stolen horses, would drive them hard to reach water. The loose animals, on reaching the Pecos, would plunge into the stream to quench their thirst, and would drink until they became sick and died."[20]

Another possible origin of the skulls was recounted by early Trans-Pecos settler and historian O. W. Williams: Capturing a herd of horses from Indians in the 1840s, a small detachment of Texas Rangers or soldiers killed them at the Pecos River crossing, then unnamed, to prevent the Indians from reclaiming them. Someone later lined the banks with the skulls to mark where the ford drops without warning from the creosote plain.[21]

No one knows when the first Anglo-Americans approached Horsehead through a haze of sand, but Dr. Henry Connelly and an escort of one hundred men probably crossed the Pecos at the site as they transported seven wagonloads of bullion to modern-day Oklahoma from Chihuahua in 1839. As only Salt Crossing and Horsehead lay along their route, they likely braved the War Trail ford.[22] In 1840 a man named Fellers died while trying to cross,[23] and in 1845 a California-bound emigrant drove a cattle herd through,[24] establishing Horsehead's reputation for treasure, sudden death, and access to the West.

The opening of the western frontier in the late 1840s spawned numerous surveys for a practical wagon route. Captains John C. Hays and Samuel Highsmith and a company of Texas Rangers came first, skirting Horsehead Crossing in September 1848 in a perilous attempt to pioneer a road to El Paso.[25] The discovery of gold in California brought a human flood through Horsehead in 1849. Wagon planks, cattle carcasses, and oxen bones began to drift downstream in the swift waters, and L. B. Harris temporarily operated a ferry—in the form of a waterproof wagon bed—to help emigrants across. Other gold-seekers buoyed their wagons by tying empty water kegs underneath.[26]

Coincident with the gold rush was the expedition of Major Robert S. Neighbors and Rip Ford, who reached Horsehead April 17, 1849. Neighbors reflected on the practicability of Horsehead as a wagon ford. "The banks are low, bottom firm and hard, and the water more shallow than at any point touched by the road," he wrote in a letter dated June 4, 1849. "Yet the depth is too great for fording, and a good ferry boat will be requisite."[27] Ford added: "The stream is not fordable above the [Castle] mountains. The Horse-head Crossing has been used by the Indians for many years. . . . Current not very swift, and horses, in swimming, are borne down but a little distance."[28]

Captain John Murchison and a detachment of one hundred men reached Horsehead in 1849, as did Brevet First Lieutenant Francis T. Bryan's thirty-man surveying party, which had left San Antonio and followed emigrant and Indian trails for almost a month before the Pecos gully suddenly slowed their progress on July 9. Bryan recorded:

> Spent to-day in crossing the Pecos, which was accomplished by making a raft of spare wagon tongues and hounds [wagon support bars], floated by empty water-casks. Everything was thus safely taken over. The Pecos here is a muddy stream, of a dark red color, and, running through the plains, has very much the appearance of a canal. The prairie does not change in appearance in the least as you approach the river, and one is immediately on the river before he is aware of its proximity. The crossing which we used is known as the 'Horse-head crossing'—no doubt from the number of horses' heads which lie scattered near. . . . The banks where we crossed were low, and tolerably firm; but this must be the case only in dry weather. In other places where we approached the water, horses sunk to the girth in the boggy soil, which was of most tenacious clay."[29]

Lieutenant Nathaniel H. Michler and a reconnaissance party skirted Horsehead on the east bank after a January 1850 blizzard,[30] and John Russell Bartlett approached from the east nine months later in surveying the U.S.-Mexico boundary. Scouting at the crossing, Bartlett noted that the east bank was only half the height at this location as elsewhere, allowing "an easy descent," though the opposite bank was steep enough to require leveling with spades. The channel was approximately one hundred feet wide with a maximum depth of four feet[31]—shallow enough for spring-mounted wagons to cross without deluging their contents. Transferring all provisions to such wagons, Bartlett's party crossed the mule-drawn vehicles without incident.

But they encountered disaster in attempting to get the low-set springless wagons across. With a teamster riding a mule in the team of one such wagon, the normally sure-footed animals were swept into swift water, and the leaders turned to swim downstream as the others "began to rear and prance in the water." When the driver of a second half-submerged wagon tried to pass, the current caused the vehicles to collide and the teams to come abreast. "Every moment we expected to be swept away, in which case our lives would have been in great danger," said Bartlett, who was in the first wagon, "as it would have been no easy matter to extricate ourselves from the close wagon." A man on the far bank leaped into the river and attached a picket rope to the lead mules, while several men mounted their horses and sprang into the river, "some to urge the mules toward the shore and others to extricate the two wagons." It took the concentrated effort of the entire party—men on shore pulling on the rope to turn the heads of the lead mules, horsemen in the river urging the teams forward, teamsters lashing the animals—to bring the wagons to the far bank.[32]

Despite the difficulties, Horsehead was about the only crossing available, a fact that led J. H. Young to include the site on his map of the West in 1853.[33]

Likewise it was a rare source of drinking water in the arid Castle Gap region, although accounts of the water's quality differ widely. *Conquistadores* called the Pecos *Puerco*, dirty or piglike, or *Salado*, salty,[34] but when Major Robert S. Neighbors and Rip Ford reached the crossing on April 17, 1849, they found the water good. Ford reported, "The Pecos is a deep, muddy stream, with many bends: the water is cool—has an agreeable taste," though he noted, "the addition of a small piece of roasted prickly pear will cause the deposition of a chocolate colored sediment, leaving the water quite clear."[35] A few months later, however, the surveying party of Colonel Joseph E. Johnston and Lt. S. G. French had a drastically different opinion. "[The] bitter waters carried a mechanical solution with more impurities than perhaps any other river in the South," wrote French. "The only inhabitants of its waters are catfish; and the antelope and the wolf alone visit its dreary, desolate shores; it's avoided even by the Indians."[36] Likely the quality of the water varied seasonally: Cora Dawson Smith, who lived a few miles from Horsehead at the turn of the twentieth century, could not recall a time when the water was suitable for human consumption,[37] but in 1900 former Pecos County Sheriff Will Rooney found the water "wonderful,"[38] and the John O. Carrs claimed that it was "good enough to drink and water their horses" in 1908, 1909, and 1910.[39]

As more emigrants sought new beginnings in California, the government appropriated $200,000 for improvements to the southern route west of the Rio Grande and dispatched a road-building crew led by James B. Leach. Leach's wagon train reached Horsehead and the Pecos on September 29, 1857, and found "a swift and turbid stream about one hundred feet wide, flowing between abrupt precipitous banks, varying from four feet to ten feet in height above the surface of the stream, the waters of which are about ten feet in depth." Inverting two wagon beds over eight barrels, the party crossed their provisions, "the boat being drawn from bank to bank by means of ropes in the hands of the crew. Nothing was lost. . . . The wagons and ambulance were then crossed safely in the same manner, all of the labor being accomplished by the hour of 4:00 p.m. The mules and horses were then driven in, not without some difficulty. They all crossed safely."[40]

The Butterfield Overland Mail did its part in keeping the route to Horsehead well-defined. The first westbound stage rumbled onto the stage stand a quarter of a mile above the crossing in the early morning of September 26, 1858. There, buckskin-clad Henry Skillman, who had been awarded the first contract to transport mail between San Antonio and El Paso in 1850, took the reins. Well-armed with revolvers and bowie knives, the famed frontiersman defied Indians and desolation up and down the Pecos on the Butterfield line in the fall and winter of 1858. In 1859 Skillman ferried across Horsehead as the route was altered to go through Fort Stockton thirty-four miles southwest.[41] Butterfield employees did not always elude Comanche depredations, however. A war party plundered the lonely stage stand of its stock and provisions in 1859, leaving attendants stranded without food until the next stage arrived several days later.[42]

As mail stages and emigrant wagons floated across Horsehead in ever-increasing numbers, the Texas legislature recognized the need for a bridge and granted a charter for its construction in 1860, but the project was abandoned when the Civil War broke out.[43] Crossing Horsehead soon became even more difficult; when the wagon trains of Noah Smithwick and a Dr. Ferguson of Dallas reached the crossing in the spring of 1861, the ferry had been destroyed, water was flush with the banks, and they were forced to trudge down the Pecos to another ford.[44]

Fearing a military operation by six thousand Confederate troops on Forts Franklin and Bliss, James H. Carleton dispatched Yankee troops to Horsehead in late 1862.[45] No confrontation resulted, but the war took troops from Indian duty, and in the 1860s Comanche warriors savaged wagon trains and herds braving this crossing on the War Trail.

The problems of the Samuel Riley Dawson party in the vicinity of Horsehead in 1864 were typical. In Castle Gap on July 28, Dawson's two-year-old daughter died and was buried. Making camp immediately afterward beneath the castle-like boulders, the travelers were besieged by Indians who stole several horses. The emigrants had traveled many miles through arid countryside from the last water source, and the siege tapped their final kegs. Only the brine of the Pecos and Horsehead gave them hope. In a do-or-die effort, several men slipped past the Indians, rode to Horsehead Crossing, and returned with full canteens. Thereafter the war party let them continue unmolested, although the Dawson party did lose one more horse when an Indian woman they had captured escaped on horseback.[46]

Just one year later a similar fate befell a 123-family wagon train which stopped for the night in Castle Gap. Marauding Comanches swooped down on the caravan and drove away all 1,050 head of cattle. When daylight came, the work oxen were driven to the waters of Horsehead, where the thirsty animals stampeded into the river. "The hindmost crowd(ed) the foremost into the treacherous quicksands," R. J. Newton later recalled, "and only nineteen steers, and nine and a half yoke, out of one

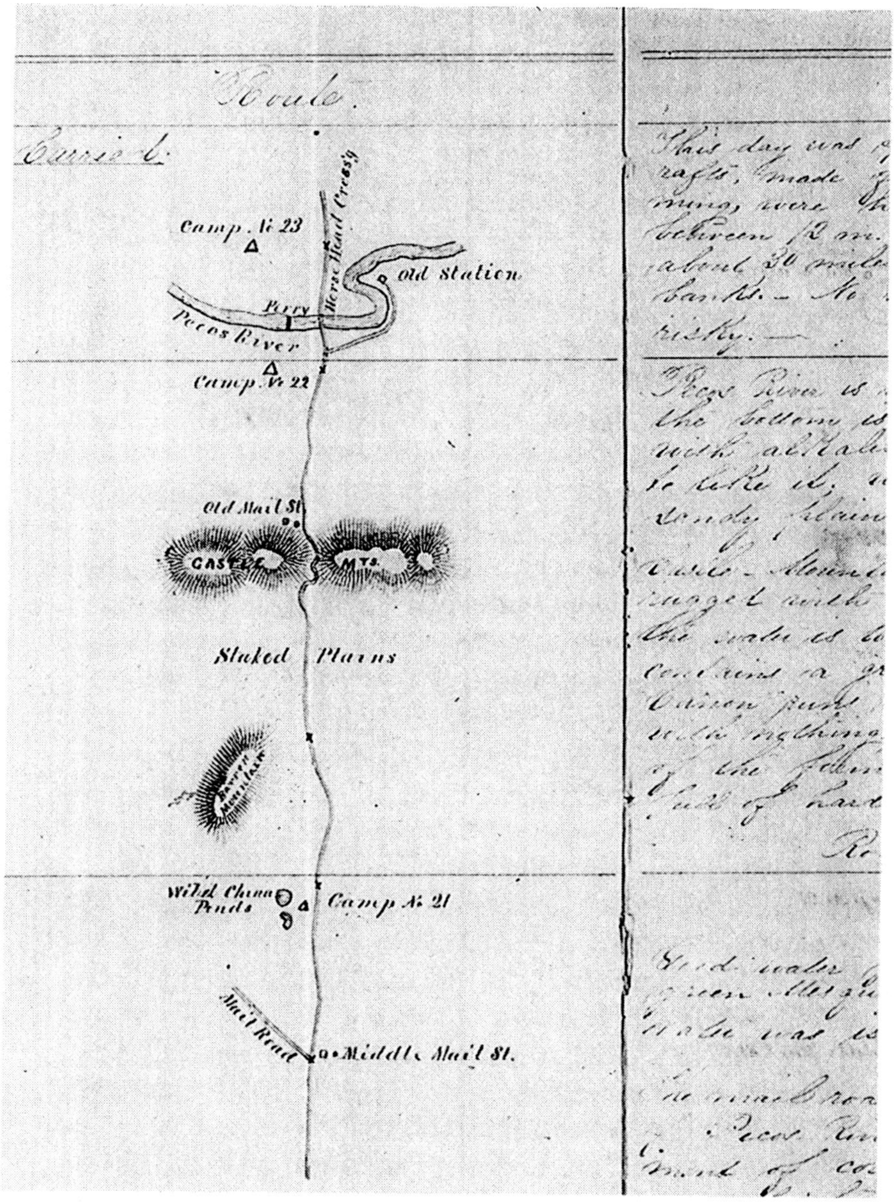

Colonel Thomas B. Hunt's 1869 sketch of the route through Castle Gap and to the Pecos, showing the locations of the Butterfield mail stations, Horsehead Crossing, and the ferry on the Pecos (National Archives).

hundred twenty yoke were saved. Two hundred and twenty-one of our oxen died in the Pecos."[47]

Travelers tried to guard against such catastrophes. Eight men from a settlement near Fort McKavett, skirting Horsehead on their way to the salt fields at Juan Cordona Lake in 1866, took extreme precautions. Watering their oxen at the head of the Middle Concho, they set out toward the Pecos along a seventy-five-mile trail of animal bones, discarded household goods, and broken wagon parts. On the third day they met two men on foot bound for the Middle Concho and filled the walkers' canteens for the long trek east. Well before the oxen could scent the waters of the Pecos, the Fort McKavett men lashed each yoke to a wagon wheel to prevent the animals from rushing into the river and drinking until they died. At Horsehead Crossing they took additional precautions, because "for one square mile, one could have jumped from one carcass to another without touching a foot to the ground," caravan member John Carlile later reported. Tying ropes about an ox, four men allowed it to approach the stream and drink only sparingly, then secured it to a wagon wheel and repeated the procedure with another bovine. Only after they had made camp did the men finally release the oxen and permit them to drink their fill. Although they avoided disaster, even this group witnessed the harshness of Horsehead when a pack of wolves came snarling into camp and killed their dog.[48]

In this barren, sun-scorched land, where water holes were days apart, anyone deprived of oxen or a mount was in desperate straits. More than once a group of Comanches besieged emigrants while other warriors slipped inside camps to make off with supplies and stock. One woman recalled, "Before we reached that stream [the Pecos] the Indians slipped in and stole all our horses. We were driving a number of loose cattle in order to have fresh oxen in case our teams gave out. The poor men were compelled to trudge through the deep scorching sand on foot and drive the cattle." Finding the Pecos a raging torrent, they buoyed a wagon bed with empty water barrels and ferried across.[49]

Cattle drives became a common sight at Horsehead in the

1860s, and with the cattle came intensified depredations along the Comanche War Trail. Few herds crossed unscathed, and the trail bosses and their guards sometimes bore fitting surnames—Peril, Gamel, Gamble. Nineteen-year-old William A. Peril came first, driving a thousand head of cattle from the Texas Hill Country through Horsehead to Presidio del Norte, Mexico, in 1864.[50] There the Chihuahua merchants who had commissioned the drive paid Peril in gold doubloons, which he delivered to the Texas cattlemen. In late fall that year, W. R. St. John, G. T. Reynolds, and S. Huff took a herd from Central Texas to Horsehead and up the Pecos to market in New Mexico—a round trip of three months.[51]

Trail drives to New Mexico were spurred by the American government's Indian policy. By the fall of 1864, almost nine thousand Mescalero Apaches and Navajos faced starvation several hundred miles upstream of Horsehead at Bosque Redondo Reservation, after attempts to make the Indians self-sufficient through agriculture failed. With three thousand Indians destined to die from malnourishment and nightmarish living conditions,[52] the government was forced to seek beef.

Charles Goodnight and Oliver Loving staged a heroic cattle drive in the spring of 1866 and firmly established the legendary trail through Castle Gap to Horsehead and up the Pecos to Fort Sumner, New Mexico, but they paid a great price. Three hundred beeves dropped of thirst. Scores were left to die on the banks of Horsehead Crossing, and hundreds more plunged into the Pecos River. A year later on the same trail, Loving himself suffered a fatal wound in a fight with Comanches.

When Goodnight and his cowboys first approached Horsehead Crossing in the spring 1866 drive, they drove the stronger animals—approximately two-thirds of the herd—ahead. After three days without water, the cattle became uncontrollable and stampeded blindly into the crossing. "Those behind pushed the ones in the lead right on across before they had time to stop and drink," Goodnight later recalled. "I was in the lead and as soon as they all cleared the river, I turned them back and they readily went in again, drinking as they swam back. They crossed in such volume and force that they impeded the current, and the water was halfway up the bank in a perfect flood."[53]

Goodnight returned to assist Loving in herding the remaining five hundred head to the crossing, but the wind shifted and from miles away the scent of water drove the animals mad with thirst. "They were virtually crazy and would go either to the water or not at all," Goodnight recounted. "All hands on one side could not turn them. The point of the river for which they were headed was like a ditch, with banks from six to ten feet high. When they reached the river they never halted, but poured right over the bank and the remainder of the horses went with them." For two days cowboys tried to pull the animals from the quicksands of the Pecos—"the graveyard of the cowman's hopes," Goodnight called it—but the unscalable banks and grasping sands claimed more than a hundred head. In 1867 hundreds more were lost to stampede and Indians at the crossing.[54] Goodnight, however, did not give up easily, and in the next eight years he watered thousands of beeves at Horsehead.[55]

Other men also found markets in New Mexico. In the summer of 1866 Charles L. Pyron encountered a herd of ten thousand beeves headed up the Pecos.[56] That December, John Chisum—known as the "Jingle-bob King" because he marked his cattle with ear slits so deep the lower halves dangled—successfully drove six hundred steers by Horsehead and along the Pecos to Bosque Grande, near modern-day Roswell, New Mexico. He was not always so fortunate. He once started toward the Pecos with 1,100 steers, purchased at eighteen dollars a head in Coleman County, and reached Fort Stanton, New Mexico, with a herd of only six. In 1872, his cowboys were forced to drive four thousand steers up the Pecos to Bosque Grande by foot for fifteen days, after Indians made off with all but the four horses ridden on night guard.[57]

Goodnight's most direct competition, however, was Andy M. Adams of Fort Union, New Mexico, who contracted with the government in the spring of 1867 to drive Texas steers to Fort Sumner at 2.5 cents per pound on foot. But no cattleman ever met with greater misfortune, and the Pecos ford in the midst of the Comanche War Trail proved the focal point of disaster. Trail boss George W. Hepburn and nine cowhands left the Middle Concho with 656 Adams beeves on April 17 and reached Horsehead Crossing the night of April 23. Before the veil of darkness had lifted the following morning, a Comanche war party of fifty to seventy-five warriors ambushed the cowboys and drove away 365 head of cattle. A few hours later thirty-eight steers were recovered, but a second raid by Indians on the twenty-sixth cost Hepburn fifteen horses.

Twelve days later Adams's second herd fell prey to Kickapoos long before it reached the Pecos, but the cowhands of his third and largest herd, driven by Joel D. Hoy, endured the most scalp-raising nightmare of all. Hoy, with his wife and four children riding beside him in a light spring wagon, left Spring Creek on May 15 in the dust of 1,014 beeves. When the animals scented water upon reaching Castle Gap nine days later, they charged uncontrollably to Horsehead. The following afternoon, 150 Indian warriors attacked Hoy at the crossing, divided his herd and mounts, and drove them across the river. Three cowhands were wounded, as well as Hoy's wife, who loaded guns and tended to the injured until she collapsed from a wound in the thigh. In desperation Hoy and the able men pulled and pushed a wagon carrying the wounded upstream to the abandoned Butterfield stage stand. There the war party besieged them, and when one man tried to escape by swimming the river, he drowned.

At the same time, a herd driven by Ben Gooch and his hands reached Horsehead and became similar victims. The two groups endured three days of desperation before being rescued by a hundred-man prospecting party, led by Jacob Schnively and Colonel William Dalrymple,[58] which had left Coleman County on May 1, 1867, to search for gold "in the Sierra Nevada Mountains on the Rio Grande River." As they approached the Pecos, they saw fifteen or twenty men clad in white fleeing on horseback through the creosote downstream—Indians wearing linen shirts stolen from a wagon train.[59]

The gold hunters outfitted Hoy with a wagon and work steers so he could continue to Fort Sumner, and Hoy managed to recover sixty steers which the Indians had dropped. Still, the losses were staggering—954 steers, 23 horses and mules, and 4 oxen. But that was not the end of Adams's misfortunes. His fourth herd left Llano on May 15 in the charge of twenty-seven-year-old Orville A. Oatman, who hired ten cowhands to drive eight hundred beeves to the Pecos and New Mexico. On May 28, for the third time in a month, 100 to 150 Comanche and Kiowa warriors struck at Horsehead Crossing. This time they got the entire herd and the remuda of fifteen horses and mules. The cowboys survived by taking refuge in a rock-lined sinkhole but were left in straits when the Indians burned two wagons containing $2,650 in supplies. Fortunately, the cowhands came across a steer wounded by an arrow and butchered it.[60]

As reports of such depredations by Indians filtered back to civilization, the U.S. Army took measures to protect emigrants and cowboys against attack. The scouting party under Lieutenant Peter Martin Boehm of Camp Charlotte, near the headwaters of the Middle Concho, found Indian signs (but no warriors) at Horsehead and Juan Cordona Lake on June 18–19, 1867, and a second detachment of twenty-one men was dispatched from the camp five days later to provide the first military escort of a cattle herd to the crossing.[61] On July 29, Captain George H. Gamble and forty members of the Ninth Cavalry stalked Indians along the Comanche War Trail to Horsehead and thwarted a possible attack on two large cattle herds bound for Fort Sumner.[62] The Ninth Cavalry became a frequent sight at the ford during the last three months of 1867,[63] and in April 1868 a company of infantry briefly set up stakes where cattle carcasses defined the boundaries of the moat.[64]

But the raids on wagon trains and herds continued. Cattle drover Judge Bourland of Llano County, for example, lost his herd of 1,700 beeves and almost his life during an attack at Horsehead sometime in the 1860s; an arrow ripped through his coonskin cap and pierced his skull.[65] In that same period warriors drove away the herd of James Ranck of Mason in the sands between Castle Gap and Horsehead.[66] W. E. Cureton lost eleven saddle horses to Indians at the crossing in the fall of 1867,[67] but Ben Ficklin fared better that same season and was not bothered as he carried the mail from San Antonio across Horsehead to El Paso.

In 1868, Ben Gooch of Mason County and Robert Casey lost most of two herds and their work oxen in an Indian raid that demonstrated the fortitude of Casey's wife. Emigrating to New Mexico from Menard County with 1,800 beeves and a small flock of sheep, Casey, his wife, and their five children joined forces on the trail with Gooch's cattle outfit. Camped at Horsehead Crossing, the groups were startled at dawn by Indians on the attack. Low on ammunition, the cowhands were forced to watch helplessly as the beeves were herded across the creosote sands. But Mrs. Casey refused to yield her flock so easily, and when warriors dismounted to drive the sheep away, she ran out from the wagon, pounded on a tin pan, and called her pets by name. The familiar summons for salt and shelled corn turned the sheep toward the safety of camp and upended their would-be herders.[68]

W. C. Cochran didn't lose a single steer to Indians as he drove a herd up the Pecos to New Mexico and Colorado in 1870, but when the cowhands reached Horsehead on the return trip, forty Indians stampeded the horses and left only two mules secured to a wagon. The men had to trudge on foot for days to reach Fort Concho at present-day San Angelo.[69]

G. F. Banowsky also encountered Indians while trying to drive three thousand cattle from Mason County to Colorado in 1871. Camping at Horsehead near the ruins of the stage stand, the cowpunchers heard war cries and dived into the adobe refuge to escape the arrows as their attackers drove away steers and horses. By the time the storm of dust subsided, Banowsky's herd consisted of a single yoke of oxen.[70]

Enough perils accompanied Horsehead even without the Comanches. Cattle died by the thousands along the waterless trail to the east, and those which survived often went mad at the scent of water, like Goodnight's first herd. Four hundred head driven by Rube Grey of San Saba County plummeted over the canal-like banks to drown or succumb to quicksand,[71] while deadly salt playas between Castle Gap and Horsehead Crossing also became crowded with carcasses.

Even if emigrants and cattle drovers escaped the hazards imposed by Indians and the terrain, they still had to contend with outlaws. Few places in the Old West were as infamous for their gunslingers and horse thieves as the Pecos from Horsehead to the New Mexico line, and along that stretch desperados commonly preyed upon westward-bound pioneers, freighters, and the earliest ranchers. The gun became a way of life and death for the good and bad alike, eliciting such epitaphs as:

> On the rocky banks of the Pecos
> They will lay him down to rest
> With his saddle for a pillow
> And his gun across his breast.[72]

The very word "pecos" even entered the vocabulary of the cowboy as a verb denoting brutal murder: to "pecos" a man was to gun him down and roll his body over the bank of the Pecos River.[73]

Horsehead itself was a favorite place for outlaws. For example, twelve members of a Mexican gang waited two weeks for a likely prey in the summer of 1868, then stole four horses from cattle drovers at the crossing. Nine of the outlaws were captured by Captain Gamble and the Ninth Cavalry on August 31, but the other three escaped toward Mexico with the horses.[74] In July 1871 Samuel Farkswell and William Henry were imprisoned at Fort Stockton after being charged with stealing horses at the crossing from a Mr. Peacock.[75] Jesse Evans and another member of his gang, Charlie Graham, hid out at Horsehead in June 1880 after they robbed the Fort Davis store, had a $1,100 bounty levied on their heads, and eluded a citizens' mob which claimed Graham's brother, Bud.[76]

Despite the treacherous Pecos and the outlaws and Indians which ruled its shores, a succession of true-to-life Gil Favors were to "move 'em out" toward Horsehead in the final three decades of the nineteenth century. Sometimes the herds were vast; Captain Joseph Rendlebrock and men from Company G, Fourth Cavalry, escorted a single herd of twelve thousand steers from Fort Concho to Horsehead and up the Pecos in the summer of 1872.[77] In 1874 alone, 110,000 beeves trampled the crossing's banks.[78]

When Colonel Ranald Mackenzie defeated the Comanches and Kiowas in the Texas Panhandle in 1874, the War Trail to Mexico effectively closed for those tribes. But Apache raiding parties still occasionally terrorized Horsehead through the late 1870s. In the fall of 1877 a stage driver was slain and telegraph line cut along the route from Fort Concho to the Pecos, and on November 11, Mescalero Apaches bearing mail sacks and telegraph wire were sighted near the crossing. The same warriors likely stole four horses three days later from a Mr. Keasy, who grazed cattle on the open range near Horsehead. On December 19, fourteen Apaches swooped down upon a cattle outfit at Horsehead and drove away fourteen horses, and though cowhands reclaimed two of the animals, they were stolen a second time by the Indians. Fort Stockton's forces were dwindling to the point that not enough horses were available for pursuit, and the raiders had ridden far down the War Trail toward Mexico before a Pecos County sheriff's posse could be organized.[79]

As Indian raids faded into history in the late 1870s, the first permanent ranches were established near Horsehead. In 1879 Henry Byler and Dawson Word formed the TX Ranch, which encompassed forty miles of riverfront on each side of the Pecos and grazed thirty thousand cattle. Headquarters were a mile upstream of the crossing.[80]

Even without the threat of war lances or outlaws, Horsehead remained treacherous to wayfarers heeding Horace Greeley's admonition. Walter Smith, who later herded sheep along the Pecos, rode through a raging blizzard to cross Horsehead in 1883,[81] and that same decade the menacing channel claimed the ox of an English immigrant when the hobbled animal wandered from camp in search of water and plunged over the bank.[82] En route from Brown County to Fort Davis in 1887, three-year-old C. C. "Cal" Childress faced Horsehead on its own terms—clinging to his grandfather's back as the man swam across. But the wagons required more preparation: "We tied the wagon beds down to the frames, swam the horses across, and took the ropes and then pulled the wagons across," Childress recalled in 1968.[83]

Horsehead also lured some of the legendary figures of the Old West: then-freighter Judge Roy Bean, who failed to be discouraged by river damage to his wagons when his whiskey survived intact[84]; beekeeper Honey Allen and his combs bound for the land of milk and honey in New Mexico[85]; Buffalo Bill Cody in 1882[86]; Black Jack Ketchum in the early 1890s.[87] Horsehead even proved to be the point at which Robert Powe cast a bull branded "Murder" into a herd bound for Montana in 1896; five years earlier, shaken cowhands on a roundup east of Fort Davis had burned the mark across the ribs of the animal after an outsider gunned down Powe's father in a dispute over who owned it.[88]

The land of the Pecos was raw and untamed in the late 1890s, and while most settlers still avoided the greasewood plains, a few far-sighted men saw potential grazing land in this "bad man's hell." Samuel Toliver "Tol" Dawson, who as a four-year-old in 1864 had survived Indian attack in Castle Gap and the waters of Horsehead in heading west from Buffalo Gap, was one such man. His parents had taken him as far as Socorro, New Mexico, before returning to Texas to settle Odessa. Dawson and his wife also lived briefly in Jones County, where a daughter, Cora Hollis Dawson, was born in 1893. When Cora was four he began ranching adjacent to Horsehead on the east side of the Pecos.

"He had cattle and horses," she remembered in 1982. "There

were no fences. They dug a well down between Castle Gap and Horsehead Crossing. They didn't have any way of getting a well besides digging it by hand."

With a permanent residence fifty miles away in Odessa, Dawson seasonally ran livestock between Castle Gap and Horsehead Crossing until the Four-Section Act in 1903 forced him to stake a claim. "You could settle on four sections, but you had to put a house on it, make improvements, and live on it as much as six months," his daughter recounted. "He paid a dollar an acre with forty years to pay it out. He took up four sections, and half a dozen of his kinfolks more or less took up four sections each, so they finally ended up with about thirty-two sections."

The squirming Pecos formed the western boundary of the Dawson Ranch, and throughout the summers of her childhood Cora Dawson roamed its banks. The ancient wagon road from Castle Gap ran directly through the ranch to the river, which carried so much water in the early years of the twentieth century that Horsehead was used but infrequently. "Horsehead Crossing was half a mile above our property. There was lots of water and lots of people drowned there. One fellow that worked for my daddy drowned there—he tried to cross it on horseback and something went wrong. There was plenty of quicksand too. I helped get many a cow out of that riverbed."[89]

In 1904 high water left cattle drover Sam McGlothing no choice but to bed down his cattle six months at Horsehead before he could cross them.[90] Cliff Newland, T. R. Long, and the Curries of Glasscock County, meanwhile, crossed ten thousand sheep on wagon beds tied end-to-end across the river that same year. "It was deep, and where you went off, the bank was just as straight up on [the east] side as a wall," said Newland, adding that a person could trail the wagon road no closer than two hundred yards to the crossing. "They had a place that was cut down in there just wide enough [for] wagons to go down.... You went downstream a little and come out. Generally, there was a little gravel island ... and there was a little quicksand. If you stopped the team to water, it would be stuck to 'em—not enough to hurt 'em. . . . Right there at Horsehead there was a vacant circle, an open place—there wasn't a tree."[91]

In 1910 Cora Dawson married J. W. Smith, a cowboy who broke horses on the Dawson Ranch, and the newlyweds took up fulltime residence in a land shunned by man for centuries. Prior to her death in 1982, Mrs. Smith was likely the last surviving person to have crossed Horsehead in the old days of ambushes, gunfights, and non-mechanized travel. Even decades later, her eyes blazed vividly with memories of the crossing: "Wagons could get down to the water there—you couldn't see the banks because the river was too full," she said. "We had a neighbor lived across there, and we had a cattle mixup—there weren't any fences. We used to have lots of fun running our cattle back and forth across the river." When she crossed Horsehead by wagon, she took the same precautions as the earliest emigrants. "We tied the wagon bed down to the running gears so it wouldn't slip off, wouldn't float off. The horses could swim it—there wouldn't be much of them sticking up, but they'd go through there. We went across on wagon a good many times."

Mrs. Smith sometimes found arrowheads, broken dishes, and other artifacts at the site of the stage stand and in the flats between the river and Castle Gap. "I never did find anything of value; I never did look for anything. I guess we would have found plenty if we had known what we were looking for."[92]

By then the horse skulls long since had decayed and the graves noted by Goodnight had become lost. No longer did a mass of wagons approach from Castle Gap, though there were occasional emigrant vehicles. But the bones of bovines still evidenced Horsehead's violent past.

John O. Carr and his wife crossed Horsehead three times between 1908–1910 en route from Sherwood on Spring Creek to a ranch near El Capitan in the Guadalupe Mountains. "What they talked about more than anything else was the dustiness, the drudgery," said their son Billy Carr. "Even at that date, they ran across straggly Indians involved in thievery." With Horsehead a three-day trip by one-horse hack from Sherwood, the Carrs relied on its waters to provide a comfortable camp. "At that time the water was good enough for them to drink and water their horses. Usually there was a lot of grass around there and the horses could graze. It was three more nights to Guadalupe Peak. I remember Dad talking about doing a lot of prowling when they'd camp at Horsehead Crossing. He talked about seeing lots of bones and Indian artifacts."[93]

Herman Zeitler of Girvin, born in 1915, remembered the bones, too, from living on a farm two miles west of Horsehead at age eight or nine. "There used to be lots of antelope there, but the water turned bad and they all starved," he said. "They said you could walk on skeletons there for miles."

Zeitler also recalled bands of gypsies at Horsehead during the 1920s. "They used to come through here in wagons, thirty-five or forty of them, and they'd cross there. They'd go in the house and just take anything they wanted. Cowboys crossed there too, because there weren't any roads in this part of the country." In Zeitler's time the Pecos ran half-bank full in the summer and overflowed in winter, and quicksand still was abundant. The surrounding land, as well, was much the same as it had been for centuries. "It was all open country. Everybody just ran their stock down there—there weren't any fences until way up in New Mexico."[94]

The cattle whose hooves had trampled out a broad roadway between Castle Gap and Horsehead during the peak years of the Goodnight-Loving Trail were long since gone, but a few small herds still swam Horsehead well into the 1920s. Buck Kelton drove a Scharbauer herd from Midland County to Horsehead and beyond to a ranch south of Fort Stockton in 1923, while the Cowdens used the ford to transport cottonseed cake from Girvin to their holdings east of the Pecos as late as 1927.[95]

With a history so rich, it is not surprising that Horsehead Crossing has had its share of treasure stories—lost bullion, misplaced rifles, stashed booty. Like its sister site of Castle Gap, Horsehead has attracted treasure hunters from afar who believe gold is waiting near the twists of the Pecos. Fueled by the belief that Mexican Emperor Maximilian's legendary treasure disappeared here rather than at Castle Gap, seekers have dug in the riverbanks more than a century for a fortune in silver and gold bullion, vessels, and coins. The Horsehead variant of the legend asserts that decades after it was cached the treasure was seized by Claude "Dave" Shepherd, outlaw, ex-con, and son and nephew of two former Jesse James Gang members who supposedly served in Mexico under Maximilian. According to folklore, in March 1867 the two elder Shepherds guided fifteen wagons guarded by thirty soldiers up from Mexico into Texas en route to Galveston. A gunbattle erupted after a drinking bout at Horsehead Crossing, and only the two men survived. Inside the wagons they found fifteen iron chests containing $200,000 in coins, which they cached in shallow caves along the river. The brothers took up residence in Missouri but returned frequently to the Pecos to replenish their finances until they were killed in an agricultural machinery accident in Jackson County, Missouri, in 1887.

In July 1909 Dave Shepherd supposedly came to Horsehead and enlisted the aid of land developer W. P., or W. R., Draper and a railroad foreman to search for the treasure. Blasting open every crevice in the cavernous bluffs of a gully known as Rattlesnake Draw on the northeast side of the Pecos, the men spilled out rattlers and finally rusty boxes containing four thousand silver and gold coins.[96]

Whether or not Shepherd or Maximilian's wealth-laden wagons ever existed is lost in lore, but that has not deterred generations of treasure seekers. Legend speaks not only of Maximilian's riches, but of several mule loads of gold cached nearby, as George Brown of Coyanosa (born in 1912) attested to,[97] or the twenty-seven wagonloads of wealth Herman Zeitler heard had been cast into a well on the Pecos's banks.[98] Legend even suggests that an armory of firearms, purchased in New Mexico in 1904 by Frank Ingram at the culmination of a cattle drive, lies buried in buffalo robes at the crossing.[99]

One person who firmly believed lost treasure lurked at Horsehead was Arkansas City, Kansas, resident George W.

Viehle, whose desire to solve Horsehead's secrets was exceeded only by his own tall tales. According to Paul Patterson of Crane, "He'd been down in Chihuahua City, Mexico, talking to the descendants of the Apaches who were supposed to have ambushed some of those Missourians that robbed and took Maximilian's gold. He had a lot of Geiger counters and equipment. He was an old man then, and said he had found $50,000 worth of money for the government—buried treasure somewhere else. He was a nice old fellow; everything was going along real smooth. And then one day he said, 'Would you think I was crazy if I told you I talked to Billy the Kid day before yesterday?' " Patterson grinned in recollection. "I didn't answer that one. But in a minute I said, 'Well, it'd be kinda remarkable, because most people think he got killed in 1881.' "[100]

Actual finds have been somewhat more modest than the legends. I. C. "Tiny" Earp of Crane, who roamed the Pecos from the time he was a boy in 1936, found some evidence of Horsehead's brutal past. "I was helping a fellow . . . work sheep one time. He and his son and I were riding together and we found an old pistol down there real close to Horsehead Crossing. When we first saw it, it looked like it was all intact. But it had lain in that old salt and gyp down there so long, that as we picked it up it began to disintegrate."[101]

In the late 1920s technology and floods did what Indians, outlaws, and the harshness of the wilderness never had been able—they forced the abandonment of the crossing once lined by skulls. And with frightening swiftness, all signs of Horsehead Crossing faded, becoming lost in channel-altering deluges, terrain-wrenching sandstorms, trail-concealing creosote. When Billy Rankin first rode to Horsehead as a young man in 1928, it already had become an uncertain crossing. "It had straight up banks and even though I was riding a river horse I wouldn't dare to go on across it," he recounted.[102]

Horsehead quickly moved from geographical presence to western lore, and some who didn't cross it when they had the opportunity now wish they had. Paul Patterson, born in 1909, recalled, "My brother John, Jimmy James, Hermon Carter and a fellow named Walter Edwards—the cook—we took five hundred head of horses from Rankin and Mertzon to Orla. We crossed the bridge at Girvin and if it hadn't been for a jackass we might've had to cross at Horsehead. That was 1931. We were dreading, hoping we wouldn't have to go fifteen miles upriver and cross at Horsehead, but I wish now we'd've done it. That would've been something historic. These horses were as wild as snakes, and we had an old jack that didn't want to lead us on. They whipped him at Big Lake when we left the stockpens and beat him at Rankin. He held these horses up at the bridge there at the Pecos, and man, we were really looking for an out of some kind. But this old jack, he just kept pecking along and directly we heard his feet pattering on this bridge. Those wild fillies just began to follow him by twos and we never spilled one."[103]

A marker was placed on the Pecos in 1936 to designate the historic ford, but then and now some swear it is in the wrong place. Horsehead's a half-mile downstream, they'll say, or the same distance against the flow, or maybe a quarter-mile north or three miles south. Aerial photographs still detail the wagon roads of a previous era approaching the Pecos from either side, but they are not apparent from the ground.

Finding real evidence of the crossing takes effort. Long after its location had become an enigma, treasure hunter Cliff Newland unearthed traces of the crossing's historic past when he found a cut in the bluffs which had been partially filled by a fresno crew. Digging into the sand, he unearthed cattle bones, and nearby, in an area where the true old-timers claimed a saloon and grocery store once had been, he discovered a pint whiskey bottle, faded to a rich pink.[104]

Today Horsehead Crossing is but a phantom. The waters which once raged between its banks are slow, sullen, green with moss, and polluted with oilfield residue. The shores once trampled by hooves now glint silvery from mineral deposits and bear salt cedars. Creosote and mesquite still crowd its rim, but the howls of coyotes have replaced the war cries of Comanches, and blowing sand rasps through the flats where emigrant wagons used to rumble. The skulls of Horsehead have disappeared into dust and legend.

A solitary man dwarfed by the sea of white at Juan Cordona Lake.

Juan Cordona Lake

The animal which became trapped in the mire served as a monument to the white mineral of Juan Cordona Lake.

It was the 1920s, and Cowden Ranch cowboys rode hard across Pecos country sand dunes in pursuit of a mustang that was

too fast for their lariats. Then a rider noticed the chase was leading them to the salt lake Juan Cordona, the bed of which was nothing but muck this time of year, and he shouted an idea to his companions.

They headed the mustang down the banks of the lake where it would have to yield to their ropes. But the mustang splashed onward into the shallows and made for the far shore. Reining their mounts to a stop, the cowboys watched helplessly as the stallion struggled farther into the mire which finally pinned it wither-deep.

The cowhands shook their heads; Juan Cordona Lake had claimed a gruesome sentinel which, preserved by the salt, would testify of nature's dominion to future generations.[1]

Situated two miles north of the Pecos River and fifty miles southwest of Midland, the lake consists of two basins, the larger of which is two and a half miles by three-quarters of a mile in size. A neck eight hundred feet wide connects that basin to one half as big. Sand dunes rise thirty-five to fifty-five feet above Juan Cordona's white flats on three sides, but on the fourth the terrain rises only five vertical feet, except for island knolls, between the lake and the Pecos.

The lake amid desert seems barren, but its life-sustaining salt brought men from afar even in prehistoric times. Through the gateway of Castle Gap fifteen miles east they came from Central Texas; along the crooked Pecos they came from both north and south; and from the Chihuahuan Desert to the southwest they approached along an ancient route. Viewed from the air, the lake in centuries past would have resembled the hub of a wheel with spokes—trails—leading to it from all directions.

Formed by capillary action over a bulge in the subterranean salt dome, the lake lay within a great forest eighteen thousand years ago. Pine, spruce, and piñon crowded the stream courses of the Llano Estacado and Pecos country and left their pollen to fossilize in the lake bed and banks. When the climate changed 11,200 years ago, the pines and spruces yielded, leaving only piñons to shade the first known inhabitants of West Texas—

Midland Man. One of these prehistoric Indians, who actually was a woman, did not completely disappear; her bones lay fossilizing for millennia until they were unearthed in Midland County sandhills forty-five miles northeast of the lake in 1953. In a mid-1950s effort to recreate the environment in which she lived, paleontologists Dr. Fred Wendorf of the Laboratory of Anthropology in Santa Fe and Dr. Ulf Hafsten of Norway recovered fossil pollen from playas on the Llano Estacado and Juan Cordona Lake that attested to the coniferous environment of which the basin once was a part.[2]

Midland Man, or other nomadic hunters of her kind, well may have scraped salt from the lake and worn footpaths to it from all directions. For not only did the basin supply a vital bodily nutrient, but it provided a means whereby meat could be preserved. That dual benefit is what enticed the Jumano Indians to beat out a trail to the lake from their *pueblos* and croplands at modern-day Ojinaga-Presidio, where the Rio Conchos tumbles into the Rio Grande. By foot, it was a journey of twelve days to the good gravel crossing on the Pecos four to five miles east-northeast of Buena Vista and adjacent to the basin. Once across, they cut salt for domestic use and for barter with the tribes of the Rio Conchos and, hunting lances in hand, began scanning the prairie and mesaland east of the Pecos for *cibola*—buffalo. That shaggy beast generally did not range south and west of the river; the treacherous waters of the canal and severity of the terrain proved natural barriers.

The Jumanos' route to Juan Cordona came to be called the Salt Trail and the Pecos ford the Salt Crossing. From the confluence of the Rio Grande and Rio Conchos at present-day Presidio, the trail went north up Alamito Creek, cut through the Davis Mountains at Paisano Pass, skirted Kokernot Springs near Alpine, passed Leoncita Spring, Leon Water Holes and then Comanche Springs at present-day Fort Stockton, and went down Diamond Y Draw to the Pecos. The same route and others were used by Indians astride horses starting in the late sixteenth century. Travois ruts remained apparent as late as 1884.[3]

Where something of value lies, greed often brings bloodshed, and Juan Cordona Lake apparently followed suit. The battles over salt are unrecorded but likely date to ancient times when Jumanos would encounter Apaches at the site. Numerous Indian artifacts and weapons uncovered by amateur archaeologists testify to skirmishes at its shores.[4]

Saddle stock first traveled the Salt Trail in 1583 as 115 horses and mules transported the expedition of Spaniard Antonio de Espejo, who explored Arizona and New Mexico before turning south along the Pecos. Near Salt Crossing he came upon three Jumano hunters, who detailed "many watering places in creeks and marshes" which he would pass en route to the Rio Conchos and Mexico.[5]

In 1684 Captain Juan Dominguez de Mendoza struck the Salt Trail at present-day Presidio and followed it toward the Pecos. Three times Mendoza mentioned the *camino*, or road, which he said was "level without stones, covered with much pasturage and with mesquites and other kinds of wood." In mid-January Mendoza reached the Pecos to hunt and explore a "great saline" situated one league (2.63 miles) across the river and "abundantly supplied with salt in white and good grains."[6] That description and recorded distance north of the Pecos, as well as the fact that he had been following the Salt Trail, identify the saline with Juan Cordona Lake. However, Mendoza's additional notation that it lay between "a high hill and a mesa" led J. W. Williams to believe it was a smaller saline known as Soda Lake near modern-day Girvin.[7]

Spain continued to show interest in the salt supplies well into the 1700s, for a marker bearing the name of King Philip V—the country's ruler from 1700 to 1746—reportedly was discovered at Juan Cordona Lake in 1932.[8] And in 1760, when Captain Rabage y Teran of the *presidio* at present-day Menard sent forty-one men westward toward Santa Fe, they reached the Pecos and rediscovered two salt lakes, one undoubtedly Juan Cordona.[9]

To the Spanish and then Mexican colonists who settled in

the Presidio-El Paso region as well as south of the Rio Grande, the salt deposit assumed just as great an importance as it had to the early Indians. It became the principal supply for all of northern Mexico, and in early spring and late fall—when the end of rainy seasons left more salt atop the lake—they came over many of the same Indian trails with seventy-five to one hundred carrettas pulled by oxen. These wooden-wheeled carts, entirely void of metal, had tongues made of tree trunks, while the felloes of the wheels were lashed in with rawhide. Upon reaching Juan Cordona Lake, the Mexicans camped and established temporary settlements on the southern shore.[10] Although they traveled without fear of Indians, with whom they bartered, folklore accounts persist that the Mexicans sometimes fought among themselves. Some old-timers in the Crane area still tell of human skeletons being unearthed from the salt.[11]

Many English-speaking colonists undertook the arduous journey westward for salt and used the lake's northeast shore as a base of operation,[12] but it wasn't until after Texas proclaimed itself a sovereign nation in 1836 that Juan Cordona Lake received its name. Throughout its recorded history, the basin has been referred to as Cordona, Cordova, Cardona, or Cardova, and some have claimed its namesake gained a grant to the site from Spain or Mexico. However, State of Texas General Land Office archives clearly show that Juan Cardona held rights to the lake by virtue of a headright first class grant issued by land commissioners of Bexar County, Republic of Texas, on February 6, 1838.[13]

Qualifications for eligibility for such grants give clues to the life of Cardona, whose handwritten name on the document has been misread into varied spellings of the lake. He had arrived in Texas prior to March 2, 1836, and was a married man. Possibly he was the Juan Cardon to whom Mexico granted a league of land in Sterling C. Robertson's Colony in present-day Bell County on December 27, 1834.[14] With that, history closes its books on Juan Cardona, for prior to applying for the league (4,423.4 acres) and labor (177.1 acres) due him from the Republic of Texas, he apparently sold his rights. Juan Cardona neither chose the land nor, in all probability, even saw the place that would bear his name.

His assignees, William H. Steele and Ludvic, or Ludovic, Colquhoun, presented evidence to the Bexar County land commission in February 1838 that Cardona was eligible for the grant, and they received Headright Certificate #151. Steele and Colquhoun, having right to any league and labor of public land in then-vast Bexar County, set their sights on the salt deposit, commissioned a survey, and registered their claim with the Republic of Texas.[15]

On May 22, 1838, Steele sold his interest to I. Pickney Henderson, who in turn sold his share to Colquhoun on March 8, 1845.[16] Though Colquhoun was sole owner after 1845, he never tried to establish dominion, for the lake continued to be frequented by Indians, Mexicans, and Texans. He may have realized his inability to secure such a remote and traditional salt source against free access.

In January 1839 the Republic of Texas Congress considered nationalizing salt lakes between the Rio Grande and Nueces River. Some lawmakers wanted to halt the acquisition of mineral sources like Juan Cordona Lake by private citizens, but the measure did not pass; most legislators were of the opinion that "the land and lakes in question was not within the limits of Texas yet" and the republic could not easily establish sovereignty.[17]

When the Mexican-American War erupted in 1846, Juan Cordona Lake became a battleground of controversy. In the 1848 Treaty of Guadalupe Hidalgo ending the war, Mexico gave up all claim to the state of Texas. However, under Mexican rule the state owned minerals with free access to the public, and an oral tradition still known in the Crane area holds that Mexico retained rights to Juan Cordona Lake's salt.[18]

Since the treaty itself does not address the matter, Mexico probably never gained legal rights, but the Mexicans of Chihuahua unquestionably considered it their privilege by precedent to take salt from the lake. They continued their twice-a-year trips to Juan Cordona through most of the nineteenth century.

In 1848 the Chihuahua Trail, a trade route between Chihuahua City, Mexico, and San Antonio, opened and followed the Salt Trail from Presidio to Fort Stockton. From their base in Presidio came several commercial freighters, known as "trail drivers," among them Juan Cano, Sr., John Davis, William Brooks, John Burgess, and August Santleben.[19]

Cano began freighting salt to Presidio prior to the Civil War,[20] while Burgess and his partners Brooks and Davis have been remembered in an oft-told tale of Indian encounter in the Trans-Pecos. Near present-day Alpine at Charco de Alsate, or Kokernot Springs, Apache chief Alsate and one hundred warriors supposedly attacked the freighters' wagon train when it was bound for Juan Cordona Lake or returning from it. Folklore has blended with fact to garble the details: some say it happened prior to the Civil War, others in 1867, and a few maintain it was after 1873, when Big Bend Apaches were relegated to reservations. Even the names of the freighters are in question: varying accounts hold they were Burgess, Davis, and Brooks, Wolff and Hagelstein, or Mexican freighters. Since Burgess, Davis, and Brooks sometimes combined their operations with others at Presidio del Norte to carry grain and corn to Fort Stockton, it is even possible that all those freighters were involved.

In one version of the story, Burgess and his associates were en route to Fort Stockton and Juan Cordona Lake when the war party attacked and besieged them for almost a week. One man muffled the hooves of a race horse with rawhide and escaped at night toward Presidio del Norte, ninety-five miles away. He rode his horse to death and walked the last twenty miles, then returned with a cavalry troop to rout the Apaches and allow the freighters passage to the lake.

Another account holds that Burgess and Davis arranged for a meeting with Alsate at the spring after finding themselves hopelessly besieged. They suddenly produced concealed weapons and threatened to slay him unless he withdrew the war party. He took Burgess's overcoat to seal the arrangement and retreated with his warriors as the freighters continued on to Juan Cordona

Lake. Alsate was wearing Burgess's overcoat when he rode to Presidio del Norte, where Burgess's wife recognized her husband's garment and believed him murdered. The chief and his band were captured and put on trial. Burgess, however, made a timely arrival with salt while court was in session, and Alsate and his warriors were set free.[21]

Of all the trail drivers on the Chihuahua road, none left as detailed an account as August Santleben, who in *A Texas Pioneer* described gathering salt to sell to San Antonio-area ranchers. Returning east in 1872 after taking government cargo to Fort Davis, he crossed the Pecos at Horsehead and went fifteen miles upstream to the site he called Pecos Salt Lake. Santleben described the basin as bordered by "numerous sand-hills, some of them fifty feet in height. The water of the lake, which covers an area of about fifty acres of land, was only about eighteen inches in depth, and its surface was a glittering sheet of white salt about four inches thick. Evidently the sun's rays had evaporated it to that depth, and the substance was sustained by the fluid beneath that was densely impregnated with nitrate of soda."

Making camp on the south shore where no dunes could conceal approaching Indians, he hobbled his mules and allowed them to graze. Then he and his men waded into the lake to scoop the mineral, which was unstable on the surface but of the consistency of "wet snow" below. In the absence of sacks, they shoveled salt waist-deep into their prairie schooners—twenty-four-foot wagons with fifty-eight-inch front wheels and seventy-inch rear wheels, tires six inches wide, and a capacity of seven thousand pounds each.

On the second day Santleben saw thirty Indians on the horizon and had his entire well-armed party accompany the mules to the Pecos for water. This left the wagons, harnesses, corn, and other supplies unguarded, but the war party, evidently suspecting a trap, did not enter their camp. Santleben's men corralled the mules that night rather than leaving them hobbled.

Loading the wagons took three days; then Santleben cov-

Sand dunes crowd the banks of Juan Cordona Lake.

ered the salt with tarpaulins and started for Horsehead Crossing through the sand. Within only five miles, however, he realized he had overloaded the schooners and removed two thousand pounds of salt from each. He continued to Horsehead without incident, crossed, and went downstream toward Fort Lancaster.

In the San Antonio area, Santleben reaped considerable profits, selling his load of fifty thousand pounds for $2,500 to "Knox's Ranch and . . . Griner, Wish and Rheiner. All these persons were sheepmen who valued it more than other salt on account of the large proportion of salt-peter it contained." Believing he was the first to haul salt for commercial purposes from the lake, he also realized the market easily could have been glutted. "Otherwise," he said, "a lucrative business might have been conducted by hauling it from the lake, because the sun would have constantly replenished the salt and furnished an inexhaustible supply for an indefinite period."[22]

Throughout the years that freighters were hauling salt along the Chihuahua Trail, others were coming from Central and East Texas for the mineral. Finus Henderson, then seventeen, carried a load back to sell in his native Bell County during the Civil War.[23] In the spring of 1866, eight men who lived near Fort McKavett in present-day Menard County followed the southern overland route to Horsehead Crossing, then turned upstream to Juan Cordona Lake, which party member John Carlile described as "a marshy swale where salt, sand and water were mixed." Shoveling the mass into heaps with wide strips of lumber so the sandy water would recede, the men allowed the sun to dry the remaining salt before loading the wagons sparingly for the trip through the dunes. A wagon wheel nevertheless broke on the return journey, and crude repairs had to be made.[24]

Central Texas settlers soon afterward began boiling away the brine of Lampasas County's Salt Creek to obtain the mineral, negating further expeditions to Juan Cordona Lake from that area.[25]

When Charles Goodnight and Oliver Loving formed the Goodnight-Loving Trail in 1866, they passed the salt basin in herding beeves up the Pecos's east side. Upon selling the steers at Fort Sumner, New Mexico, Loving went on to Colorado with the breeding stock and Goodnight and three cowboys turned back down the Pecos with $12,000 in gold. They lost most of their supplies when a pack mule stampeded and were forced to ride by night and hide by day to avoid Comanches. They were so beleaguered by the time they reached Horsehead and entered the seventy-five mile arid stretch to the east that they did not even flee when they thought they sighted a war party ahead. "It was useless to stop; we had to go on," said Goodnight. "The mass looked like about twenty Indians and the boys were . . . pale as death. . . . I looked at the boys and thought to myself: 'Here you are with more gold than you ever had in your life, and it won't buy you a drink of water, and it won't get you food. For this gold you may have led three men to their death—for a thing that is utterly useless to you!' "

Switching saddles to speedier horses from the mules they had been riding because of their stamina, the riders bunched together with the mules at Goodnight's flank so he could open a lane through the warriors with gunfire. Within another mile they noticed the line ahead remained unbroken, an unusual configuration for Comanches readying to attack. Then to their relief they realized the mass was only a wagon pulled by a six-yoke oxen team. It was driven by Rich Coffey, bound for Juan Cordona Lake to sell his load of watermelons to the Mexican carretta caravans and to return with salt. Outfitting Goodnight and his hands with provisions, Coffey went on to the lake but failed to meet the carrettas because it was not their traveling season. He buried the melons in the sand and returned home to Coleman County with a wagonload of salt.[26]

Coffey, known as "Old Rich" or "Uncle Rich," became a familiar sight to emigrants along the southern overland route and cattle drovers on the Goodnight-Loving Trail. Twenty-one times he made the four hundred-mile round trip to Juan Cordona Lake from Coleman County, occasionally traveling alone and several times losing men to Indians when he brought a contingent. A

Brown County native, he had moved in 1861 to the confluence of the Colorado and the main Concho in Coleman County. He and his family first lived in the open and then in a dugout before he built a stone house. He gathered Juan Cordona's salt for his cattle and horses and bartered it for corn meal and flour in Weatherford and for items and services from other open-range ranchers. Though he experienced tragedy and hardship in his quests for salt, "Uncle Rich" always retained his sense of humor. Learning his three sons had initiated a William Tell-like game called "hat shooting" in which the target holder was decided by the drawing of grass stems, he sternly halted the goings-on. "Hats are too hard to come by," he said.[27]

Coffey befriended more than Goodnight and his cowhands along the route to Juan Cordona. More than a dozen men led by gold seeker Jacob Schnively were attacked between Horsehead Crossing and the Middle Concho by sixty to two hundred Indians. After a running skirmish the men dismounted to take cover in a gully, leaving their thirty horses and mules to be captured or killed. Though the Indians withdrew, the men now were afoot in arid Comanche country; three of the party saw no choice but to strike out for the nearest ranch seventy-five miles away on the South Concho. Their only provision was buffalo meat lashed to their belts. They walked a day and a night before reaching Spring Creek, where they heard ox bells at daybreak; it was the camp of Coffey, who was bent for Juan Cordona Lake. "Uncle Rich" fed the men and headed his wagon out to rescue their companions.[28]

Others continued to haul salt eastward to barter or to sell. "A large lot of superior Pecos salt for sale in sacks at Fort Concho [present-day San Angelo], Texas," proclaimed an advertisement in the January 21, 1870, *San Antonio Herald*. "For particulars apply to A. Bayless, Fort Concho."[29]

Cavalrymen found in Juan Cordona Lake a commodity as precious as it was to Indians and ranchers, and by 1873 freighters had gained a contract with the U.S. government to supply salt to Fort Stockton thirty-five miles distant.[30] Meanwhile, Mexican freighters had contracted with hunters east of the Pecos to provide them with buffalo meat, which they cured at the lake for the journey home. Phillip Halker Pruett, headed down the Pecos from Santa Fe with forty shorthorn cattle in the fall of 1876, encountered 250 wagons from Mexico City and Chihuahua at Salt Crossing, all bent for Mexico with dried buffalo meat.[31]

Juan Cordona Lake owner Colquhoun, probably frustrated at his inability to capitalize on his vast mineral resource, sold his 22,372,900 square varas to Annie James on January 4, 1867. Mrs. James likewise never sought to establish sovereignty over the lake,[32] a decision whose wisdom became quite apparent in 1877, when Judge Charles H. Howard halted free access to his salt lakes west of the Guadalupe Mountains and began marketing his salt in Chihuahua. Howard precipitated something which the owners of Juan Cordona Lake wisely had avoided—a war between Mexicans who had hauled salt from the basins since time immemorial and the Americans who suddenly would deny them. Approximately fifteen men were killed and as many as forty wounded before the Mexicans were forced to accept that only Juan Cordona Lake remained open to them as a source of salt.[33]

Completion of the Texas and Pacific Railroad through Texas in 1881 brought domestic salt from far-away markets, but the Juan Cordona basin continued to be important to ranchers. Grazing 3,600 sheep on the Pecos flood plain between Pontoon Crossing and "S" Crossing in the 1890s, Walter Smith and A. D. Locklin cut salt from the lake, piled it on a sled, and transported it by wagon to their flock downstream.[34]

Freighters continued hauling salt from Juan Cordona Lake well into the twentieth century. The last of a breed, these men acquired colorful nicknames such as Burro Jack and Salty Bill. Burro Jack, the earlier of the two, freighted salt in a wagon and trailer pulled by eighteen to twenty donkeys.[35] Salty Bill Latham frequently made hauls in 1913 and 1914 with a three-wagon outfit of one lead, two trailers, and a thirty-six-burro team. The entire population of the now-ghost town of Upland, just east of Castle Gap, lined the road to watch every time he passed through.[36]

Ancient foot and wagon routes often evolve into modern

roads, and Salt Trail followed suit. During Pecos County Judge Homer Powers's term from 1906 to 1910, he had a road surveyed to Salt Crossing,[37] and a bridge eventually was constructed at the prehistoric ford of the Jumanos.

Free access to the lake finally ended when the Cowden family—W. H., Jax M., G. H., and W. H. Jr.—bought the 3,963-acre Juan Cordona league on February 19, 1920, to establish a vast ranch around the 1,100-surface-acre lake.[38] Introducing sheep to the creosote flats as had Smith and Locklin three decades previously, the Cowdens suffered considerable losses due to predators. Coyotes running in packs herded the flocks into Juan Cordona Lake, where the sheep bogged helplessly and were slaughtered. On repeated mornings Jerry Gene Cowden and other horsemen witnessed the eerie roundup and fired numerous rounds of ammunition, but sheep losses still mounted to the hundreds. "A lot of people call a coyote a dumb animal," Cowden reportedly observed. "Ain't nothing dumb about him. Sucker done figured out what's out there and a way to use it to his advantage."[39]

The Pecos country witnessed other unusual episodes involving animals. Riding the river near Juan Cordona Lake in the early 1920s, one of the Cowdens saw an elephant in its waters. He later learned it had fled a circus that had stopped in the town of Fort Stockton.[40]

From the time they first began ranching the Pecos country, the Cowdens cut salt from the lake to supply their livestock and to barter for labor or material items.[41] But it was not until 1932 that the ancient shores of the basin finally witnessed the first long-term mining operation by an individual.

He was Max Omo, and his was a name to be forever remembered by the oil drilling industry, for it was he who, in soliciting a market for his mineral, first suggested using salt water to drill through the salt section of the earth. Previously, recalled old-time cable tool driller W. W. Allman of Crane, operators of rotary rigs tried drilling deep wells with fresh water, which would dissolve the subterranean salt and lead to vast problems. Accepting Omo's challenge, a rotary rig operator purchased a load of salt from Juan Cordona Lake, mixed it with fresh water and drilled. It worked—not only in the salt section but through other formations as well. Today, the use of brine in rotary drilling is a common practice. "He was the ordinary man selling salt who gave 'em a billion-dollar idea and didn't know it," said Allman.[42]

Omo, a native Texan familiar with the Great Salt Lake in Utah, had moved to Crane in the town's infancy on January 2, 1927. Contracting with the Cowdens in the spring of 1932 on a percentage-of-salt basis, he set up his operation on the west side of the lake and moved his German immigrant wife, Marie, and family into a sheet iron and wooden house built into the side of a sand dune overlooking the basin. An innovator and man of logic, Omo knew the prevailing winds regularly would drive the brine from the northeastern pool to the southwestern basin and leave a deposit of salt before receding.[43] "It was a funny thing out there—the wind would start blowing from the east and then you'd see the tide coming," said Alton Evans (born 1905), who worked with Omo in 1937.

> It would make you think of the ocean, kind of bringing it in every day or two. Water would pile up on the west side, and then when it drifted back it would leave salt. That's the reason we didn't fool with any other section. When the wind began blowing we'd just get ready, because we knew the tide was coming in. There was an extremely high content of salt, and it was a pretty good salt. It didn't really have any bad minerals. It wasn't for human consumption because there would have been one or two minerals that would've had to have been taken out. But for cattle and sheep it was ideal. You could smell that salt—it wasn't a bad smell, because it didn't have any bad ingredients. Standing there smelling of it would make you think of the sea.[44]

Omo, who had as many as a dozen workers during prime season in May and June, employed a variety of mining methods.

First, he used a sled as Walter Smith had four decades previously; wading out in rubber boots, Omo's workers raked salt into heaps to allow the brine to recede and shoveled it onto a barge of oilfield scrap iron. He then dragged it ashore by cable attached to an anchored pickup and dumped its contents to dry. Omo later learned to dig parallel trenches one hundred feet long and three to four feet deep to permit the brine to recede from the salt deposit. Finally he developed a beveled sled, pulled by cable attached to a tractor on shore, that scooped the top three to four inches of salt.[45] "If you'd get down too deep you'd get into the soil," said Evans. "And also we didn't go any deeper than that because in a day or two here would come the water back, and it would deposit a lot more salt. And then it would retreat again and then we'd get out there again in a day or two. Sometimes, the water would come back before we were ready for it."[46]

Omo placed the raw salt in tow sacks to ship to ranches inside a hundred-mile radius the initial two years, then developed a steam engine screener comprising a series of barrels with different-sized holes in the sides. As the barrel tube revolved, the mineral would be sifted into fine, medium, and coarse grades. The fine he sold for fifteen dollars a ton to sheep ranchers to be placed in troughs or mixed with feed, while the medium went to cattle ranchers. The coarse, meanwhile, was sold to individuals at twelve dollars a ton for freezing ice cream.

Packaged in 120-pound lots in tow sacks, the salt was delivered by truck to ranches or drilling rigs.[47] Under contract to Omo, Howard Evans carried one-hundred-sack loads "for fifteen or twenty cents a sack" to oilfields near Big Lake and Kermit on a 1935 flatbed truck.[48]

To the Omo family, the dubious honor of becoming the first permanent residents of Juan Cordona Lake was a trial by fire. Never before had man tarried as much as an unnecessary minute at its shore; now it became home for parents and their infant children. Crane and the nearest conveniences were hours distant by primitive road. The Omos had neither running water nor electricity, and they faced difficulty bringing in ice before it melted. They hauled water three barrels at a time and found the coolest place to keep a jug was in a truck cab. Omo's wife Marie cooked on a wood-burning stove fueled by mesquite. Summers were intensely hot, winters cold, and sandstorms common. Drought left the basin dry, yet heavy rains one season flooded it for months and forced Omo to halt his venture temporarily and move his family into Crane.

Marie gave birth without anyone attending her in May 1933, though Omo had gone to Crane in the middle of the night to get a doctor. The children had no shade on the treeless shores, prompting their father to build them an open-sided shelter. Scorpions, vinegarroons, and tarantulas invaded the house, and numerous rattlesnakes discouraged the Omos from visiting the still-visible Salt Trail extending toward the Pecos. The air always was filled with the taste of salt. Summer nights brought the only respite from the environment, as a cool breeze swept over the brine. But even then there were dangers: packs of coyotes frequented the shores and once attacked the dog at the steps of the house.

Such a life wore heavily on Marie and the children, and Omo moved his family into Crane permanently in early 1936. He continued mining the lake during the prime season for the next two years, but he sustained a back injury which cost him the lease in 1939.[49]

In 1936, ten-year-old I. C. "Tiny" Earp rode horseback to Juan Cordona Lake and began a lifelong association with it. The son of a Cowden Ranch employee, he explored the basin often the next few years, continuing to do so after his family purchased land immediately westward in 1945 and moved into a house a mile and a half from its banks. In 1964 Earp leased the Juan Cordona league itself and began ranching its boundaries. He recalled:

> As a kid, when we were living there in that old two-story adobe house, we would work that salt lake pasture. There was a fellow that worked for McElroy

> Ranch Company—back then large ranching operations neighbored with one another. He had brought his horse and bedroll and was to stay till the work was over. He hunted Indian artifacts and had a great collection, and in the process of gathering cattle around that old lake, he reported that he had found an Indian grave and wanted to go back and dig it up. Well, of course there weren't any roads to speak of close to the area, but we all got in an old pickup and went back over there when we got through working that day. He had a little screen and shovel and he dug up several Indian bones and various artifacts like points, arrowheads, obsidian. I didn't care anything about the arrowheads—I liked the bones, so I took the bones and carried them to school.

As a ten- or eleven-year-old, he also found signs of later visitors to the lake:

> I would ride with my father around that salt lake and we would find a lot of stuff obviously old-timey—freight wagon equipment that had been broken down or left, a buggy hub, old camping equipment like cast-iron stoves, relics, and pieces of harness. Also, along the outside perimeter of that lake, there's a gyp formation in some areas, and whenever cattle or wagon wheels crossed it repeatedly, it would wear an indentation in the face of it and leave the normal curvature. On two or three occasions I've found what I thought to be some of these old wagon roads where the freighters hauled their salt out of that lake. They would be in the general area of the two well-known camps, one on the north side and the other on the south side.

Earp also determined that freighters did not always herd their teams to the Pecos for water:

Desert plants at Juan Cordona Lake.

These people that came in and mined that salt obviously had to have water for their teams as well as for themselves. They could carry enough for themselves, but if they carried enough for their teams they could haul less salt. And so they hand-dug wells down to what was evidently pretty decent water for their mules and horses. There's still evidences of where they'd dug those wells about thirty feet deep on the southwest side of that lake. Back at that time this country hadn't been stocked heavily and there was an awfully lot of grass. I'm sure it rained in cycles like it does now, and the soil

Corroded oilfield cable on the bed of Juan Cordona Lake.

> held up enough water to where there was a small volume at the thirty-foot level separated from any formation water that would have been contaminated by that lake. Somebody put a windmill over one well; the anchor posts and wooden casing are still there.[50]

Considerable petroleum deposits were discovered beneath the lakebed in the middle of the twentieth century, bringing men and technology to the site. But the mire continued to prove treacherous. Sheep and cattle in search of water often bogged and died; a similar fate almost befell a ranch specialist and agriculture agent summoned to the salt lake pasture to examine Earp's sheep. When their pickup became stuck in the sand, the men considered the several miles back to the ranch house and then remembered the gas plant and possible telephone directly across the lake. "They decided just to walk across," Earp recalled. "They got out a hundred yards or so and they started bogging down—they didn't know how boggy that thing was. The remarkable thing about that old lake is you can ride or walk over the surface of it and it will hold you up. But if you start bogging down, turn around and start back out, you'll bog down in the place that you just walked over without bogging at all. It's real frightening running into those kinds of things." After a desperate struggle the men made their way back to shore and were rescued by Earp, who would later become involved in a similar episode.

During dry spells, when footing was firm, Earp rode horseback across the basin in working livestock. One day, trying to save himself a two-mile ride, he urged his horse down the bank and onto the lakebed. When he reached the midway point, "my horse started bogging—and bogging badly enough where it really scared me. I was proud of the horse and feared for his safety as well as my own. And so I stepped off this horse to get my weight off him so he wouldn't have to manage that, and I began bogging down also. I was in front of this horse trying to stay out of his way and he was lunging all the time and bumping me every now and then. I ended up trying to outrun that horse; we were both trying to outrun one another across that lake. That's the last time I ever crossed it. I always rode around it after that."[51]

Juan Cordona Lake is peaceful today, except for oilfield activity, and its salt is no longer vital to a seasoning-rich world. Yet its final chapter is far from written, for even the pumpjacks are only temporal, and the ancient basin will far outlive the petroleum reserves below. Man may again scrape life-sustaining salt from its bed.

Fort Stockton Sutlery

On dark nights west of the Pecos in Fort Stockton, say those who should know, the black-draped form of a faceless spirit paces the rooms of an old adobe house in a foredoomed quest for peace. The existence of *el hombre vestido de negra*, the man in black, is not often questioned by those of Indian-Mexican ancestry who live near the crumbling building at Nelson and Sherer streets, only the identity. For much of the century they have seen him stand at the rock cone of the water well or wander the neighborhood. Some supposedly have actually laid hands upon him with terrifying results, while others have seen or heard evidences of his presence: moving lights and the sounds of upheaval and of shovel striking gravel. Eyewitnesses say he possesses definite mass, yet has no face, and wears a black hat and long dark coat almost like Lincoln.

Literally a walking shadow, he is a *bulto* to those familiar with Mexican-American folk religion in the vicinity of the Texas-Mexico border. That Spanish word, which translates as a "figure" or "shape," is used in reference to the carven image of a Catholic saint elsewhere in Spanish-speaking America, but near the Rio Grande boundary the concept incorporates man's fear of death and the ultimate destiny of those whose lives held evil deeds or whose work was left incomplete. The *bulto* must right that unrighted wrong, fulfill that unfulfilled purpose, pay that unpaid debt, seek out that special something or someone. If successful, *el bulto* can escape purgatorial condemnation and enter hell or heaven; otherwise he or she must wander forever.

Though it has no face, it does have the power of speech. It is never seen if it is heard, nor does it ever speak if seen. Too, though it is ambulatory, *el bulto* always appears or disappears during momentary shifting of the witness's vision or the blink of an eye.

El bulto's dress, actions, and words provide clues as to its purpose, say those initiated in folk religion. The two colors it may wear, black or white, literally spell the difference between evil and good. *Bultos* of children or women are always in white, which symbolizes warmth, brightness, and good. Though without peace, they nevertheless may effect good in those to whom they appear. *La Llorona*, the crying woman in a white gown, is the most well-known of all *bultos*. Having killed her children, she is fated to wander until she finds and restores them, but she still can serve as a positive force by eliciting reverence and fear in those to whom she appears.

Black, meanwhile, always has been associated with mourning, death, gloominess, darkness, the unknown, and, especially, evil. When the *bulto* of a man is so adorned, it indicates that a

Fort Stockton sutlery, the so-called "Oldest House in Fort Stockton."

hideous, undisclosed deed was associated with his life. Perhaps he was the victim, perhaps the perpetrator, but he will never find freedom unless he reveals it.

Also, a soul may not have attained its final state if the person did not receive last rites in the Catholic church or a Christian burial and is awaiting proper prayers or entombment. Or a *bulto* may persist to warn of imminent danger, as in the case of the El Paso fire station at which some persons claim a dead fireman appears as a prelude to every deadly fire in the city.

But in a society in which poverty is commonplace, the most romantic concept associated with *bultos* involves concealed treasure. Treasure and spirits long have been interrelated in many cultures; supposedly, the body of a man was buried with pirate booty so his ghost would oversee it. But a *bulto*'s intent may be to reveal the treasure rather than guard it. Possibly a person died without having last rites performed and seeks to have his or her

FORT STOCKTON SUTLERY

soul prayed out of purgatory by revealing a money cache to be directed to a priest as payment. Or, the treasure may be predestined for a certain type of individual to whom the *bulto* bears the responsibility of revealing it.

Regardless of the *bulto*'s purpose or responsibility regarding the treasure, this spirit holds no dominion over it. On the contrary, in border culture the treasure assumes a personality and identity all its own and even dictates the actions of the *bulto*. Too, because of its desire to be found by a good person who is not self-serving or bent upon inflicting evil upon others, it reveals itself through flames or light, the brightness of which is dependent on its size.[1]

Some say the Fort Stockton *bulto* is Francisco Pancho Robles, a reputed sorcerer who died in the house in the 1920s. In his last days, boils covered his body, and the old *curandera* who read his palm insisted that he burn his books of *la magia negra*, black magic, in order to gain peace. Robles denied having such books, but he grew weaker and more racked with boils—and others took it as a sign of his impending damnation for following the Prince of Darkness. Finally, a week and a half later, he supposedly called again for the *curandera*, nodded weakly to her accusation that he was ensnared by *la magia negra*, and consented to have the witchcraft books burned. But he already had walked with demons too long, believe some, and within three days he died, never to rest in peace.[2]

But there are other candidates for the identity of the *bulto*. Within the rooms of this house persons have died of disease and age after a life amassing money. Before its walls a notorious gunslinger suffered a fatal bullet wound; supposedly, other killings occurred in the adjacent arroyo and men were hanged in the back yard.

In all the Pecos country there is no more likely place to be frequented by a spectre than this edifice overlooking Comanche Springs. The building dates back to 1859, when Company H of the First United States Infantry founded Camp Stockton near

Comanche Springs and adjacent to both the Comanche War Trail to Mexico and the San Antonio-Fort Davis wagon road.[3] In order to provision the troops, a sutler's store was established at the post's southwest corner; constructed of adobe brick two feet thick, it rested on a native stone foundation and had a roof of stripped sotol branches. Provisioner J. D. Holliday, a civilian who owned the land on which the post lay,[4] could look northward past the hand-dug well and watch the passing of emigrant wagons, Butterfield stages, cavalry troops, and even the U.S. Army camel corps.

A visiting general sketched the post in 1860, noting the positions of the tent grounds, commander's and officers' quarters, commissary, bakery, hospital, and sutler's store. The store's shape—rectangular, built on a north-south axis—and location near a draw clearly identify it with the ancient house on Nelson and Sherer streets.[5] The southernmost section is the oldest portion of the building, which today is twenty-five paces long and five paces wide; the rooms nearer the well were added as multigeneration families outgrew their confines.[6] Built to help man cross the frontier, the building now may testify to those who have spanned the chasm between death and life.

Camp Stockton became Fort Stockton on May 3, 1860, but U.S. Army occupation continued less than a year. Within a week after the Civil War erupted on April 12, 1861, U.S. troops under Brigadier General David E. Twiggs abandoned Fort Stockton. Captain Bill "Cood" Adams and the Confederate Cavalry's Second Regiment, Texas Mounted Rifles, soon crossed the Pecos at Horsehead Crossing and occupied the site. In March 1862, however, Confederate hopes to take the West were left buried in the snow of Glorieta Pass, New Mexico, and the Rebels set the thatch roofs of Fort Stockton afire and retreated east of Horsehead.[7]

That same year, J. D. Holliday sold the land on which the post and sutlery lay to George H. Giddings, a native Pennsylvanian and once an emissary of Abraham Lincoln, who nevertheless was to fight with the South at the Battle of Palmito Ranch.

During the war, Fort Stockton's buildings disintegrated as emigrants and Indians used wooden portions for campfires. Only the adobe sutlery remained intact.[8]

The fort was not immediately reoccupied at war's end, and Indian depredations went largely unchecked along the nearby stretch of the wagon road between San Antonio and El Paso. In early July 1866, an eastbound stage from El Paso was attacked by Apaches at Valera, or Barrilla, Spring on the eastern slope of the Davis Mountains. A man named Davis was killed by an arrow, and two other persons sustained wounds when the stage's occupants, unable to outdistance the war party, made a stand. Repelling the attack by day, the six survivors crawled away by night to find themselves afoot in arid country frequented by Indians. With another stage not expected for several days, they set out across the virtual desert for the abandoned sutlery forty-two miles eastward. Thorns shredded their clothing and rocks cut into their feet, but at Leon Springs they found water to sustain them the remainder of the way to the empty fort. There they hid for days inside the sutlery, their only food a quart of corn picked from the dirt floor and boiled in an oyster can. They were rescued by the next westbound stage and taken to El Paso without further incident.[9]

With such reports filtering back from the Trans-Pecos, two companies of the Forty-first U.S. Infantry reoccupied Fort Stockton early in 1867. Though the sutlery still stood largely undamaged, only rubble remained of the original fort;[10] Colonel Edward Hatch and the Ninth Cavalry's companies A, B, E, and K arrived in July to rebuild the post. These troops were "buffalo soldiers," negroes so named by Indians because their curly hair resembled the fur of the buffalo. Commanded by white officers, these troops were important in guarding the Trans-Pecos frontier after the Civil War.[11]

Meanwhile, the sutlery became a home for pioneers. Maria Manuela Sosa likely was born in that structure to Pedro Sosa and his wife on Christmas Eve, 1867; hers was the first birth recorded in the town of Fort Stockton. The elder Sosa, of Ojinaga, Mexico, had come to the site to work as a stonemason on the new fort.[12]

Peter Gallagher of Wicklow, Ireland, also probably lived in the building while he constructed a store immediately west of the modern courthouse plaza. He soon acquired most of the Comanche Springs holdings and platted the St. Gall townsite which included the sutlery and other historic portions of present-day Fort Stockton.[13]

About the adobe house history was woven: the state legislature created Pecos County in 1870 and saw it organized in 1875; voters selected Fort Stockton as county seat over St. Gall in 1881, by a sixty-four to twenty-nine tally; the army post closed for good on June 26–27, 1886, when Company P, Sixteenth Infantry, and Company G, Third Cavalry, marched away.[14]

Native New Yorker Joseph Friedlander probably served as last provisioner in the adobe building in the period 1872 to 1876,[15] after which Aniseto Pina acquired it for use as a private residence. Pina's wife Matilde became known as a living example of goodness and was the bulwark of the city's first Catholic church; she attended Mass at six o'clock each morning and even handled duties of the priest when he was away.[16] She never regarded anyone as a stranger and took many persons into her home, among them Annie Riggs, herself a strong force in the Catholic church and a notable figure in turn-of-the-century Fort Stockton. But Annie's presence in the adobe house brought violence, for she was the divorced wife of a notorious gunfighter, Barney Riggs.

Barney Riggs, born in 1856 in Arkansas, had a tendency toward violence that took him first to Texas, where as a teen-ager he accidentally killed a man, and then to Arizona. With a yearning for gunfighting, he treaded a narrow line between hero and outlaw. In the early 1880s in Willcox, Arizona, he killed a man in a dispute over a woman. Though some claimed the slaying was justified, he was convicted of murder and sentenced to Yuma Territorial Prison for life.

Barney soon became a trusty, and as such he happened to be in the secretary's office one day in 1889 when an alarm indicated a breakout in progress. Frank Hartley, a sentry, reached the entrance first to see a convict pressing a knife against the back of warden Thomas Gates as he held him from behind. The inmate threatened to kill Gates if anyone tried to stop him, but Hartley nevertheless fatally shot the man, who in his last act stabbed his hostage severely but not mortally.

Always attracted to battle, Barney seized a pistol from the commissary office and ran outside to find a second escapee shot but a third leveling a pistol on Hartley. Barney shot the man down, then turned to slay two other convicts involved in the breakout attempt. For saving the life of the guard, Barney received a full pardon, placing himself in the unique position of having slain one man to get into prison and three to get out.

Upon release, Barney joined his family in Fort Stockton in 1890 but continued to walk along both sides of the law. Never one to back away from a direct confrontation, he once put an end to rumors he had shot an enemy in the back by exhuming the body and displaying it in a saloon. He was still a man with an ungovernable temper and steady nerves when Annie Frazer Johnson married him in 1891, in a union nurtured by family intermarriages. Annie, devout and persevering, could do little to change Barney for the better, even when they lived in neighboring Reeves County where her brother Bud Frazer was sheriff. Not only was Barney arrested a number of times for carrying a weapon, but he was tried and acquitted in 1893 on a charge of assault with intent to murder. Reportedly he had fired at a man and then pistol-whipped him outside the Riggs home.

His gunslinging peaked in 1896, after Deacon Miller killed Sheriff Frazer and ordered the dead man's family and Barney to leave the city of Pecos. But Barney was not one to back away from a fight, not even when he learned Miller's henchmen Bill Earhart and John Denison were out to kill him. As he neared town with his family that day, he stopped in the brush and donned a bulletproof vest, knowing that the two men sometimes wore such themselves. "I'll just shoot them in the head," he vowed. A few minutes later at the Orient Saloon, he did exactly that.

Barney's violent disposition was a burden on his marriage from 1892 on, and Annie later looked upon those years as being filled with his "cruel treatments and outrages." Annie and the four sons she bore him always were subject to his moods and beatings. She later claimed that on February 13, 1902, Barney torched the furniture, threw her to the floor, and tried to douse her in coal oil and set her afire. When five-year-old Ernest, rock in hand, cried for him to stop, Barney threatened to kill all of them. As he went into another room to get his gun, Annie and the children fled into the night. Matilde Pina took them into the house of adobe, and though the Riggses had a brief and volatile reconciliation, they were divorced on March 27, 1902.

Meanwhile, J. R. "Buck" Chadborn, who was married to Annie's daughter by a previous marriage, became sympathetic with Annie and drew the gunfighter's wrath. On April 6, 1902, Barney, who had begun to suffer from rheumatism, thrashed Chadborn with his walking cane at a livery stable. The next day, while Barney was standing in Mart Adams's saloon, he glanced across at the nearby Pina house and saw Chadborn pull his mule-drawn hack to a halt before it. Barney, who had been hoping for another reconciliation, let his temper flare and started out the door. Sheriff Bob Neighbors stopped him and demanded he leave his pistol in the saloon. Underestimating a foe for the first and last time, Barney acquiesced and headed defenseless toward the adobe house. Chadborn was loading Annie's belongings into the rear of the hack when he looked up and saw Barney approaching. The gunslinger shook his finger at Chadborn, cursed him vehemently, and when he got within arm's reach, drew back his cane to strike him. The younger man lunged for the hack seat, found a gun, and shot Barney in the chest. Barney fell, then struggled up, plugged the hole with his finger, and staggered more than thirty yards before collapsing at the arroyo. His nine-year-old son Barney Jr. ran to him, and Barney made him promise to slay Chadborn someday, a deed the boy later considered but decided against. Annie ordered Barney taken to the Koehler Hotel where, cursing Chadborn to the end, he died the following day.[17]

Death came to the adobe house through disease as well as

violence. During the 1918 Spanish influenza epidemic, the Pina home was an outpost hospital for the stricken from area ranches. A yellow flag signifying quarantine flew over the house for weeks; in all, more than one hundred persons died throughout the city, many of them at the old sutlery.[18]

As the one-time sutlery continued to shelter generations of the Pina and then the Manuel Ramos families and their tenants, a variety of activities within gave it an aura of mystery. Iron resounded against anvil in the blacksmith shop of Aniseto Pina's son-in-law, Pancho Robles, an echo that still reverberated a half-century later in the memories of those who knew his nocturnal obsession with witchcraft and horrible death. "*Si,* he practiced *brujeria*—the occult," recalled a *viejito,* an elderly man who knew Robles and married into the Pina family. "Pancho Robles was accused of being a *brujo*—an occultist—because he used to read a lot of books concerning what you today would call devil worshippers. Every time he had a chance he would get and read something about devil worshippers, and that's why a lot of people said that he was a practicing one."[19] Robles's niece by marriage, Angelita Garcia, was more blunt: "Maybe he gave his life to the devil."[20]

Some claim that same room on the northwest corner where Robles supposedly kept his satanic books continued to be infiltrated with the occult even after his death; there, from the 1930s until approximately 1950, resident George "Choche" Garcia operated a cobbler's shop rented him by Manuel Ramos and allegedly experimented with marijuana. In border culture, to be under marijuana's influence is to be possessed by *el diablo*; not even a bullet can stop a person so powered by evil.[21] "George Garcia, the shoemaker, got in the habit of dressing up in black, wearing a big black hat and cape, and going outside and scaring people," said the *viejito*. "He was maybe practicing the occult too."[22]

"I would say that Mr. Choche Garcia would have been more inclined to deal with the occult," noted Joe Primera of Pecos County Historical Commission,

> because he was always a little bit odd and wore strange clothes. I remember they were always in black, and a black hat and big old wide brim. He was very pale-complected and very thin, and if you saw him in black he was going to catch your attention; he was going to scare the heck out of you. When you went to his shop he never said anything, a very quiet person. He was always outside at night. Maybe he was out to meet somebody; maybe he couldn't sleep. I always like to give everybody the benefit of the doubt. Maybe he was in something that was not legal. As young kids we used to go by there and we'd see him walking around there; he might be maybe in his pajamas. It looked white to us. We would throw rocks and then he would turn around and make some kind of sign, and I guess we assumed it was a ghost. We took off; we were excited; we never stopped for anything because we were afraid.
>
> S. L. Gonzalez, Sr., also mentioned that he thought George [Garcia] was always a person who couldn't sleep and that he used to walk around in front of the house and that people could have mistaken him for a ghost.[23]

Too, the house reportedly once contained a gaming operation, with resulting arguments not infrequent. "Manuel Ramos used to like to invite friends to play poker . . . and had some . . . gaming that was supposed to be against the law," said Primera, reporting information passed along to him. "I'm sure they had quite a few fights over the pot."[24]

Designated a Texas historic landmark in 1966 by the Texas Historical Commission,[25] the house was bought by the Fort Stockton Historical Society in 1967. A fence was erected in 1968 to secure it against vandalism,[26] and a shed-type roof was built over it in the mid-1980s to protect it from weather. Crumbling and out-of-time, it is without occupant for the first period since 1867.

Or is it?

Many of those who live nearby believe it is the dwelling place of *fantasmas*, or ghosts.

Aniseto Pina's grandson, the late Seterio Pina, who was born in the house in the nineteenth century and lived there many years, long was acquainted with the man in black. Seterio also was aware of moving lights and a suitcase about which *el bulto*'s purpose revolves. "I don't know when I first became aware of the whisper that he lived there," said Seterio in 1970. "I guess when I was quite young. I don't know who he is, or how long he has survived—longer than me anyway. There is a light sometimes seen, not every night, but sometimes. It is not as bright as a flashlight, or even a lamp—about the size of a candle and it flickers and sometimes it stays awhile and moves about, and sometimes it is only a glimpse. There was something about a suitcase, that maybe he is looking for a suitcase he left sometime, buried under the floor. I just don't know. . . . I never met or saw him, only the whisper. Who knows?"[27]

A descendant of Seterio who desired anonymity verified that his ancestor told such stories. "He lived there until he went into the army in about 1918. He said there were some unusual things happening there. He told me many times, 'A light moves from room to room—there's a light there.' He told stories that there was a man who came out of the water well, or was close to the well—something to do with a suitcase."[28]

While Seterio could not understand the purpose of the suitcase in *el bulto*'s wanderings, others initiated into border culture believe they do. "He has hidden something and wants to reveal it," said one. "Somebody should follow this ghost, find out what it's trying to show us. If somebody would follow, the ghost surely would lead them to whatever it wants to show."[29]

Equally enmeshed with *el bulto*'s objective is the well, which once tapped a current of Comanche Springs eighteen feet down. Many have seen the man in black standing before it, and some believe he lives within it. One thing of which witnesses are sure is that the abyss, brimmed by an open cone of rock, easily could accommodate the body of a man—or spirit. Researcher Lee Harris was told by witnesses that as he rises from the well he "breathes smoke [and] some kind of light flashes in his eyes like fire. He is so sinister-looking when you look him in the face, and they never notice how he has the light in his hand, whether it's a candle or flashlight—just that it's a light."[30]

Mrs. Harris interviewed one man who knew just how sinister the man in black is. "I don't know who he is, or what he wants, but he is there," said the man.

> I remember one day, there was a man—a mean S.O.B. He was a barroom fighter. People feared him and stayed away from him when he was drinking. God, he was mean! He was about twenty-two or twenty-three years old and I was about eleven or twelve, but I stayed away from him. Well, he closed down a tavern—I mean stayed late drinking until they closed the doors. He was walking up the trail—it was not a street then—and he saw a man walking ahead of him. He liked to fight and so he called out to this man, "Hey! Wait up! Who are you?"
>
> The man didn't answer or turn around. So he called out a couple more times. The man ignored him. So he overtook the man in a hurry and grabbed him and turned him around. He looked into the man's eyes and stood still. He could not move. The man stood there and looked at him and then spat right between his eyes. It was this ghost—he walked away and went into the old well. The barroom fighter went home in a trance and never spoke another word. He died that morning. I went to the funeral . . . you should have seen his face.[31]

Another Fort Stockton man, born in 1921, encountered *el bulto* under similar conditions. One night when he was sixteen years old, he walked a path toward a vacant field just north of the house. Entering the field, the teen-ager saw the adobe walls ahead as well as an adult male approaching through the shadows. "Hello!" shouted the youth from a distance. The man did not answer but continued nearing. As they came within twenty feet of one another the teen-ager extended a Spanish word of greeting, "*Queibole*!" The next instant, "I blinked—and he disappeared," the man recalled, adding that he was convinced he had seen *el bulto*. "I think the reason he disappeared was he got close to me. I did not imagine what I saw in the path there."[32]

Many witnesses of *el bulto* request anonymity to avoid possible ridicule, such as the *viejito* of Indian descent who moved next door to the house, then occupied by Aniseto and Matilde Pina, at the age of five in 1892. He was nearing manhood by the time Barney Riggs was shot, a slaying he remembered. Marrying into the Pina family, he came to live in the house and later returned for overnight stays after it was acquired by Manuel Ramos. He first realized the structure housed spirits in the 1930s. "When I slept there during the night I could hear furniture falling, dishes being overturned," he said in detailing the culture's phantom sign of hostility within a place. "It was furniture full of something falling. I heard a lot of noises of the house. It was *el diablo*—the devil."

But he was also aware of *el bulto*. "I have seen it. A man comes out in black. He is not very old. He is still strong. He used to live there. He wears a cap and is dressed in black, all black. I never did see his face because he was always at a distance. He just appears and stands there or sits on the water well and then goes away. I wouldn't be afraid, because one minute you would see it, and then you wouldn't see it. And when you did see it, he wouldn't do anything. It's been happening a long time. I have seen him almost every night."

He also was familiar with the white-clad *bulto* of a woman at the site. "My *compadre* Domingo Pena [born circa 1908], the father of my daughter-in-law, saw a woman in white when he was little, nine or ten years old. 'Mingo was walking by the house and saw a lady kneeling, and she gestured and said to come kneel beside her. She had a crucifix. 'Mingo became frightened and ran off. He went to tell others about this, and when they came back there was nothing there."[33]

Angelita Garcia, the granddaughter of Aniseto and Matilde Pina, also became acquainted with the man in black after moving into the structure upon her marriage in 1936. "I think it was a ghost because we heard lots of noises—like a cabinet coming down with all the dishes. My uncle, Pancho Pina, slept in there and he heard the same thing. We'd get up and then we wouldn't hear anything. A man used to have a shoe shop there [George "Choche" Garcia]; one time he told me he heard something, but couldn't describe what kind of noise it was, and said that he saw a female dressed in white."

Immediately upon the death of her aunt in 1945, Mrs. Garcia had a visual encounter with the man in black as she returned with relatives to her then-home situated across the street from the adobe house. "It was between 12:30 and 2:00 at night. We were driving south on Nelson Street when we saw that man. I think it was a bad spirit—it was a ghost. It was sort of like a man dressed in black. He was standing by the well close to the door in front. I couldn't see his face. He was standing looking through the door into the house. I got out of the car and went into my home, and my cousin, who lived west of the old house, turned at the well—and he was gone."[34]

Over the years *el bulto* apparently revealed himself only to those he chose, and sometimes it was a terrifying encounter. One night in 1959, around 9:30, a Fort Stockton woman and her stepmother exited a small house a hundred yards east of the adobe structure in an otherwise vacant field. Walking toward their home, the two women looked toward the adobe house and saw a figure dressed in black, the only white being the V of his shirt. But as they looked more closely they saw that this man was headless—and approaching them swiftly. They turned and ran in terror all the way to the *padre*'s quarters at the Catholic mission as the headless *bulto* chased them. When the priest came to the door they turned and saw the *fantasma* had disappeared.[35]

Those initiated to border folk religion say a headless *bulto* signifies the person died violently and that his head was not buried with his torso. He is doomed to wander unless he directs someone to the missing skull and reveals his murderer.[36]

El bulto definitely had his head a few years later when Angelita Garcia's daughter Elida saw him standing by the well one night. "He was just like a shadow, dark, but looked like he had a suit on," she said. "He was standing like he was getting some water or something, or just looking down in the well. We all saw him at the same time, my sisters and my brothers. He looked like a man—and then he was gone. I know it was a ghost because he disappeared." Elida Garcia had a second encounter with a *bulto*—this time a woman in a white gown—at the adobe house in 1978. "I was riding around with my boyfriend at night when I saw it. It disappeared also."[37]

Testimony has come from persons not enmeshed in Mexican-Indian culture; even local law enforcement officials have become involved. The Fort Stockton Police Department's part-time night dispatcher from 1969 to 1973, Mary Lou Harris, handled several calls regarding unusual occurrences at the house. "There were three reports of lights, and the callers would be pretty scared," she said. "It was basically before 1 a.m. They described them as dim, moving from room to room, or window to window, or moving around the house—something like a weak flashlight or candlelight. It didn't seem to be a strong light. They did report hearing things also." However, officers dispatched to the site always found the house dark and quiet. "They got to asking me, 'Are you sure those people called? We're getting tired of going up there and seeing nothing,'" recounted the former dispatcher.[38]

Rose Duarte, who assumed duties as chief dispatcher in 1977, often heard callers describe a man in black at the house:

> Most of the calls have come after dark between 10:30 and 11 p.m. It's always a man dressed in black—that's what they describe. He's wearing a black coat, black pants, and a hat. He looks all black. You

> can never distinguish his face and I can tell you that for a fact—because I saw him too.
>
> I work part-time at the hospital as a nurse, and our shift ends at 11:30 p.m. and by the time report's over and I get in the car, it's pretty close to 12:00. In October 1982 I left the hospital and drove behind the house and saw him—standing at the southeast corner of the house on the outside of the fence. To me, he looked like Abraham Lincoln—you know, that little hat and everything black. The coat wasn't a long one; it was short, heavy. And he had a black pair of pants. I don't remember seeing any shoes. His face was dark, black with a big collar around it. All of that is what seemed so strange—people don't wear something like that and the person was facing me and I was unable to see his features. He was all black. To me, that was a spook.
>
> I got pretty scared seeing him stand there. I'd gotten calls on that same thing and it just clicked and I said, "Well, I'll drive around." I drive pretty fast and it doesn't take that long to get around the block, and I knew if it was [a prankster] I could see him run. But there was nothing.

Ms. Duarte noted that reports of *el bulto* at the house come in spurts. "For two or three months they'll keep calling and calling, then they'll break off and you won't hear of the man in black. When they do call, the only thing they say is, 'We just saw somebody down there; the man is just standing there.' He stands there and that's all he does."[39]

To some witnesses, *el bulto* reveals himself audibly. In 1959 Epifano Gonzales, who was staying overnight in the house, was awakened by the rumbling of a wagon just outside. Though he was sleeping near the door, when he rose to look out into the night he saw only darkness.[40]

Succeeding generations are raised on tales of *fantasmas* in the adobe house, as in the case of Greg Ambris, who lived next door from 1960 to 1969:

> When my mother used to hang clothes outside she would always see people, hear steps and voices arguing at that house. I'd come in from work and she'd tell me, "There's always noise there; there's always noise." And I'd say to her, "Mother, how can you hear voices when there's nobody living there?" And she would say, "Oh yes, son, you can hear them." She always said that man was always watching *la Llorona*, that she could always see the man at the window looking outside. To her he was like a shadow, and he was tall, a Spanish guy. At nighttime she also could hear people as if they were taking water out of the well.
>
> My uncle used to say, "Be careful." I said, "Why, uncle?" He said, "See that house? Nobody knows about that house but your mother and I." I said, "What do you mean about that house? Is it scary?"
>
> Later, we got to throwing rocks at it, and one time we opened the front door. We were going to go in when my uncle stopped us and told us, "Don't go in that house—it's a dangerous house." We asked him, "What do you mean, Uncle, it's a dangerous house? Is somebody living there you don't want us to know about?" He said, "No, you might go in there and find something you don't want to see, that God doesn't want you to see. Maybe *el diablo* lives there."

As the years passed, Ambris became a witness himself:

> About 1967 or 1968—just before my mother died—she would tell us that at nighttime she would hear that front door open and a man gathering his animals, bringing them into the house. I said, "Mother, the man couldn't have animals." She said, "Oh yes, son."

Photoillustration of *el bulto* based on eyewitness accounts, made by author at the sutlery.

One night I stayed up—at first I thought I wasn't praying enough—and I heard it, and I heard the lady *la Llorona* crying. And then when I worked nighttime, I'd come in at two or three in the morning and always saw a light in the house. It was like lanterns moving from room to room all night long till morning came—and I knew nobody was there. I thought maybe it was because of the stars but Mother said no, that somebody was in there.

But I'd say, "Mother, there's not anybody in there. But there *is* a light. You can see it, like somebody turned on the lights and lighted up the whole house. But nobody lives there." She'd say, "Oh yes, son—that man lives there."[41]

Though Gloria Dupre of the Fort Stockton Police Department never saw *el bulto*, she heard many stories of him through her grandfather and her great-uncle, one-time owner Manuel Ramos. Ramos came to their house frightened one night in 1963 when she was still a child. "He was really scared because he said this person had spoken to him, wouldn't leave him alone. He was afraid and he would ask back, 'Who are you? Who are you?' He also said he could never see his face, other than it was dark, that he seemed to be in a shadow. He did know it was a man, but he couldn't make out facial features. It was not a void—there was a face there—but he was in the shadows and just blended in so deeply. He also said he got a sensation of it getting very cold in the room, the chills type of thing. I can still visualize clearly my grandfather scoffing at him: 'You're getting old—you're just imagining things.' My grandfather went over and stayed with him three nights until finally he did supposedly see what my great-uncle was talking about. And he came back and told us, 'It's true! It's true!'"

Ms. Dupre gained a mental image of *el bulto*'s appearance through descriptions given by family members. "He has a top hat and collar, but it's not as vampirish as you might imagine. It's more like a tuxedo, a long-tails type outfit to where you couldn't distinguish actual leg movement yet you could hear footsteps. What I visualize is how a hangman used to dress."[42]

Indeed, a folklore account persists that hangings were conducted immediately behind the house. "Dad said something about it being like a courthouse, way back in the 1800s," said Rose Duarte. ". . . His grandfather, or his grandfather before that, said to him [that] he believed there was a place where they had sort of a court . . . in the back where they hung people."[43]

Ms. Dupre also heard stories of other supernatural occurrences at the structure. "There are tales of a woman dressed in white on horseback. They'd hear the sound of the horse and look around and see it approaching. The next thing they'd know it was no longer approaching, but leaving. It never actually came. There are also stories that from within the house comes a shoveling sound, like that a shovel makes when it strikes gravel."[44]

The latter, within border folk religion, is the sound of treasure revealing itself in much the same way it does visually through lights or fire. "*La fantasma* is there because of the treasure and would certainly rest after the treasure is found," said the *viejito*, who long dowsed for it. "I have tried to find the treasure, but I didn't find it. It is not hidden in the well; it's hidden somewhere in the house and it's real hard to get to. Many people have looked for it, even using machines, but they haven't found it because they don't know the location." He added that only the individual destined for it ever would find it.[45]

Were the treasure to be unearthed, say those who should know, it might lend a clue to the identity of the man in black. Just who might have cached a bonanza?

During the nineteenth century, Aniseto Pina was a wagon freighter, farmer, government mail carrier between Fort Stockton and Haymond, and water tank builder. He also owned acreage and possessed many mares. Undoubtedly he was a man of means for those days, and in a region void of banks, he probably cached much of his wealth.[46] Because of that, some old-timers suggest that he left a treasure in his adobe house. Still others, however, recall a tale that suggests a treasure belonging to his son Pancho.

Supposedly, Pancho Pina knelt over a can in a dark corner of the house one night to count the silver and gold pieces derived from his eight sections of land southwest of Fort Stockton. A live-in housekeeper walked in upon him to gape at the wealth and inquire, "What are you doing, Don Pancho?" He quickly concealed the coins and shrugged, "*O, nada*—nothing, nothing." But he already had seen the knowing look in the housekeeper's eyes and realized she now shared his secret. He fired her within a matter of days.[47]

Treasure alone, however, may not be the only reason *el bulto* wanders restlessly about the house. "Just a man in black would indicate an evil deed done and a desire to reveal this deed in order to be set free," said one man. "A treasure would be indicated only if there was a fire or flame. There was a candle mentioned—a small flame—and the treasure would be equivalent to the fire. In this case it would be a small treasure, which would indicate the deed would be the thing that would merit the spirit coming and haunting instead of the treasure. So it's the deed that needs to be discovered much more than the treasure."[48]

When the sun is snatched away by the horizon, the old men with deeply carved features and the *niños* alike ponder the mystery. They are sure *el bulto* is there, but of all who walked the house and its grounds in recorded history, just whose wandering soul is it? Seterio Pina, born in another century, believed the man in black had existed even before him, but those who are convinced *el bulto*'s purpose is enmeshed with unrevealed treasure are sure his identity is either Aniseto or Pancho Pina.

"Pancho Pina, lots of people say that he had some money [buried at the house]," said Angelita Garcia, his niece. "Maybe his ghost, too, is looking for the money."[49]

The *viejito* concurred: "Aniseto made real good money and was in a pretty good position to put money away, but *la fantasma* is Pancho, Pancho, Pancho Pina. Pancho died in the house [in the fourth room deep, in 1937]. The ghost had not been seen before he died. I did not see it when I was little. Manuel Ramos reported seeing the ghost after Pancho Pina died. He is the one that told me about the house; he saw *fantasmas* and told me."

The *viejito* also claimed another spirit has frequented the site since the death of Ramos in 1969. "In front of the house is a well, and there's a rock by the house which an old man comes out and sits on. We believe it is Manuel Ramos. I did not see it before Manuel died."[50]

Yet another *fantasma* which postdates the initial appearance of the man in black is that which Roy Garcia encountered as a ten-year-old. Playing at the house, he suddenly came face-to-face with long-dead George "Choche" Garcia, the cobbler who had paraded about in black.[51]

Greg Ambris came to believe a long-ago murder at the house spawned *el bulto*. "When my mother was a little girl there was a man living there that shot his wife—a long time ago," he said. "He went crazy. My mother said that when he died, he never rested; he was looking for his wife. That's the story of the old house; that's why it's spooky. They call it 'the spooky house.' They always see a man or a woman crying or a man looking out the window to see if he can see his wife. My mother knew the truth because she was good friends with the people."[52]

The name of that supposed murderer has not endured the folklore-shrouded decades, yet S. L. Gonzalez verified that killings did occur at the house, and the *viejito* remembered several slayings in the adjacent arroyo.[53]

Despite a variance of opinions as to *el bulto*'s identity, those who saw the sores of hell cover the body of Pancho Robles the reputed occultist do not doubt it is he. "It's Pancho Robles, the one that had the *magia negra*—black magic—books," said Angelita Garcia (born in 1913), the niece of Robles's wife.

> That room [on the northwest corner] where he lived had a chimney he used to keep the bad books in. I don't know what books he had, but he had three or four. It was black magic books, something like the devil.
>
> My uncle Pancho was real sick. For two or three weeks he got worse and worse; he had scars all over his face and body, sores like he was burned. Lola—she was a *curandera*—came and read the palm of his hand and said, "If you get rid of those books, maybe you will rest in peace." The lady told him to burn those books, to find someone to burn the books, because he couldn't get up from the bed. I was scared when the lady told

my uncle to send somebody to burn those books, but he said he didn't have any books. He knew very well he had those.

I was afraid of him. One time my aunt told me to stay with him and give him some water or something. I stayed with him, but I would sit on the well while he was in the room sick. He had a bad look, but I think the reason why he had that is because he read those *magia negra* books. When he was sick, lots of people were scared to see him because he had that look—he was like someone who fell on the fire.

A week and a half after the *curandera* came, he finally had the books burned; I don't know who burned the books, but maybe the same lady. He didn't want to get rid of those books, but he had to. I remember the day—it was on Thursday—when he sent somebody to burn those books, and [then came] Friday and Saturday, and on Sunday night he passed away in the house. I think it was in 1926 or 1927. In that room where he had those books is where the ghost disappears. Lots of people think that it might be Pancho Robles because some people knew he had those books. That lady who read his palm said, "If you don't burn those, you're not going to rest in peace." No one saw the ghost until after he died. Maybe he gave his life to the devil.[54]

The *viejito* believed it possible for a priest to free the house of its spirits; indeed, the Catholic church has a rite of exorcism in which a church bell, the Holy Book, and a religious candle are used together to expel a demon from a structure. Too, say some, a *bulto* may gain peace through prayers and a blessing delivered by a priest.[55] But such rites are extremely rare in the Catholic church and apparently never have been performed before the adobe walls.

Though there are numerous witnesses to *el bulto*'s presence in the structure, there is also counter testimony. Manuel Ramos's son Remie, born in 1932, lived in the house from childhood until 1949 and again in 1952–1953 and never experienced anything supernatural. "I don't know where people got that," he said. "It was my home—let me put it that way—and I never did see anything unusual. I slept in that house many, many nights all by myself, and I was never bothered by any thing or body. I've heard people say that you see ghosts, but it's just something I never did believe in. I sure don't."[56]

Furthermore, Remie and Chino Duarte[57] disputed others' statements that Manuel Ramos was aware of the man in black. "He never mentioned anything," said his son. "As a matter of fact, the last few years that he was there, he was there all alone, and he never mentioned a thing about seeing anything or hearing anything."[58]

Likewise, Domingo Garcia never noticed anything unusual in the house despite moving next door in 1969, though in 1978 his daughter saw a moving light.[59] Nor did Mrs. Charlie Gonzalez observe supernatural occurrences from her home across the street,[60] or Juanita Arcives in the more than half-century she lived within a block of the adobe walls.[61]

However, *el bulto* seems to make himself known only to those he chooses, and many residents around the old sutlery believe this borderland poltergeist draped in black still awaits, fated to roam restlessly forever unless the predestined individual unshackles his bonds.

Site of Arthur Hayes's discovery of the lost wagon train near Old Flag Mill in Winkler County.

Lost Wagon Train

Rising from the creosote and scrub mesquites east of the Pecos, the dunes which stretch two hundred miles north from Horsehead Crossing are governed by the wind. They shift at its command, burying and exhuming, and in 1901 the endless cycle revealed an anachronism in southeast Winkler County: a large wagon train which had been burned.

Arthur E. Hayes of the Half Circle U or Cross O and Bob Brown of the Figure 4, on their way home to Monahans after driving TX Ranch cattle up the Chisholm Trail, stopped at Flag Point, a one-time Comanche camp at a spring bordered by willows. While Brown cooked supper, twenty-three-year-old Hayes wandered into the free-drifting dunes nearby and discovered numerous wagons partly buried. He solicited the aid of Brown, who initially was uninterested, and together they counted forty wagons, "twenty wagons on either side of what was apparently a V-shaped camp," said Hayes. They decided six-oxen teams had pulled the vehicles. But it was the gold-digging equipment that most aroused their interest, for it supposedly was made of steel manufactured only in San Francisco; they believed the wagons had been returning from the California gold fields, and that perhaps the ore had sunk into the sands.

But what had happened to the wagoners?

Hayes noted three clues: the formation of the wagons, their burned condition, and their presence in what was once Comanche country. Because the wagons were in a "V" and not a circle, he suggested the emigrants had been unprepared for attack; too, the charred relics indicated they had not abandoned the wagons simply because they had bogged. To Hayes, there was only one answer—massacre.[1]

But in this land of enigma, establishing documented facts about such a supposed event was like trying to grasp a sandstorm. Indeed, for more than a half-century before Hayes's discovery, explorers had been awed by these hills of silicon where men might ride within and never find their way out. In 1849 Captain Randolph B. Marcy described them as "a most singular and anomalous feature"[2]; a few months later Lieutenant N. H. Michler called them "really an object of curiosity"[3]; and in 1854 Brevet Captain John Pope noted they were "a curious and interesting geologic formation."[4] And to thousands of westward-bound emigrants in the nineteenth century, they were threatening as well as demanding.

Marcy, ordered by the U.S. Army to find the best wagon route west, escorted a wagon train from Fort Smith, Arkansas, to Santa Fe and returned east by way of Guadalupe Pass and a ford near Emigrant Crossing. Sighting the sands September 22, 1849, on the second stage of that march, he described them as "a chain of sand hills . . . running from north to south across our course, about twenty miles to the east of us." A Comanche warrior who served as his guide told Marcy that the only practical route through the dunes, which held abundant water, was via a fifteen-mile pass.[5] Nevertheless, Marcy balked at entering the wasteland and dispatched a lieutenant and dragoons to look for a better route to the south; the following day they returned to report that within the succeeding forty miles southward "was no place . . . where they could be crossed with wagons." On the contrary, the region "seemed to be one continuous succession of white sand hills, from twenty to one hundred feet high, in which . . . horses sunk to their knees at almost every step."

Marcy was left with no choice but to follow the course suggested by his Comanche guide. On September 25, 1849, they forged northeastward through the sands in present-day Winkler County. About them rose white drift-dunes, hewn by the wind into myriad "conical hills, destitute of soil, trees or herbage." With thirst becoming a matter of concern, they sought springs which reportedly lay a half-mile off the trail; riding into "the

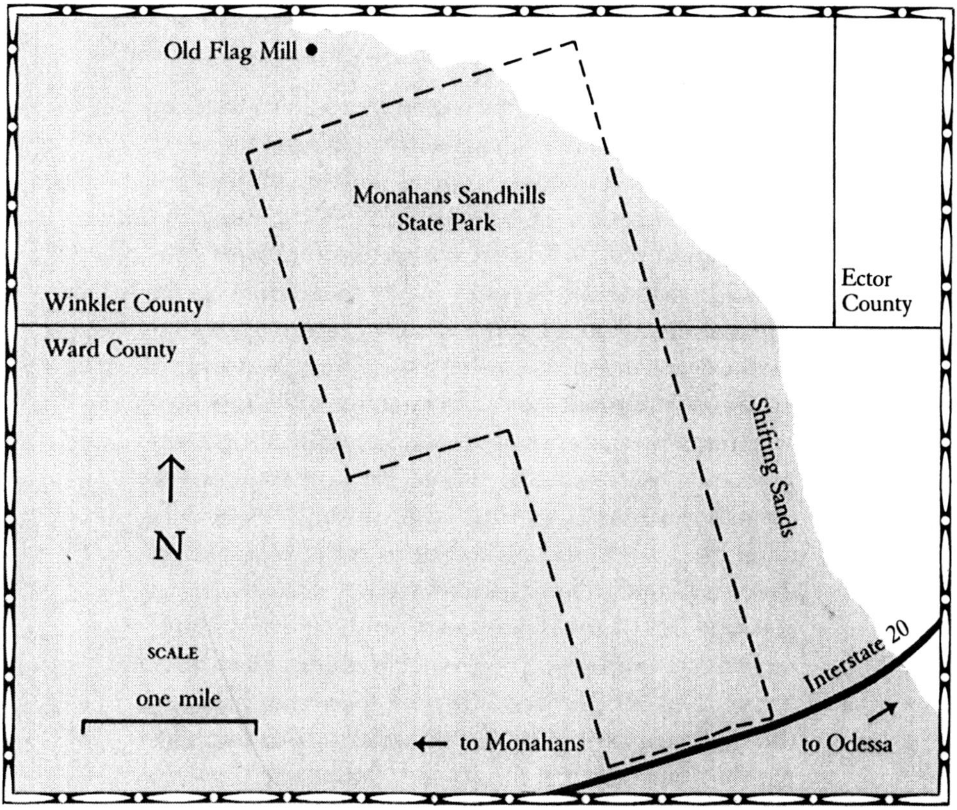

midst of this ocean of sand" they found several deep pools of pristine water at "the very last place on earth where one would ever think of looking for it," said Marcy.

The next day Marcy's contingent sustained difficulties; the wheels bogged so badly Marcy had to abandon half the wagons and double-up the teams. After reaching the final pool of water five miles later, he ordered the animals unhitched and driven back to pull the remainder of the vehicles. On September 28 Marcy finally attained solid ground again; it had taken three days to navigate a seventeen-mile course through the sands.[6]

The journey was no easier for succeeding expeditions. "A difficult undertaking it was to cross our wagons," said Lieutenant

Nathaniel H. Michler, who reversed Marcy's route three months later in exploring between San Antonio and the Pecos:

> . . . We found, for the first twelve miles, low ridges of sand, running parallel to each other, plains of the same kind interspersed between them, with small hillocks. The sand was here of a black color. Then come the white sand hills. . . . They are a perfect miniature Alps of sand—the latter perfectly white and clean: in the midst of them you see summit after summit spreading out in every direction, not a sign of vegetation upon them—nothing but sand piled upon sand. They form a belt two or three miles in width, and extend many miles in a northwest direction. But a matter of the greatest surprise is to find large water-holes among them: they are found at the base of the hills, are large, deep, and contain most excellent water, cool, clear, and pleasant. The water is permanent. A great deal of vegetable matter and young willow trees are found on their banks. This was the first water we found since leaving the "Mustang springs"—a distance of sixty-seven miles without any: during this entire distance we saw no indications of any whatever. Instead of going above the sand hills, we crossed them, following a large Indian trail . . .[7]

Surveying the thirty-second parallel for a proposed railroad route to the Pacific in 1854, Brevet Captain John Pope cursed the trail through the dunes as "dreadful" and "miserable" from the initial struggles of his eight- and ten-mule teams March 26. He described the sandhills as comprising "white drift-sand, thrown up into innumerable conical mounds, totally destitute of all vegetation. . . . When amongst the 'Hills,' one would suppose there had been a heavy fall of snow. . . . One would suppose that this region of sand is the last place where water could be found; yet, however incredible it appears, there is an abundance of water in these hills, contained in basins of the finest sand." The site of such a pool situated thirty-six miles from Immigrant's Crossing and a half-mile off the main trail foreshadowed Arthur Hayes's discovery five decades later. "From the great quantity of fragments of abandoned wagons," recorded Pope on March 26, 1854, "this place has been evidently a general camping-ground."[8]

To Pope, it was no mystery why wagons had been left amid the dunes:

> They are in reality impassable for heavy-laden wagons. . . . From the Pecos river to the level prairie east of the Sand Hills, the road passes through about thirty miles of the heaviest sand. It is the worst road to be found in New Mexico, on the Rio Grande, or, indeed, anywhere else. It cannot be too strongly urged upon emigrant parties never to attempt travelling by this route, except in the rainy season, from August to the middle of October, as the distance without water from the Sand Hills to the first permanent water to the eastward, is sixty-seven miles, thirteen of which (immediately to the eastward of the hills) are through sand so deep and heavy as to be absolutely impassable for heavy laden teams. With animals perfectly fresh, and lightly loaded wagons, it requires all our exertions to overcome the difficulties of this dreadful road.[9]

Through the remainder of the nineteenth century westward-bound pioneers battled the sand, drawing upon Marcy's 1859 *The Prairie Traveler: A Handbook for Overland Expeditions* for a description of the route he took in 1849. The passage of a decade had not blunted his memory of the effect of the dunes on wheels, and he advised "travelers with loaded wagons to make half loads."[10]

Even when emigrants adhered to his suggestion, the trip was brutal, as Elizabeth Mitchell Moorhead learned when she crossed in the 1880s. "The wagons had narrow tires, and she said they had to get out all their quilts, fold them, and put them under the tires so that the mules could pull," recounted J. Conrad

The West Texas sands at Old Flag Mill, where a wagon train massacre is said to have occurred.

Dunagan of Monahans, who interviewed her in Pecos in the 1960s. "And when they got over that piece of quilt they'd run back and get it and take it up and put it under the wheels for the next stretch."[11]

Undoubtedly, Arthur Hayes realized the severity of the sandhills forced the abandonment of wagons occasionally, but he believed the fact that those he came upon had been burned proved a massacre had occurred. From that day in 1901 when he rode into Monahans to tell of his find, the legend of the "Willow Springs Massacre" grew in stature. He did not initially say he uncovered human remains at the site, but later he amended his account. "So many years have passed that the human bones have decayed, so I could get only pieces," he noted.[12] Eventually he determined to his satisfaction, if not to that of historians, that the wagoners were among the three hundred to five hundred emigrants who passed through Yuma, Arizona, in the spring of 1873 en route back east from the California gold fields.[13]

Ultimately, a legend evolved from Hayes's initial allegation of a massacre. Supposedly, the caravan consisted of Dutch emigrants returning from the California gold fields with three million dollars in gilded ingots. To ensure the treasure did not fall into the hands of Indians, a contingent buried it off-trail when they made camp each night. Finding recent signs of Indians when they reached the Pecos country, the wagoners sought to avoid confrontation by striking out across the sandhills; they did not realize warriors frequented the dunes. Stopping for the night at a willow spring, the emigrants buried the ingots in the sand some distance away. In an ensuing attack Indians killed the pioneers and burned the wagons, leaving the ingots lost.[14]

Hayes, who held fourteen law enforcement commissions throughout West Texas prior to becoming justice of the peace in Monahans,[15] allowed much of his life to revolve around the alleged massacre at Flag Point. Not only did he dig at the site himself, but he dispatched area youngsters to prowl the blowouts and acquired finds made by others. Obtaining an unusual gold wire necklace from an Indian grave at Flag Point, Hayes publicized its description throughout the nation. An elderly woman in Pittsburgh, Pennsylvania, responded that her sister had owned a similar necklace when she had headed west in the 1849 gold rush; though the sister later had written from California that she would be starting home soon, she was never seen or heard from again. A Mrs. Waldon, the Pittsburgh woman's daughter, worked her way to Monahans with Ringling Brothers Circus and declared that the necklace was identical to her aunt's. It led the older woman to become convinced her sister died in the Willow Springs Massacre.[16]

Though Hayes never gained unquestionable documented proof such a massacre had occurred, he exploited the legend by displaying artifacts taken from the site in his justice of the peace/notary public office. He charged twenty-five cents admission to his display of saddles, ox bells, miners' picks and lamps, pots, kettles, meat cleavers, firearms, bullet molds, and arrowheads. But, in seeking the color and notoriety of Judge Roy Bean, Hayes apparently was not above deceiving his museum guests. L. B. Stevenson, a Monahans veterinarian, said that as a youth he gathered sandhills relics—not necessarily from the vicinity of Flag Point—and sold them to Hayes; the justice of the peace in turn included them in his collection, thereby implying they were from the site of the Willow Springs Massacre. "He would buy those things from us, and I imagine that he let those things embellish his story and imagination that those things came from the wagon train," Stevenson said. "I think he liked to let his imagination grow maybe."[17]

The collection became further garbled in succeeding decades with the addition of outside items; eventually it was claimed by Monahans Sandhills State Park and by Museum of the Big Bend at Sul Ross University in Alpine. "I think we have a core group of materials that we can say with assurity came from the Hayes collection and may have been associated with Willow Springs," said Ken Perry, director of Museum of the Big Bend. "The heavy things are perhaps the kinds of things that might have been on a wagon crossing West Texas or traveling overland in the mid-1800s."[18]

The original wagon train, however, long since has disappeared from the Flag Point vicinity, as artifact hunters and treasure seekers carried the major wagon parts away and shifting dunes claimed lesser items. But an eyewitness account endures, thanks to Ward County resident Edd Cox who, as a twelve-year-old in 1929, scoured the site for artifacts. "At that time there was no way in to those sandhills really except afoot or on horseback, and a horse couldn't do much in it," said Cox. "So we younger fellows went in, spent some time and hunted arrowheads and skeletons. You could dig you a hole and get water any time you wanted to. We carried food, stayed all night some. You could have

A mortar, presumably discovered near the lost wagon train and later included in the Hayes collection. Now displayed at Monahans Sandhills State Park, the vessel was used to crush ore in gold mining procedures.

loaded a truck with things out of the sandhills like corn grinders, and of course those wagons you couldn't have put on two or three trucks. Arrowheads were fairly plentiful. You had to hunt for them—you didn't just go pick them up. But after every sandstorm some were uncovered."

Cox sold the artifacts to Hayes or Micki Bland, a Monahans

woman, for "practically nothing. If we'd find a pretty good arrowhead we'd get fifteen cents for it. Another person would buy our lunch and give us a dollar, dollar-and-a-half a day [to hunt], and lots of times we'd find several arrowheads. He got them all."

But Cox alone retained memories of the caravan out-of-time. "The first time I was ever there—from Monahans, northeast probably about eleven miles—we had walked in to a windmill they call Flag Mill that was close to this. That was almost on the north side of the sandhills; in fact, that was just about as far north as we ever went. There was a flat, kinda—there's always those valleys where the wind has blown it out and piled it up. A bunch of sand hills had made a semi-circle on the south side of that flat and the wagons were lined up for a quarter of a mile from the southeast to the northwest or vice versa. The ground was blown off fairly hard, and these wagons were partly buried. Probably a lot was completely buried that we didn't even see."

Constant shifting of the dunes had obscured evidences of the willow spring Hayes had noted twenty-eight years before, but, said Cox, "If there had been willow trees right by it, they wouldn't have impressed me because they were all over the sandhills, and still are." Other details Cox observed also differed from Hayes's account.

> I don't remember anything about [the wagons] being in a V. Of course, they had been there for a number of years when I saw them, but in my mind's eye they were more or less lined up, and I can feature if they were going west they were bearing a little to the north; if they were going east they were bearing to the south—*if* I have the true north in my mind right. And I believe I did. . . . I flew over there not long ago, trying to get it in my eye like it was when I was a boy. But it's changed a lot. Of course, when you're walking and flying an airplane you get a different perspective. . . . If I'd've been interested enough in it [as a boy] I could've determined whether the wagons, by the tongues and

so forth, were headed in one direction or the other, but I didn't. Also, I've tried to think about [the number of wagons] in years gone by. It's possible that we could have counted. But it's also possible we couldn't have, because this was a good while after this happened and more than twenty years after it was located. Probably some of it had been carried out before I saw it.

I can remember some of the wheels were standing up, but they'd be buried in the sand maybe halfway. Particularly, one of the things that I remember was that these were what we called butcher knife wagon wheels. Now the butcher knife was a narrow wagon wheel about two inches [in width]. Quite a bit later they made a wheel that was wide and would not bog up in the sand like a butcher knife. But these were narrow, and they were tall. The hind wheels were a little taller than the front wheels. I never thought to measure one, but I wouldn't be surprised if they were not five feet six inches or eight inches tall.

The most unusual detail Cox noted about the wagons was that they were charred. "I've been questioned before about whether they were burned, and I'm pretty sure they were because the wood was burned off the single trees and double trees. The iron was still there."

Though Hayes believed oxen had been the modes of power, Cox was certain the wagoners had used teams of mules or horses because trace chains were present rather than oxen yokes. "The single tree has hooks on it that hook into the trace chain, and the single tree has particular kinds of hooks that I would recognize anywhere. If I found one now I would know what it was immediately. And I can remember the parts of the single tree, the parts of the wagon. I would imagine that these horses were worked two [abreast], and if they were working four [to a wagon], they were working in front, not four abreast."

But puzzles remained. Cox recalled, "Later they came up

A saddle which was unearthed in the sandhills, possibly at the site of the abandoned wagon train. Once part of the Hayes collection and now in the charge of Monahans Sandhills State Park, it is displayed here by Edith Grissom.

A grove of willows in the dunes near Old Flag Mill, where a wagon train was found half-buried in 1901.

with the theory that maybe there was not a massacre, that the sands were so difficult to make time in that they abandoned the wagons, and then later they were burned. So some of them questioned me, 'Do you particularly remember any harness?' And I can't say that I do. I can remember wood from the wagon, the iron from the wagon, the wheel, found it very easy to determine that there were wagons there, but I can't definitely say that I remember finding any of the harness. So I couldn't say whether or not the wagons might have been left intact and burned later."

Regardless, Cox as a boy became aware of how easily a wheel could bog in the sand. "The first time I was there a couple of boys named Haines and I decided we would bring home one of the rims of the butcher knife wagon wheels, which was a little higher than our heads. We had quite a ways to go and over pretty good sand hills. This was a hind wheel, and we rolled it, what I would guess, a couple of miles. It rolled pretty good where the shinnery was, but it was very difficult where there was sand. We finally abandoned it and left."

But the dunes could yield artifacts as well as claim them. "It was very common to find human remains," said Cox.

> I don't have any way of connecting any of those to the wagon train. Most of them would be on top of the ground, and most of the time it wouldn't be a complete skeleton. I never did find a complete skeleton, but I did find a skull or two. Once we found what had been a grave, with human remains we supposed to be a woman. The bones were in fairly crumbly condition, and in this little place where they were we found a gold cross. On one side of it was Christ nailed to the cross, and on the other side was an image of a woman holding a baby. I'm just nearly positive that Judge Hayes got that. Through the years I've felt like that probably came from an Anglo woman—I wouldn't think the Indians would have had anything like that. It wasn't at the [wagon site], but it may have been within two or three miles of it. . . .

Now you can't find any traces of the wagons. . . . When roads began to be built there, oil people and pickups carried that stuff out immediately and stripped it. . . . I don't know where any of the old train is. A few years ago the Colorado River Municipal Water District built a big line and dug up a couple of wagons which had been completely covered in the sands. They probably didn't have anything to do with the train, but the historical commission here tried to get the parts. They were hauled off and we never tracked them down.[19]

A similar burned wagon train, apparently unrelated to that at Flag Point, was discovered in northwest Ector County dunes in 1940 by Avery H. "Rusty" Russell of Odessa. Bulldozing right-of-way for a pipeline, Russell felt the impact of a metal object against the blade and unearthed the wagons as he plowed onward.

At the age I was then, I didn't care about the possibility of an Indian raid on a wagon train—it was just a bunch of old debris. But they'd burned the wagons, and what they hadn't burned had decayed. There'd be a section of wooden axle that was charred on the outside end, and maybe three or four spokes left on a wheel with the rest of 'em burned off at different stages. They very definitely had been burned, but they hadn't been just piled up and burned. It was like someone had set them on fire and went off and left them, and wherever the fire went out is where it wouldn't be burned.

Of course, the old tires were iron. They were lying there and when you hit one of them it'd bend until the blade pushed it out of the sand. I just pushed those wagons back, this side and that. I didn't get outside the pipeline right-of-way. If I had there's no telling what I'd've found. I've been trying for the last forty-five years to remember where that wagon train was at, but I can't get it back in my head.[20]

The sands which both reveal and conceal mysteries from the past were known intimately by Rex Pigmon, foreman of the Vest Ranch which encompasses Flag Point and myriad Winkler County dunes. Born in 1927, he spent much of his life walking, riding, or driving the sandhills, yet never came upon evidence of a massacre at Willow Springs.

> I've been over it horseback and known every inch of it ever since I was twelve or fourteen years old, and I've never seen anything. My granddaddy, he had come out here in 1887 and homesteaded. He started ranching this country when he was eighteen. He was in here horseback all the time and he never saw anything either. Now, I have found lots of arrowheads. As a matter of fact, I'd come out weekends when I was going to school and look for arrowheads to sell to old Judge Hayes for a nickel apiece. Also, I was riding horseback one day and I came down through one of those low places and there was a piece of pipe sticking up out there. I got down and scratched around it, and there was a sight on the end of it. I dug it up and it was an old musket, one of those old black powder guns. It was blown up, had a split in the barrel.
>
> I've also found wheels and harnesses, but it'd be just a piece here and there somewhere. In 1947 I found a wagon rim and rolled it into a mesquite tree and stood it up. That's the last I ever saw of it. I've found a hack over there too. It stayed there for years and years until a seismograph crew found it and hauled it off.

Pigmon's failure to corroborate the legend of the Willow Springs Massacre and the wealth buried in the sands has not deterred treasure hunters from converging on his ranch.

> They've been looking for it here ever since I can remember, ever since I was a kid. They have all kinds of gear. Boy, they're really hunting. "Rex, we find this,"

they say, "we're sure gonna split it with you." And I say, "Well, I'm not too worried."

When I was a kid, twelve or fourteen years old, there was an old colored gent who had lived there in Monahans all his life. They called him Negro Sam. And he wanted to go look for that gold, so he conned me into driving a team for him. He was going to walk on ahead with some kind of hoo-doo stick and find it, and boy, I was thrilled to death. But in order to get our wagon in there we had to strip it down; all we had was wheels on running gear because mules couldn't pull a wagon in there. We stayed in there all day, but shoot, we couldn't find anything. But there's always gonna be lost gold around somewhere. It might be there and it might be fifty feet underground. I imagine a man could spend a lifetime out there looking.[21]

Old Flag Mill, the site of Hayes's discovery, lies within a half-mile of the northern boundary of Monahans Sandhills State Park, which consists of six sections of free-drifting dunes in Winkler and Ward counties. From the visitor center, park employee Edith Grissom of Monahans watched numerous treasure seekers embark only to return empty-handed. Yet, acutely aware of the wind's ability to alter the terrain and uncover items long hidden, she could not disregard the possibility that riches and answers might yet be found. "There's no telling what they might uncover someday," she said. "From the evidence . . . it's obvious to me that there was a massacre; the Indians were known to do things like that. . . . But you'd think if that many people were missing that it would have been in the papers."[22]

J. Conrad Dunagan undertook a serious study of the so-called Willow Springs Massacre:

I went out to Old Flag Mill with an old-timer named Fern Tatom who had cowboyed in that area in his youth. He said that when he was young, there was so much wagon iron left in the hills that you didn't dare lope a horse because he might step on a buried piece of wagon iron and ruin his foot, or fall and hurt himself or his rider. We picked up a few old square nails which could have been used in part of the wagons, and a few bits and pieces of harnesses which might have been of that antiquity. That would've been over a hundred years since the supposed massacre. But they could have also been from a little pigpen, though undoubtedly a great deal of wagon iron was left out there.

Serious historians have all told me if there was a massacre of that kind, it [the disappearance of emigrants] would have found its way into the newspapers of the day. And they can find no evidence of any such thing. The early explorers who passed that way in the period of the gold rush did not mention any evidence of anything like that. There's no question about there being a large number of abandoned wagons, but it's obvious as to why they were left—they simply couldn't get through the sandhills.[23]

The last surviving eyewitness of the intact relics, Edd Cox, also wondered if Indians were responsible for the wagons' demise:

I didn't see anything to indicate there was a massacre there. Like I said, at that time it was not uncommon to find human remains at the sandhills, and I don't remember any at that particular site. I couldn't even *absolutely* swear that those wagons were burned, because when something rots it has very much the same look as it does when it's been burned, particularly when it's been burned a good many years before that.

There's no doubt the wagons were there; that's been substantiated by a number of people. Now how they got there, where they were going and what they

> were doing, I can't tell you. Judge Hayes felt they were attacked and people were killed and the Indians stole the teams. But I believe there's some good evidence that would indicate the wagons were abandoned there and that the people took their things and left, that they just bogged down in the sand and couldn't make it.[24]

But what of the probable fact that the wagons were set afire?

The answer lies only in the wind, which moves this land a grain at a time, creating legends only to conceal the evidence which spawned them.

Charcoal sketches of William Caldwell Sublett and his wife, Laura Louisa Denny Sublett, drawn prior to 1900 from miniature photos they exchanged early in their marriage (courtesy Ethel Pitt Harris).

The Lost Sublett Mine: The Man and His Diggings

The gold nugget at his fingertips would baffle succeeding generations. As large as a robin's egg, it gave bulk to a chamois bag of gold coins, perhaps eight hundred dollars' worth—undeniable evidence of a treasure he had found where such could not possibly have existed. But on the sixth of January 1892, he lay dying of pneumonia in a rented room above a restaurant operated by a Chinese immigrant in Barstow, a Ward County, Texas, town situated near the Pecos. But for his eighty-acre, $160 homestead sixty-eight miles away near Odessa and a rickety five-dollar camp wagon and hundred-dollar team in the Monahans wagon yard, all the possessions he had claimed in his fifty-seven years crowded near: a suit of clothes, the straight-bladed skinning dirk at his belt, and a .50-caliber Sharps rifle, a sixteen-pound single-shot breechloader which had felled countless buffalo and fended off Comanches. No one attended him, and only his children and a few friends would mourn him. Indeed, some would even curse him, for William Caldwell Sublett would carry to the grave the secret of the Lost Sublett Mine of Trans-Pecos Texas or southeastern New Mexico.[1]

The story of Sublett and his lost diggings epitomizes the blending of history and folklore which is common along the Pecos in West Texas and southeastern New Mexico. Few "historical" accounts have been more debated in the region, or any lost treasure sought more fervently, with the possible exception of Maximilian's wealth. Yet, unlike the latter treasure, whose very existence is questionable and for which documentation is sketchy at best, Sublett's source of gold undoubtedly existed; eyewitnesses, including his children, saw the ore. But as the last breath passed his lungs, his secret mine in the Guadalupe Mountains eighty miles northwest or in the Delawares or Rustler Hills or possibly some other range disappeared as well.

A telegram from a Ward County law officer notified Sublett's twenty-year-old daughter Jennie and her husband Sidney Pitt of her father's illness, and they immediately took a train from their homestead near Odessa. But by the time they reached that lonely little room on the West Texas frontier, he had died and desecrating thieves had ransacked the room, taking the nugget and chamois bag, the dirk, the Sharps rifle, everything except what they may have sought the most—a waybill to the mine. Left without a cent for his own burial, this man who apparently discovered such golden wealth and who launched generations upon obsessive quests for it would have been buried in a pauper's grave but for his children, who returned his body to the Ector County Cemetery in Odessa. The epitaph on the three-foot tombstone, chiseled at Granbury, Texas, and shipped west by his older daughter Ollie and her husband Sam Knight, speaks volumes, in consideration of the succeeding century:

> Their bodies are buried in the dust.
> But their names shall live forever.

And indeed, whenever tales of lost treasure and mystery are woven, Sublett's name invariably surfaces. Around the campfires of Pecos River nights he has become known as "Old Ben" Sublett, a hard-drinking and crusty prospector who, virtually abandoning his motherless children, limped off year after year into the Guadalupe crags or another canyon-slashed range and ultimately found gold where it could not have lurked. For a hundred years now, Sublett and his mine have been swallowed up in the folk tales of the region's natives and of credulous gold seekers from afar, inexorably entwining reality with fantasy. But what about

William Caldwell "Will" Sublett, the man of history? And what are the facts of his mine?

Will Sublett was the son of Caldwell Sublett and his wife Nancy, who may have been part Indian; both of his parents were born in Kentucky and moved to Tennessee, where, possibly in Franklin County, Will was born on September 25, circa 1834,[2] the second of six children. Sometime between 1836 and the winter of 1838 little Will moved with his family south to Alabama, and by 1840 the Subletts were settled firmly in the northern district of then-Benton County in the northeast part of that state.[3]

During this period of his boyhood, perhaps even in his latter Tennessee years, Will learned he possessed the inexplicable ability to witch water. Dowsing was ancient even by the time Will nurtured his gift; possibly traceable back to Biblical days, it was well-established in Europe by the Middle Ages and accompanied immigrants to the Western Hemisphere, although the skill was regarded with some skepticism.[4] Will came to prefer the "V" of a green peach branch, the forks of which he held in his hands as he prowled the countryside in search of underground water sources which theoretically would exhibit a "pull" on the stem. He learned to keep the branch in a crock of water between dowsing ventures; when it leafed out he would see it planted and cut another such branch for his use.[5]

Other events not normally associated with boyhood also enveloped Will. Family tradition holds that as a youngster he and an older friend, a South Carolina native with the surname Rylee, were adopted into the Choctaw Indian tribe, in which the Sublett boy gained some knowledge of Indian sign language.[6]

Will apparently received a good education for the 1840s, for he was still attending school at age fifteen or sixteen.[7] That he was literate as well as religious was evidenced by his daughter Jennie Pitt's recollection that he often read to her and her siblings from the Bible.[8]

By the time Will entered his teens in 1847, his father had been elected Benton County sheriff and the family probably resided in Jacksonville. That Will's boyhood was spent in relative affluence for that era is suggested by his father's declaration of $1,500 in real estate in the 1850 Benton County census and the fact that between December 15, 1847, and March 16, 1857, Caldwell made thirteen purchases from estates.[9]

Will turned sixteen in 1850 and, though still in his parents' household, already had taken up farming, a virtual necessity in the nineteenth century.[10] However, once Caldwell Sublett retired as sheriff, likely soon after October 1854,[11] he began a new project which involved Will as well. In a region obviously void of hospitals they began caring for the sick and afflicted in their home. In January or February 1857 Caldwell and Will entered bills against the estate of Benjamin C. George, who had been under their care during his fatal illness in December 1856. Will requested fifty-five dollars for "attention while sick eleven days and nights at five dollars per day and night" for the period ending December 14, 1856, and twenty-five dollars for "travelling with corpse" on December 21, 1856.[12]

By that time Will was twenty-two and had grown into a slender, wiry man with tawny hair,[13] possibly already sporting the squared blonde beard displayed in the one surviving likeness of him. His eyes were dark and beady, his cheekbones well defined, his nose small and thin, his forehead high, and his ears laid back against his head. He probably had developed many of the character traits that marked his later life. He was not in the habit of swearing in the presence of ladies; "Mercy!" was his favorite expletive. He made friends easily and kept them. He became known as a dependable man of his word; if he said it, it was so. As he grew into middle age, people called him "Mr. Will" out of respect; he was never known as "Ben." He seldom drank (though some later tale-tellers claimed he was a drunkard); only at Christmas did he imbibe his special brand of eggnog that put him in demand at family gatherings. At opportune times he enjoyed repeating quotations, one of his favorites being, "Never take the horseshoe from the door."[14]

In his twenties Will began yearning for the rugged life of

the frontier, a calling which never deserted him. And so, according to family tradition, sometime after the winter of 1857 he set out for the wide-open spaces of Texas with his boyhood friend Rylee.[15] By January 1860 Will had drifted down to San Marcos in the Texas Hill Country. Sam Houston had just assumed the governorship and in his inaugural address had reminded Texans that they faced a "frontier stretching . . . but little short of two thousand miles," half of it "exposed to Indian depredations" so frequent that they no longer elicited sympathy in the state's interior. Houston believed federal troops were inadequate in Indian wars and that Texas Rangers best could combat the Indians on their own terms.[16] On January 5, 1860, he authorized Ranger Captain W. C. Dalrymple to muster sixty men into duty, and within four days created additional Ranger companies under Captain Edward Burleson and John H. Connor.[17]

Will Sublett enlisted under Captain Burleson in San Marcos on January 20, 1860. Though the wide-open frontier and the proximity of anarchistic Mexico held the threat of bloodshed, Will's time as a Texas Ranger private was relatively quiet; he patrolled from San Antonio to Camp Colorado in northeast Coleman County in late winter and possibly scouted into the Wichita Mountains of southwestern Oklahoma in March. He also was stationed at Fort Belknap, three miles south of present-day Newcastle in Young County, and elsewhere in North Texas, and in July he went on a long scout to a site his commanding officer called "Camp Mountain Pass, C.N."—forty miles north of Fort Chadbourne.

What Will did gain in his Ranger duty, which ended in San Marcos on September 9, 1860,[18] was experience in coping with the frontier. It led him within a few months to seek further adventures in the West, departing sometime after December 3, 1860, when he filed a claim with the state comptroller's office for $125.05, presumably for Ranger service,[19] but before Sam Houston was removed from office in February 1861. Will, an avid supporter of Houston, believed as he rode toward the setting sun that the governor and twice-president of the Republic would keep

Texas out of the conflict which was already threatening to divide the nation.[20]

In later life Will told his daughter Jennie he spent the next eighteen months "on the frontier,"[21] but exactly where and what incidents befell him are matters of conjecture and hearsay. Some say he prospected the Rockies,[22] others that he trapped in the White Mountains—Sierra Blanca—of the Mescalero Apache country of southern New Mexico Territory. Years later, one-time buffalo hunter Charles Dixon claimed that he heard Sublett say he had learned the location of his gold source from Indians during that trapping venture,[23] but Dixon's account is marred by errors: he claims Will made the statement in Midland in 1892, although Will died the first week of that year, ninety miles away, after a bout with pneumonia.

Whatever happened in young Will's eighteen-month period "on the frontier" has been lost to history, but on May 23, 1862, the Texas comptroller's office finally authorized payment of his military claim.[24] When Will returned to the state's interior, Sam Houston was long since deposed and the nation and state were rent by the War of the Rebellion. Will, with no family or roots in Texas, headed northeast to Arkansas, where his parents had moved prior to the 1860 census. On August 4, 1862, a few weeks before his twenty-eighth birthday, he joined the First Arkansas Cavalry, Confederate States of America, at Fort Rector on the Mississippi River. Of his participation in the war, he reflected later in life, "I went, but it wasn't the same as it would've been if I'd heard all the songs and stirring speeches. It was not like it would've been if I'd've seen the thing coming." Duration of Will's enlistment was to be through war's end, amended the next year to "three years or war."[25]

Will served as a private with Gordon's Regiment, Arkansas Cavalry, in Captain J. Fen. Rieff's company.[26] Unlike many of his undisciplined fellow cavalrymen, Will was experienced in the military system from his Ranger days and knew how to obey orders. His early directives took him near his father's home in Carroll County, and he first saw action in late 1862 southwest of

Fayetteville.[27] On April 18, 1863, he participated in brigade commander William L. Cabell's surprise attack on Union-held Fayetteville, and though Confederate forces were pushed back after three hours of heavy fighting and many casualties, Cabell noted that, along with the demeanor of several officers, the gallantry of "Private Sublett, of Rieff's company, deserve[s] to be particularly mentioned."[28] Of the nine hundred enlisted men in Cabell's charge, only Will was so cited; *any* mention of privates in the official reports of the Civil War is relatively rare. But apparently even Will was not immune to the hardships—inadequate sustenance, delayed pay, and battle fatigue from desperate, fighting retreats through Arkansas and Indian Territory—which seriously depleted Confederate troops by desertion; in October 1863 his name on Company F's muster roll included the remark, "absent without leave Sept. 18–1863."[29]

Will saw more hard fighting in 1864 and even may have been wounded. One of the earliest written accounts of Will and his mine in the 25 October 1929 edition of the *Pyote* [Texas] *Signal* alleged that in the Civil War he received a bullet wound which caused him to limp in later life. The authorities for this article, written thirty-seven years after his death, were three men who supposedly had known Will: Joe Graham, John Buchanan, and J. J. Amburgey (or Amburgy), who all lived in Ector County when Will did.[30] But the veracity of their recollections must be balanced against family tradition: Will's younger daughter Jennie never mentioned her father limping or having suffered a bullet wound.[31]

Sometime after General Robert E. Lee surrendered on April 9, 1865, Will, a civilian again, rode back to Fayetteville and began courting Laura Louisa Denny, the daughter of Alexander Denny, a blacksmith, and his wife Melvina, said to be a Cherokee. Will may have met Laura in 1863, when he served near Fayetteville with Cabell, or perhaps, in an era when courtships could be short, he met Laura after the war. In either case, family tradition holds that by the end of 1865, Laura, who was eighteen, and Will, who was thirty-one, had plighted their troth before God and man.[32]

Life in Reconstruction Arkansas was tough, but to the north lay bustling Saint Louis and apparent opportunity. Relatives of both the Subletts and Dennys lived in the city and surrounding Saint Louis County, so the newlyweds soon trekked two hundred miles eastward to the Tennessee border and the Mississippi River, then booked riverboat passage to "Sin Louie," as Will called it. The succeeding few years are mysteries; all that is known about their life there is that Laura gave birth to a daughter, Ollie, purportedly in 1866, and to a second child who died in infancy. Even more tragedy followed during this period—Laura developed tuberculosis, then known as galloping consumption.[33]

On the advice of a doctor, the Subletts left the Saint Louis area, probably by 1868, for a holograph by his younger daughter Jennie paraphrases Will as saying he traveled "five years in a wagon" for Laura's health.[34] The drifting brought Will back to Texas in time to be included in the 1870 census for DeKalb, Bowie County, in extreme northeast Texas.

Many settlers established homes in Bowie County in the early 1870s, lured in part by intersecting railroads being laid in the northeast section.[35] Though Will may have sought employment with the track crews or initiated a water dowsing practice, his occupation by July 1870 was "farm laborer," according to the census. His income for the year, as declared on the 1870 Bowie County tax roll, was seventy-five dollars, and his only material possessions were two horses or mules valued at $192 and miscellaneous items totaling forty dollars. It was a struggle for survival, especially since he now bore the responsibility of providing for another child, a girl born just that May in Texas.[36] The baby did not live long, and Laura herself began deteriorating rapidly, so Will loaded his wife and surviving child into their wagon and moved again to what he hoped would be a more healthful climate, though probably no farther west than Bowie County because of ongoing Indian depredations.[37] Where the Sublett family spent 1871 is not known,[38] but Jennie Cornelia was born in Bowie County on January 2, 1872.[39] That year Will's Bowie County tax bill was for four head of cattle valued at twenty dollars and for fifty-two dollars in miscellaneous property; state ad valorem tax was twenty-six cents, county tax was seventy-six cents, and poll tax was one dollar. Will, significantly, paid poll tax each year he lived in Bowie County and apparently considered it his civic duty to decide who was to govern him.

The Subletts probably remained in Bowie County until after the birth of their only son on May 5, 1873. Christened Rolth[40]—later chroniclers would corrupt the spelling to "Ross"—he was born more than a month prematurely to a mother wasting away with consumption, and Will kept the tiny baby alive by feeding him milk with an eyedropper and keeping him warm in a box surrounded by heated rocks wrapped in blankets. As Laura's health declined, Will moved his family to the home of Laura's sibling, presumably somewhere in East Texas, and at that unknown site she died on November 6, 1873, at the age of twenty-six. A negro woman who apparently lived with his in-laws volunteered to wet-nurse Laura's frail little son,[41] and when the infant was finally strong enough to travel, probably by early 1874, Will moved his motherless children back to Bowie County and resumed farming, again with no great success.[42]

Once Colonel Ranald Mackenzie had conquered the Comanches and Kiowas in the Texas Panhandle in the fall of 1874, Will felt it safe enough to move his children west to the prairies and buffalo range, presumably in the Fort Griffin region of West Texas. As Jennie later wrote, "Father said he had lost his wife and two children and the three that were left were not strong and he intended to keep us out in the open until we got well and happy camping."[43] The area he chose was one where vast herds of buffalo roamed undulating grasslands or thundered through gaps in cedar-covered bluffs which divided one watershed from another. About that time Will probably purchased his large-bore Sharps rifle—which was accurate to eight hundred yards and so deadly a good hunter could fell ninety buffalo for every hundred shots fired—and aligned himself with a buffalo outfit. Jennie later reflected on their free, frontier life near the buffalo range: "We children were happy as long as we had plenty to eat and a warm place to sleep. Our fare was wild game, bread sorghum, Eagle Brand milk and he would let us each have a little coffee. Our bed was in the wagon, or sometimes in a tent, or sometimes on the ground out in the open. I've heard him say he took us to the settlements just often enough to keep us from going wild."[44]

But such a life sometimes wore heavily on three motherless youngsters, and Will sought help from the wife of his boyhood friend Rylee at Granbury ninety miles southeast of Fort Griffin. Rylee's wife Mary, a South Carolina native then in her midforties, became the "Grandma" the children needed, and Will frequently left them in her care for two or three months at a time while he hunted the buffalo range. Though he always paid for their care and needs and made a point of being with them every Christmas, Mary Rylee and her family did the things Will could not—they taught the girls vital skills like sewing, sent them to school and church, and gave them a home they could return to when they could not accompany their father.[45]

As for Will, he almost certainly spent the winter of 1876–1877 felling buffalo, for approximately 1,500 hunters crowded the range that season. He doubtless returned the next year, when buffalo outfits took one hundred thousand hides from the Texas range in December 1877 and January 1878 alone. By the following winter, however, only a few minor herds remained, and by 1880 even these were gone.[46]

As the slaughter of the buffalo herds progressed, Comanches and Kiowas from Indian Territory launched raids on the camps of buffalo crews.[47] About this time—certainly prior to early 1879—Will and his children twice encountered Indians while they were crossing the buffalo range in their wagon; the episodes revealed his cool courage and native intelligence in protecting his family. Having served in Comanche country as a Texas Ranger, Will was wary and told his children to remain out of sight as they neared the summit of a long rolling slope. His daughter Jennie recorded the incident:

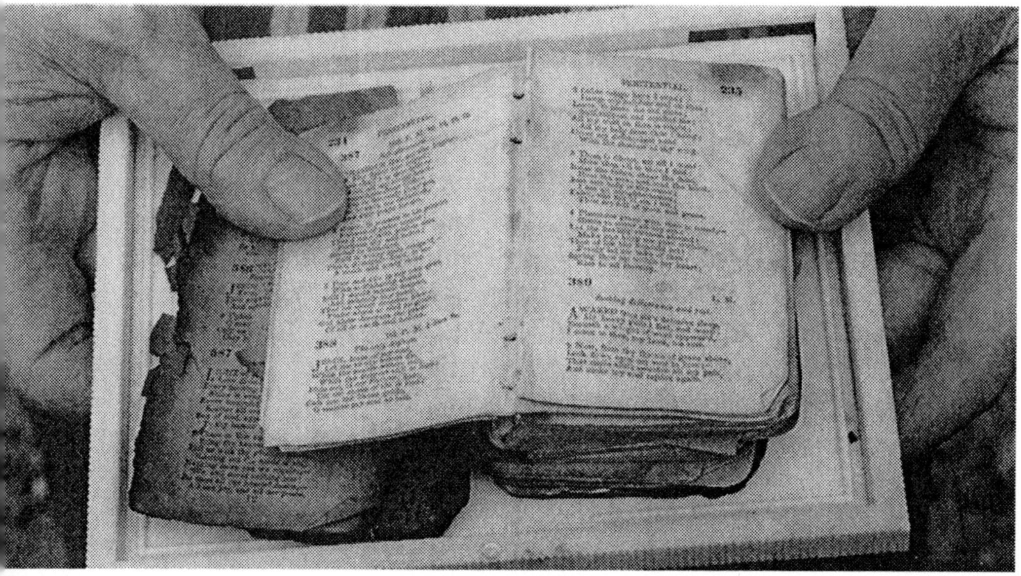

Close-up of Laura Sublett's songbook, the only extant item which belonged to William Caldwell Sublett and his wife.

[At] the top of the hill there was a large flat about a mile across. And at the far side of the flat was a creek with trees growing along the banks. . . . Sure enough when he got to the top of the hill, there was a band of Indians chasing wild horses.

Father stopped the wagon. No use to try to turn around. They had seen him and started toward us. He waved a white handkerchief, but they came right at us at a run, single file. Father sat down and shot over their heads and they turned and went off over the hill. I can remember they were coming right toward us, one right behind another, and at the sound of Father's big Sharps rifle, the leader turned and they all followed him. They

> had no way of knowing how many men were in the wagon and the little carbines they had and bows and arrows were no match for the buffalo gun.

Rather than turning the wagon and vainly trying to outdistance the Indians' mounts, Will urged the team straight ahead to the creek, where a faint road evidenced occasional patrols by Rangers. Slowing the horses to a walk, he suddenly burst upon an Indian camp. "There was a man as a lookout in a mesquite tree outside of camp," recounted Jennie. "He fell out of the tree and crawled off through the grass. Father drove right on by a big tepee. He could see the outline of someone inside. The Indians had horses tied to mesquite trees, and they were divided by colors. White ones together, black ones together, sorrels in another bunch, paint horses together, and they were all trying to break loose."

Will knew he could not camp anywhere near this water source as he had intended; he also realized he could not afford to show fear. So he walked the team on through the camp, then trotted the horses in depressions where they could not be seen. At each exposed area he would slow them, until finally darkness fell and he lashed the animals in a high trot all the way to a Ranger post. They permitted the horses to recuperate several days before continuing on and reaching another creek by nightfall. "It was dry but Father knew there were holes that never went dry," continued Jennie.

> So he walked up a ways to look for water. While he was gone my sister Ollie was holding the horses. All at once a campfire blazed up just across the creek. And there by the campfire light, we could see several Indians around the fire.
>
> When Father came back he quieted the horses down. We could see an Indian in a mesquite tree between us and the campfire. Father took his gun and leveled it on the Indian in the fork of the tree, and called out, "Is there any water down there?"

> As soon as he called, the Commanche in the tree fell out of it and crawled off in the high grass. Father said he counted four more who crawled away in the grass from the fire. After the fire died down he could tell by the way his horses acted that they had come back after their horses.

Immediately thereafter Will watered his team and then staked out the animals with long ropes tied to a wagon wheel. But he remained ever-cautious and alert. Jennie recalled:

> At first the horses would not graze out to the length of the rope, but finally [did so]. But sometime later they all at once ran back and jerked the wagon. At the same time it sounded like two other horses ran away as hard as they could go.
>
> Father got hold of the ropes and pulled his horses up close and quieted them down. After a while they got over their scare and started grazing again. Next morning Father took the horses to water, then got breakfast. While we were eating, a bunch of Rangers and two cowboys rode up. The cowboys had ridden up late in the night and had gotten close enough to scare the horses. They got scared we were Commanches and rode off and reported it to another Ranger camp [and] came back with the Rangers. They all had breakfast with us, [then] the Rangers examined the Indian camp and left.[48]

Indians were not the only troublesome people on the prairie. Once when Will was traveling alone in his wagon, about a day's ride from Fort Worth, two men on exhausted mounts rode up to his camp and, with drawn weapons, asked him to exchange horses. When Will hesitated, the pair offered him five hundred dollars in gold for the trade, and he accepted the offer. Soon after they left on his relatively fresh animals, a party of horsemen approached from the direction of Fort Worth and demanded to know the whereabouts of the men who had spurred the ridden-down horses. Recognizing the accents of carpetbaggers, Will replied, "Those are *my* horses" and stood firm as the riders searched in vain for tracks leading away through the tall grass. Will did not worry about the source of his new wealth; five hundred dollars richer for the exchange, he remained camped at the spot until the horses were able to travel, then continued his trip.[49]

While his children were in the care of "Grandma" Rylee and the buffalo herds were dwindling rapidly, Will may have begun prospecting the Trans-Pecos or southeastern New Mexico Territory. If so, he returned with nothing but calluses to show. With children to provide for and limited opportunities in frontier Texas for anything other than subsistence farming, Will found new hope in the track being laid westward by the Texas and Pacific Railroad. He had two traits which the railroad needed: the keen eyesight (and a Sharps rifle) to kill game to feed the crews of Chinese and Irish laborers, and a dowsing gift to pinpoint water sources along the route proposed for steam engines.

Exactly when Will signed on or began work on a commission basis is a matter of conjecture because records have not survived.[50] The rails, which paralleled present-day Interstate 20, reached Weatherford, twenty-three miles north of Granbury, on June 4, 1880,[51] but Will may have been hunting for the advance crews (the bridge-builders and brush-clearers who preceded track-laying crews) and scouting water along the route prior to then.

What is clear is that Will wandered far and wide while working for the railroad and in his free time began to prospect the precipitous canyons and wasteland crags west of the Pecos. Perhaps he searched in the faint hope of stumbling onto a lucky strike. Or maybe, as Charles Dixon asserted, he had gained the Apaches' inner circle and learned of gold in the Guadalupes or in another range guarding the Pecos drainage; early in his frontier life he had been friendly with the Choctaws, and a later episode indicated he did develop a rapport with Apaches. Some have suggested he was driven by stories of military payroll or outlaw booty cached along the Southern Overland Route which slashed through Guadalupe Pass, and others claim that stolen booty had been placed there by his own hands. But all these are theories. His motivation for prospecting may have lain simply in his obsession to explore new territory and in his dowsing ability.

As the rail line moved two-thirds of a mile farther from Granbury each day, logistics soon demanded that Will find someone other than Mary Rylee to care for his children while he searched for game, water, and precious minerals. Sometimes he took along Rolth, who by the fall of 1880 was a strapping seven-year-old. Family tradition holds that in preparing for one such expedition with his son, he paid a woman at some frontier locale to look after Ollie, age fourteen, and Jennie, eight. After an extended period, rumor drifted back down the line that Indians had massacred a man and little boy. The woman, having grown close to the girls, believed she had two orphans in her care and became determined to retain them. But something about the woman or her treatment of the Sublett girls aroused the ire of neighbors, who began circulating a petition to remove them from her home. Will's timely return with Rolth settled the matter.[52]

In a year the T&P had pushed 230 miles westward from Fort Worth; the pace of construction had quickened to almost a mile a day and soon would be three a day.[53] The early months of 1881 found Will and the children in Martin County at Colorado (later known as Colorado City),[54] a burgeoning town of several tents, one or two boarding houses, a buffalo bone crew camp, a newspaper, and four or five saloons. A large shanty with a tent roof housed a general store, and the sole eating establishment was in a twelve-by-fourteen-foot tent. Elsewhere lay the five-foot dugouts of cattle herders and of entrepreneurs who had pushed ahead of the railroad to prepare for the onslaught of laborers and their pay. As the tracks neared in February, March, and April 1881, the population increased to two to three hundred, the total number of saloons mounted to fourteen, and, of prime importance, railway officials situated construction crew headquarters at the site. "Colorado City was a sprawling, sorry sight in the daytime, with its disorderly rows of drab, dingy tents," remembered Mrs. J. W. Miller, who arrived in the town March 31, 1881. ". . . The open range lay all about. But the tents were lovely at night. At night the red lamp light glowed through them and you have never seen a prettier sight."[55]

It was in such a setting on the banks of the Colorado River that Will stopped his wagon and set up two tents, a tall cook tent in which he slept and a smaller one to shelter the children. By this time fifteen-year-old Ollie had developed into an excellent cook who knew how to prepare almost any item in a Dutch oven, to cook eggs by inserting straws into cracks in the ends and piling coals about them, to snare rabbits, to tend to their half-dozen chickens, and to preserve milk without refrigeration. Those things she learned from her father, who had lived out of a wagon or pack saddle for much of thirty years. By necessity he had become adept at all phases of camp life, and decades later Jennie still remembered his tasty sourdough biscuits, gravy, fried potatoes, venison battered and fried, and beans baked in a pot lowered into a hole rimmed with coals, as well as the honey or molasses he dipped out for dessert.

Such a camp with two good cooks often attracted visitors, and Will seemed to enjoy their company. If a rider approached Will frequently invited him to stop for a while; if the horseman politely refused, saying he didn't want to intrude, Will insisted by noting, "A short horse is easy curried." The insistence usually led to the Subletts sharing a meal with the stranger. But maybe Will was too affable a host; there always seemed to be five or six "hangers-on" for whom Ollie had to cook. One such man at the Colorado camp was an Englishman sporting a long-tailed coat. Feeding the Subletts' dog a bite of food that was too hot, the foreigner burst into laughter at the animal's discomfort. The act infuriated Ollie, who slipped around and placed hot coals on the man's coattails and set them afire.[56]

One reason Will solicited the company of strangers may have been an inner need to voice his belief that gold lay in the Trans-Pecos; some folklore accounts hold he was virtually obsessed with the notion. But he was not alone in believing precious minerals lurked west of the Pecos, where the Guadalupe Mountains jutted southward out of New Mexico Territory to crest at 8,751-foot Guadalupe Peak and abruptly cease at the half-mile cliffs of El Capitan. The latter fist of rock sentineled the choppy ridge of the Delawares reaching toward the southeast, the escarpment of Sierra Diablo—Mountains of the Devil—crowning the southern horizon, and symmetrical white beds of salt in a mile-deep basin extending to the twin Cornudas to the west. This northernmost expanse of the Great Chihuahuan Desert was an inhospitable land that held not only Apaches and outlaws, but also the dangers of dehydration, hypothermia, disorientation, and rattlesnake bite.

The Guadalupes long had been hunting ground and shrine to Indians, who once revered Guadalupe Peak as home of the Sun Gods. White men supposedly gave the V-shaped range its name when Apache raiders captured the *señorita* Guadalupe from a hacienda south of the Rio Grande and carried her into that one-hundred-mile forested backbone marked by gaping canyons. Even as late as 1881 both wild and reservation Apaches freely roamed its high country. Geronimo, notorious liar though he was, reportedly claimed the Guadalupes concealed the richest gold mine in the Southwest.[57] A white man also testified to riches in the Guadalupes: in 1863 the Apache Tats-ah-das-ay-go, or Quick Killer, led Captain John C. Cremony and a thirty-five man scouting patrol from Fort Sumner, New Mexico, southward to the Guadalupes and a site the warrior claimed held pure silver. Cremony wrote:

> Having arrived at the cañon, I left the command under the charge of the First Sergeant, and proceeded with Quick Killer for about a mile and a quarter, when he

dismounted and hitched his horse to a tree, requesting me to do the same, which I did, keeping my carbine ready and placing my holster pistols in my belt. We then ascended about three hundred feet until we reached underbrush and stunted trees. Quick Killer stopped a moment, examined the place well, and proceeded directly to a spot, which he unearthed for a few inches and displayed several magnificent specimens of virgin silver. I was satisfied, and possessing myself of a goodly lump, we retraced our steps to the command, none of whom were ever made cognizant of these occurrences. Wood, water and grass abound in the locality, which is in Western Texas, on the Pecos river.[58]

Furthermore, the aforementioned Charles Dixon contended that while prospecting near the Mescalero Reservation near present-day Ruidoso, New Mexico, around 1879 he fell in love with an Indian princess who showed him gold nuggets taken at diggings southward across the Texas line. She purportedly described the mine as situated two and one-half miles from "*Selas Teticua* or the Twin Mountains" which he would find in low foothills south of Guadalupe Peak. Landmarks would include a seep spring, a canyon or gulch, and a skeleton-filled cave haunted by evil spirits of ancient Indians.[59]

Such stories of Apache silver and gold in the Guadalupe region seemed more than legend; then-extant records in the archives of the Territory of New Mexico documented that Spaniards once had mined gold from the site. Unearthed by General Lew Wallace (later the author of *Ben-Hur*) during his tenure as governor of the territory, the official papers included a personal account, directed to the governor general, of Captain de Gavilan's expedition to the mine. Wallace claimed the document contained the names of every man in the party, the details of each day's march and work, and a brief description of the mine, from which the Catholic church supposedly gleaned great wealth through tithes. An account of that expedition appeared in the October 11,

1890, *Eddy Argus* and claimed that after traveling generally southward from Santa Fe several days and reaching the Guadalupes, de Gavilan's men

> crossed to the eastern slope to some low foothills, which were called *Sierra Cenizas*, or the Ashes Mountains, from their volcanic origin. From thence, about three leagues easterly in low hills, the mine was situated. It was about one league from seven pure, cold springs where the miners lived.... The rock is described as exceedingly rich in gold. The metal was found in wires, nuggets, and masses which were cut out with chisels.
>
> The gold which the property produced was shipped to Santa Fe over the route followed by the officer as described above. Another account states that afterwards, a trail was laid out from the mine to a mission to the south, supposed now to be San Antonio, Texas, and that to mark the trail stakes were driven. General Wallace was of the opinion that the Staked Plains of Texas came from the staked trail.[60]

It is little wonder that even skeptical prospectors searched the upper Trans-Pecos for precious minerals in the latter part of the nineteenth century. Frank Collinson told of meeting in the Pecos drainage a man named Miller who "was convinced that there was gold in the Guadalupe Hills and planned to continue his prospecting."[61] The October 11, 1890, *Eddy Argus* reported that "the Guadalupe Mountains is known to contain some very promising prospects. So far, no work has been done to a depth of more than three or four feet. Surface samples have been given an average assay of from seven to fifteen ounces per ton in silver and from 30 to 56 percent in lead.... Sooner or later the mineral resources of Eddy County will be developed, and that they will prove to be a source of great wealth is not for a moment doubted by those familiar with their flattering prospects."[62] In the same era the Eddy newspaper reported on mining activity in the range:

"B. A. Nymeyer [has] mining interests on silver, copper and lead ore in the Guadalupe Mountains, and F. G. Tracy will go up in a few weeks to the mountains to develop their claim. They already have a tunnel 110 feet deep and will sink a shaft this winter probably."[63]

Despite implications that precious metals lie in the Guadalupes or surrounding foothills, modern-day geologists maintain the range holds no such minerals because it is a fossil reef. But prospectors of Will's time or of any other era never let geology inhibit their search, for they lived by the axiom, "Gold is where you find it."

Such a controversy did not trouble Will when he left his children in the care of a family at Colorado in those early months of 1881 and trekked west of the Pecos with dowsing branch and rock hammer. Behind, laid out fragmentarily across a half-dozen states and maybe two territories were forty-six years of life and more than two decades of wandering, as though from the start of manhood he had searched for that indefinable something that always had remained just out of his grasp. Possibly it was a quality for which he yearned, perhaps one to help him rise above the masses destined to live in anonymity and die in oblivion. Maybe he sought immortality—not only spiritually but in the remembrances of those who had known him and those yet unborn. Somewhere beyond the Pecos he succeeded, becoming fated to be remembered in the annals of the Southwest—for discovering gold.

One wishes, from the vantage point of a century later, that Will had not been so reticent in describing the diggings' location even to his own children. But he was, and except for intimations here, suggestions there, the details of his find are left largely to conjecture and folklore. However, at least one supposed eyewitness to the mine did survive far into the twentieth century—Will's son Rolth. This frail boy grew into manhood to spend the next half-century searching for his father's lost gold, and he often detailed the one occasion when, as a youngster, he had accompanied Will to the site. Though to family members

Rolth would describe the visit in somewhat different terms, he once claimed in a 1948 Carlsbad, New Mexico, newspaper that he had been with Will at the initial discovery. The article so contradicts standard folklore accounts, especially as to the amount of gold taken, that it warrants consideration for veracity. According to Rolth's statement in that article, while searching for water for the T&P early in October of 1882, Will carried his son sixty miles north of the tracks to Pine Spring(s), at the mouth of the Guadalupes' Pine Canyon. There, 5,700 feet above sea level, where the abandoned ruins of a Butterfield stage station lay dwarfed by canyon walls rising an additional 2,600 and 3,000 feet, Will sighted a bear and cub one morning and felled the larger animal, for its meat, with his Sharps. Will then got his rope and the two trailed the fleeing cub several hours through rough country. In so doing they accidentally spilled their canteen of water.

Three o'clock in the afternoon found the pair seven or eight miles from Pine Spring and standing on rimrock surveying the northwest. In this arid mountain country where the autumn sun quickly dehydrated a man, something more important than a bear cub had risen to the forefront of their search—water. Believing he saw the reflection of sky in a pool in the gulch below, Will made fast one end of the rope and tossed the remainder over the edge. Lowering themselves fifty or sixty feet to the bottom, father and son proceeded up the gulch approximately three hundred yards to a pair of waterholes.

Rolth, who was nine years old at the time, sat down exhausted by one of the pools and removed his shoes to wash his feet. Innocently picking up a nugget from the water, he showed it to Will.

"Dad said it was pure gold," recalled Rolth.

Immediately leading his son fifty to seventy-five yards upcanyon to the spring which fed the pools, Will found six more gold nuggets. Then, carving at the vein just above the spring, ostensibly with his dirk and their bare hands, they removed twelve pounds of ore which years later assayed at $790 in gold and $12 in silver.

Pine Canyon in the Guadalupe Mountains of Texas.

Returning to camp, they awakened the next morning to hear gunshots from the direction of the canyon of gold. Hiking back to the site, they found evidence a large band of Indians or horsemen had been there during the night. According to Rolth, it was the last time he or his father ever looked upon the spot; despite stories to the contrary, Will never returned or sought to develop the mine because it would not have been "healthy" to do so. The seven nuggets upon which the legend of the Lost Sublett Mine rested, said the son, remained in Will's possession until he exchanged them for $200 in gold pieces in Midland, Texas, in 1889.[64]

This 1948 account, however, is somewhat at variance with what Rolth had told his sister Jennie decades before and with what she personally remembered: though he may have visited the mine, he was not present when their father made the discovery. Furthermore, the find must have occurred earlier, when the T&P railhead was at Colorado, for by October 1882 the railroad had been completed ten months and the need for additional water wells would have been questionable. Too, according to Jennie, their father returned to the mine for more gold several times.[65] As Rolth's senior by almost two years, Jennie well may have recalled such points of the story better. But the Carlsbad newspaper account cannot be dismissed totally, for it corroborates many details passed down through the family.

"Uncle Rolth told Mama about going down in a deep cave with Grandpa, and that was where the gold was," recalled Jennie's daughter Ethel Pitt Harris, who never personally heard her uncle describe the mine. "Uncle Rolth said he was eleven, and that they went into a little opening and then it opened out bigger and there was a cave down in there (with) water running in the bottom. They had to let themselves down there with ropes, and Grandpa got the gold out of that water. Uncle Rolth thought it was some place in the Guadalupe Mountains. Mama said she never heard Grandpa say anything about taking him off down there, but he might have."[66]

The account that Rolth gave Jennie bears similarities to his

October 2, 1947, claim that he and Will were the first white men to enter now-world-famous Carlsbad Caverns on a northeastern spur of the Guadalupe Mountains. In an affadavit witnessed by Carlsbad Caverns National Park superintendent D. S. Libbey, Rolth swore he "first visited what is now known as Carlsbad Caverns in 1883 when I was twelve years of age. I went down the natural entrance about sixty to sixty-five feet and then in the part where the bats stayed. The cave was known as the Bat Cave. My father, William Caldwell Sublett, was with me."[67]

Whether Rolth, then seventy-four, was seeking to associate Carlsbad Caverns with the Lost Sublett Mine, or whether the pair simply stumbled upon the cavern during a prospecting venture, is not known. Regardless, the affadavit carries an intrinsic contradiction: in 1883 Rolth was not twelve years of age; he was nine or ten. Too, the possibility exists that Rolth, in the twilight of a life marred by failure, may have played fast and loose with the date in seeking the notoriety that would accompany the caverns' discoverer.

At any rate, Rolth's description of a cave with gold suggests a cache rather than a mine; such would satisfy the geology critics of today. Indeed, folklore tales persist that Will's source of gold was booty he had taken in outlaw activity and concealed in the Guadalupe region. One third-hand account holds that below Guadalupe Peak in the 1870s Will and a man named Sutterhall held up a wagon bearing California gold and killed the lone wagoner. Placing the spoils on horses, the two men proceeded southeast along the edge of the Delawares, crossing its ridge near Twin Peaks and dropping into a fork of Chico Canyon. This mention of enigmatic double mountains south of the Guadalupes correlates with the "*Selas Teticua* or the Twin Mountains" sought by Charles Dixon as a landmark to Apache gold. Regardless, using a frying pan and butcher knife, Will and Sutterhall supposedly buried four caches of gold and then separated; Will, however, double-crossed his partner and relocated the caches.[68]

The episode of selling his horses outside Fort Worth indicated Will was not above taking advantage of a situation for personal gain. But as the son of a sheriff, he had been imbued with the concepts of right and wrong from boyhood and later counted the lawman at Monahans, Texas, among his friends. Too, much difference existed between aiding two fellow Southerners, albeit outlaws, against a carpetbagger posse, and taking a man's life for his hard-earned money. Furthermore, Jennie always contended her father referred to the site as a mine, not a cache.[69]

Will's wagon creaked back into the midst of Colorado City's flapping tents, 240 miles distant from the Guadalupes, sometime in late winter or early spring 1881, while the town was temporary railhead of the T&P. The date is not certain, but a Galveston newspaper made no mention of construction crew headquarters in Colorado in a description in its February 2, 1881, issue, and the first train did not reach Sweetwater, twenty-eight miles to the east, until March 12. The railhead probably was relocated to Colorado later in March, for residents heard the spikes being hammered through town on April 1; by April 28, 1881, the first train reached Big Spring to the west and headquarters likely had been moved to that site.[70] Though he was not a drinker, folklore holds that Will displayed his new-found wealth in the saloons the day he rolled in; if so, motivations of greed and jealousy to determine the mine's location probably prompted as many to plot against him as to toast his success, for Will's life did not become easier with his discovery.

Where Will converted these and later nuggets into hard money is conjectural, but it was common practice in those days for a prospector to ship his find to the nearest mint—in Will's case, the Denver, Colorado, facility. There, the government graded and refined the ore and then purchased it or minted it into bullion or coin for the owner.[71]

Will, however, always retained a nugget the size of a robin's egg and rich in gold. It was the largest such piece he ever took from beyond the Pecos, most of his finds being in the form of dust. He carried the nugget on his person inside a chamois bag which often also contained seven or eight hundred dollars in gold coins apparently gleaned from the mine. Often during the next decade he displayed that chunk of raw gold to his children. "Mama said he showed that to her many times," recalled Jennie's daughter, Ethel Pitt Harris.[72]

Now that it no longer was vital to hunt game for a livelihood and continue subjecting his children to a nomadic life, Will returned with his family to Mary Rylee's at Granbury, where his nine- and fifteen-year-old daughters could be raised as ladies.[73] By this time Mary's husband and Will's old friend Rylee was dead; he well may have been gone by the mid-1870s.[74] But there was a new man of the house now, for on June 29, 1879, Samuel Knight had married the Rylees' seventeen-year-old daughter Amanda, or Narcissa.[75]

Will immediately resumed farming, a vocation he had not undertaken since he left Bowie County shortly after Laura's death. Though family tradition holds he purchased a farm at Granbury with the findings from his mine, he must have only leased property; no record exists that Will owned land in Hood or surrounding counties.[76] The fact that he was not listed at all on Hood County tax rolls in the early 1880s suggests his stays there were temporary and that he continued seeking out the frontier and his diggings. One account claims that he hauled salt from the deposits south or west of Guadalupe Peak about this time.[77]

Bringing up two motherless daughters caused Will some problems. For one thing, Ollie and Jennie were tomboys, and he did his best to mold them into ladies. After a Granbury woman commented that the girls should not have been riding "stride," Will purchased them sidesaddles and brown bengaline riding habits. But it was less easy to discourage a budding romance between seventeen-year-old Ollie and Sam Knight, now widowed and the father of a baby girl. Will disapproved of the relationship, at least partly because Knight was twelve years older than Ollie.[78]

After approximately two years of living primarily in Granbury, Will responded to the lure of the open prairie again and headed westward, with his children, alongside the tracks of the

T&P. Discouraging Ollie's romance may have influenced his decision, but he may also have wanted to be nearer his mine. As Will's wagon rumbled toward the sunset in 1883, the arid 170-mile stretch between the Colorado River and the Pecos was largely void even of ranches. Midland, then known as Midway, consisted of a water tank and railroad car on a siding and little more. Odessa held but a section house. And when Will and his children halted their wagon thirty-nine miles west of Odessa near a boxcar depot and two abandoned buildings, it more than doubled the population of Monahans, then known as Monahan.[79]

When J. J. Amburgey and twenty-five other settlers arrived in Monahans later in 1883, they found Will and his children living in a tent near the railroad. The only other residents of the community were two railroad employees, an operator and a pumper with the last name Scroggins. The latter probably was either M. J. Scroggins or Adam Scroggins, both of whom are included in the 1884 tax roll for Tom Green County (which then included Monahans). The operator may have been a man with whom Will became close friends—a Mr. Wilson, whom later chroniclers said went by "Mike." But Will's friendship with a T&P employee named Wilson may not have come until later, or else it would be resumed, for Will's friend, an apparent widower, had a daughter the age of Jennie and a son the age of Rolth, and the two families were to become close. If "Mr. Wilson" were indeed the operator living at Monahans in 1883, he must have brought his children out to West Texas later.[80]

It was probably during Will's time in the Monahans area with its sands and desert reptilia that he suffered a rattlesnake bite in his foot or ankle. Fortunately, he was not alone, but with the nearest doctor hundreds of miles distant, well-meaning townspeople could only submerge his foot in a bucket of kerosene and fill him with whiskey. It was the only time Jennie ever saw him drunk, but the important thing was that he survived.[81]

Though it no longer was a necessity, Will did odd jobs around the settlement to occupy his time.[82] The apparent availability of great wealth had not altered his lifestyle or personality;

he seemed content to live frugally and take only enough gold from his mine to last his family until the next trip. But he may have had good reason to bring out only a small amount at a time: increasingly, men he once had considered friends plotted to wrench the mine's location from him.

Never would that be more apparent than the day several men rode up to his camp as he was en route in his wagon to his source of gold. He immediately recognized them as settlement acquaintances with whom he always had been affable, but the men nevertheless leveled their weapons on him and demanded directions to the mine. But that was a secret Will would not relinquish even to his own children. The men tied him up and denied him food and water, threatening to let him die if he refused to quote a waybill to the gold. But Will remained steadfast throughout the evening and night, and the attack of Apache raiders after sunrise the next day sent the white men fleeing. When the Apaches cut his bonds, they saw Will display the Indian sign of peace he had learned in his boyhood from the Choctaws, and they let him go on his way.[83] Or maybe they spared this aging man with iron-gray hair[84] because they long had known and trusted him, perhaps even to the point of sharing the secret of Apache gold.

If so, it was a secret bearing a curse, and Will's decision not to burden his children with it was made with great foresight. Only once, according to tale-tellers, did Will ever waver in his determination not to reveal the mine's position and dictate an unwritten waybill to another. That was with his friend Wilson, and perhaps Will empathized with this widower who like himself had been forced to raise children alone.

According to one of the earliest written accounts of the Lost Sublett Mine, a newspaper article of unknown origin reprinted in magazine form in 1916, Wilson followed Will's directions and found the diggings in the Guadalupes. Emptying his pack of supplies, he squeezed in as much gold as he could and undertook the arduous trek back without adequate food or water. When he finally reached home, physically drained by the rigors of the journey, he embarked on a drinking bout that lasted three weeks. The back-to-back episodes robbed him of recent memory, and when he sought to retrace his course to the mine he quickly became bewildered. Will, having seen how knowledge of the gold had affected his friend, refused to detail its location again.[85]

With the T&P providing passenger service from Monahans to within a few miles of Granbury, the Subletts continued their association with the Rylee clan. In early 1885 Ollie, particularly, must have spent considerable time there in the company of Sam Knight, whom Will continued to dislike. Nevertheless, nineteen-year-old Ollie wed thirty-one-year-old Knight in Hood County on May 31, 1885.[86] The age difference, incidentally, was less than that between Will and Laura. Ollie assumed instant motherhood, caring for Knight's child (the granddaughter of Mary Rylee) and raising the girl as her own. "I met this woman in El Paso and she said Aunt Ollie was all the mother she ever had," recalled Jennie's daughter Ethel Pitt Harris.[87]

Whether Will and his youngest children returned to Monahans or relocated to Odessa immediately after leaving the newlyweds in Granbury is not clear. He was not included in any West Texas tax roll until 1886 when he was so listed in Tom Green County, which then encompassed both settlements. By that time he still had not succumbed to what must have been an overwhelming temptation to embellish his life with the material. He possessed only a thirty-dollar wagon and two horses or mules valued at sixty dollars, on which he paid $2.59 in state and county taxes.[88]

It was one of the great ironies in Southwest annals: a man holding the secret to vast treasure found himself restricted by that very knowledge into removing only minute amounts at a time. Or perhaps Rolth was accurate in his 1948 claim that his father only took seven nuggets and twelve pounds of ore, all in 1882, and exchanged the nuggets for $200 in gold pieces.

Will and his children apparently moved to the ranch settlement of Odessa by at least 1887, for in that year teen-age Jennie also began to be courted by an older man: Sidney Pitt, son of

David Meeks Pitt who settled Odessa in the mid-1880s and Jennie's senior by four years.[89]

Only a hundred or so men lived in proximity to Odessa, which lay in a prairie virtually without topographic feature to distinguish one site from another. It was, as a later chronicler would describe, the land of the high sky where Spanish *conquistadores* had been able to see the horizon beneath the bellies of the buffalo.[90] Summers were intensely hot, and all the way to Canada existed scarcely a knoll to slow the onrush of frigid winter air known as northers.

However, it was apparently enough to suit young Jennie and nineteen-year-old Sidney Pitt; they eloped on December 29, 1887, when she was still four days shy of her sixteenth birthday. Though Will was disappointed at her early marriage, he did not seek to have it annulled. Ultimately, Pitt came to respect his father-in-law as an "old-fashioned gentleman."[91]

Will was not included in the Tom Green County tax roll for 1887—possibly he was away at his mine much of the time—but he may have been the "J. S. Sublett" listed in the 1888 record. No such Sublett had paid tax previously in Tom Green or ever would again. Too, specific items declared by this Sublett, a wagon and team valued at seventy-five dollars, are identical with Will's possessions as described two years before. Likely, the "J. S." was a clerical error.

Will doubtless spent time twenty miles east of Odessa at Midland, a sister ranching community. There, not only did Charles Dixon claim to have heard Will state he learned the gold's location from an Apache, but folklore dictates some of the town's leading citizens once plotted to steal the mine from him. As recounted by master storyteller J. Frank Dobie, the conspirators were pioneer banker W. E. Connell, rancher George Gray, livery stable operator Lee Driver, and horseman Jim Flannigan.[92] The names belong to men of documented history. W. E. Connell, who was first listed on Midland County tax rolls in 1887, owned the Five Wells Ranch forty miles north of Midland and in 1888 helped organize a private banking service that became First Na-

William Caldwell Sublett's daughter, Jennie Pitt, at age sixty-eight (courtesy Ethel Pitt Harris).

tional Bank, later the largest independent bank in the state.[93] Gray purchased a ranch in what later would be Midland County in 1884 and was one of the original county commissioners in 1885.[94] He paid taxes in Midland County from 1885 through 1887 and was listed alongside Will on Ector County rolls in 1889 and 1890.[95] Driver may have appeared as an unreadable name on the 1891 Midland County tax roll; he definitely was included in 1892 as L. G. Drivers. A J. W. Flanagan first turns up on Ector County tax rolls in 1888 and was doubtless the same man as the J. M. Flanigan and J. M. Flanagan in the 1889 and 1890 Midland rolls, respectively. His birthdate, as given in the 1900 Ector County census, was July 1837.

An understanding of these facts is vital in determining the historicity of Dobie's account, in which banker Connell and cattleman Gray offered Will ten thousand dollars to reveal to them his source of gold. Will supposedly laughed in reply and stated he could "go out and dig up that much in less than a week's time." The two men then commissioned Flannigan—the spellings vary—to trail Will upon his next mining trek. For two weeks livery stable owner Driver kept a horse ready for Flannigan, who finally heard Will had left Odessa by hack and followed in his wake. Through the sand he trailed him westward along the T&P seventy-five miles to the Pecos, then upriver twenty-five miles before inconceivably losing all signs of the wheel ruts and horseshoe prints. Flannigan searched desperately for more than a day until he encountered a rider who had seen Will going back downriver. By the time the frustrated Flannigan reached Odessa, Will already had lugged in a sack of gold ore. Supposedly, only four days had elapsed from the moment Will had departed Odessa.[96]

So goes the story spun by old-timers of the region in the late 1920s and written down by Dobie, who admitted he had a "constructive memory."[97] But was there a basis in fact?

That the principals in the tale existed there is no doubt. That men on occasion sought to wrest the mine from Will by various means is probable. Possibly Flannigan, with or without the prompting of Connell and Gray, was one of these. But even Dobie had doubts about the veracity of the account; indeed, he wrote to historian J. Evetts Haley on October 6, 1929, "I am still wondering if Sublett actually found a lot of gold."[98] In a letter to Haley two weeks later he was even more bewildered:

> I wrote to W. E. Connell, First National Bank, Fort Worth. He said they "might have offered Sublett $10,000"—could not remember, hardly remembered Sublett's name, could not remember a thing about his bank account.
>
> . . . Ralph H. Shuffler, director of publicity, Odessa Chamber of Commerce . . . According to him . . . Sublett went to Monahans first, where there were just two other men. Further, Sublett never did have anything! But I'll be durned if I am going to let the truth ruin a good story.
>
> I guess I shall have to put a fact or two in a footnote, but *for the story* Sublett must lug in gold nuggets.[99]

Shuffler's informants, as stated in the letter, were J. J. Amburgey and Joe Graham, two men who doubtless had been acquainted with Will.

That Will did have a source of gold, however, whether it comprised seven nuggets or thousands, is virtually incontrovertible. But the undocumented stories surrounding this man and his mine are forever subject to scrutiny. Many can be dismissed with ease; in others a basis for truth may exist.

One such account holds that in the late 1880s a partially crippled man named Stewart hired on as a guide for several T&P officials hunting the Pecos country. Camping in rugged hills east of the river, they were approached one evening by a wagon bearing Stewart's old acquaintance Will Sublett, whom they invited to share the spot for the night. After the hunters had retired, Will told Stewart he was bound for his mine at the point of the Guadalupes, and that never before had the journey so taxed him; he had turned fifty back in 1884. Believing he might never be physically able to make the trip again, he offered to take Stewart along to the diggings.

But Stewart had to refuse; he was obligated to guide his clients through this inhospitable land. The next morning he accompanied Will as far west as the summit of a knoll, from which Will tried to show him the mine's location with the aid of a spyglass. But it was fruitless from so great a distance, and Will went on alone. Three days later he returned to the hunters' camp, and in privacy he unveiled to Stewart a tobacco sack filled with gold nuggets.

In the mid-1890s Stewart supposedly told the story to Ward County Judge J. J. Walker, who related it to J. Frank Dobie in the late 1920s.[100] The episode is impossible to substantiate, yet documented facts suggest it could have happened; J. J. Walker was included on the first Ward County tax roll in 1892 and J. A. Stewart was so listed in 1894. Too, Jacob Stewart was listed as fifty-seven in the 1900 Ward County census and clearly was old enough to have known Will.

To return to verified history, in the autumn of 1888 Will was fifty-four years of age, then considered old. Laura had been gone fourteen years now and both his daughters were married and had lives of their own. Only fifteen-year-old Rolth remained in their modest rent house, likely amid scattered structures cresting a slight knoll south of the tracks. Life was slipping through Will's fingers swiftly; he no longer had vigor in his gait, and some folklorists later said he limped.[101] But between trips to his diggings he continued to occupy his time with odd jobs and trapping. Too, recalled fellow Odessan Julius D. Henderson, who was only seven at the time, Will hauled buffalo bones and wood off the prairie to sell.[102]

Nor had he forsaken his dowsing gift. To the contrary, his ability to search out hidden water sources brought him into demand as far distant as El Paso, 280 miles westward. Once, while on unknown business in that city, where the great ridge of the Franklin Mountains jutted out almost to touch the Rio Grande, Will was approached by an official of a local bank; perhaps it was there Will converted his ore into hard money. Asked by the man to dowse a well, Will agreed with the understanding he first could go by horse with pack mule to his mine, from which he would return in seventeen days. The bargain struck, Will traipsed off into regions unknown and returned at the end of the allotted time to witch the well; his chamois bag was heavy with nuggets again.[103]

The knowledge that Will could reach his mine in a week's ride from El Paso (allowing three days for actual mining) still leaves a vast expanse of territory to search. Placing a compass on a map with its point at El Paso and tracing a circle the radius of a week's ride reveals three present-day states and two nations where Will's mine may have been. But somewhere within that vastness Will had found a single cave of gold, so well concealed that no one else has been able to locate it with certainty in the century since his death.

From the time he and Laura had departed Missouri in the latter 1860s, Will had been a virtual nomad, either living out of a wagon or leasing a place just long enough to get cabin fever and again seek out the backcountry. Never had he exhibited the slightest desire to set down roots, not even after his gold strike had left him financially able to do so. But finally, on October 18, 1888, he took up a homestead under the Act of 1873. It consisted of 160 acres of vacant public land situated near the T&P Railroad either two and one-quarter or three miles east-southeast of Odessa; today that location lies within city limits. Will's selection of that site was not made without forethought, as it bordered the 160-acre homestead assumed at that time by Sidney Pitt and Jennie.[104] Likely he already had dowsed the land to verify subterranean water sources. Charged with making improvements and maintaining occupancy three years to hold his claim, he purportedly constructed a dugout for Rolth and himself[105] and finally, it seemed, had settled down.

But as one long-conditioned to self-sufficiency, Will never had needed lavish ornaments, and staking a homestead was no indication he had changed. As declared on the 1889 Ector County tax roll, the land carried a value of only $240. Nor did Will acquire extensive farm implements or livestock; his only addition that year was an extra pair of horses or mules, likely a plow team, which increased the worth of his animals to forty-eight dollars. His wagon, meanwhile, had devaluated to only ten dollars, setting his total assets at a still-miniscule $298.[106]

But age or loneliness may have curbed Will's wanderlust; in August 1889 he acquired rights to a second homestead, this one consisting of eighty acres. For twenty-five dollars, E. R. Bryan, who had settled the site ten months before, relinquished his hold on the tract which lay quite near Will's 160-acre homestead, in the same section and block.[107] This additional acreage of Will's bordered the eighty-acre homestead of Jennie's father-in-law David Meeks Pitt, thus creating a community of neighboring homesteaders knitted together by family ties.[108] Will and Rolth soon relocated to this smaller tract, which must have included better living quarters, for in later applying for a patent Rolth testified he, his father, or Bryan had occupied the land three consecutive years beginning October 18, 1888.[109] The inevitable result was for Will to abandon his 160-acre homestead, which he did by deeding the rights for eighty dollars to F. M. Tallant on December 7, 1889.[110]

Odessa remained a remote outpost for only the most hardy; in 1889 the entire county held but 120 men of taxable age.[111] But Will's descendants already were increasing in number. On July 5, 1889, Jennie gave birth to his grandchild, Marvin Milton Pitt.[112]

By the fall of 1890 Will had turned fifty-six and still needed another year of occupancy before he could obtain a patent on the eighty acres. Rolth at seventeen was nearing manhood, while Jennie was the mother of a toddler. Whether any of them saw Ollie during this period is unknown, but the T&P did provide ready transportation between their homes. Will continued his spartan lifestyle: his only possessions included on the tax roll that year were the four horses valued at sixty dollars, though a portion of the record is missing. Obviously, officials also assessed taxes on his homestead and wagon.

From the time of its creation from Tom Green County in 1887, Ector County had been attached to Midland County for judicial purposes. Finally, however, the residents of Odessa and surrounding farms and ranches decided to govern themselves. What resulted on January 6, 1891, was one of the most important events in the history of the county—the organizational election to determine a county seat and county officers. Unquestionably in so vital a milestone, the election and tallies were overseen only by the most trustworthy of citizens, not by dregs of society whose drunken stupors were exceeded only by their levels of irresponsibility. That W. C. Sublett was so chosen should forever quash the allegations of tale-tellers that he was a drunkard so lacking in responsibility that he abandoned his children to people of the community for months at a time. In addition to assisting at the polls, Will was the sole person charged with carrying the returns the twenty-five miles to Midland County courthouse. Furthermore, when Ector County commissioners on August 18 finally authorized payment to those who had helped hold the election,

Will's name preceded all others. Clearly, this man who received six dollars for his two days of public service held the respect of his peers.[113]

The second of Jennie's eleven children was born near the newly designated county seat of Odessa on March 15, 1891. Already twice parents by the ages of nineteen and twenty-three respectively, Jennie and Sidney Pitt named the girl Sarah Etta in honor of Sidney's mother. (Their tenth child Ethel Kindness, who preserved in oral form many of the vital episodes of Will's life, was not born until June 22, 1910, long after he died.)[114]

When Ector County commissioners approved their first tax roll on August 8, 1891, no one could realize that the listing for W. C. Sublette (sic) bore final testimony to a curse. For decades he had struggled to find his niche, and all the while the relentless wandering had taken the color from his hair, etched his face with lines, wrenched the vigor from his stride. In a lost canyon he had discovered wealth, but he was never able to claim it fully because of the greed of those about him. This ironic twist and his own self-denial left him with but $265 in possessions to embellish the twilight of his life. He had only his $160 homestead, five horses or mules valued at $100, and his rickety wagon, now worth only five dollars. Though Jennie later said his bank was a chamois pouch, Will did not submit its contents for tax consideration. He likely believed it his right by public consensus to overlook any gold coins it held; only one man in the entire county that year declared "money on hand."

His son-in-law Sidney Pitt, meanwhile, paid Ector County taxes on his 160-acre homestead and a few animals; in 1889 he possessed nine horses or mules worth $108 and in 1890 five valued at $75. He seemed destined never to give Jennie and the children luxuries, yet Will saw in him and in his other son-in-law, Sam Knight, men whose love for their families would grow the harder they had to work.[115]

Rolth, on the other hand, was displaying increasing signs he would undertake any venture to save earning his way by the sweat of his face. When the Texas legislature passed a law providing bounties on jackrabbit and predator scalps, Rolth struck out on the prairie of Ector County with his firearm. By August 18 he had slain twenty-nine dozen rabbits for which Ector County Commissioners paid him twenty-nine dollars, while on November 9 he received six dollars for five dozen jackrabbit scalps and that of one "wild cat."[116]

Shortly after October 18, 1891, when the three years of required occupancy on the homestead expired, Will responded one last time to the summons of the frontier. Taking only rudimentary camping equipment with him, Will headed his wagon toward Barstow, which fronted the T&P tracks near the Pecos sixty-eight miles southwest in Ward County. At his old home of Monahans, between Odessa and Barstow, Will urged his team into the wagon yard and halted. Here he camped for an indeterminate period while visiting his friend the Ward County lawman. Through this official, Jennie later came to understand why her father never shared the secret of his diggings with his children: aware of the dangers and temptations of riches, he had refused to become a prisoner of either, yet he was not so sure that his sons-in-law and Rolth could have withstood them. "I don't know, it seems to me like it's a cursed thing, that gold," Will told the lawman. "I've had people I thought were my friends try to kill me for the knowledge of it. If I was to tell my family about it, why, both my daughters are married to men that would be better to them if they had to work to make a living. If they were rich, they might not be good to them. And my son would never do another honest lick of work the rest of his life."[117] Will may have understood his son, but his silence did not help him: up to his death in 1953 Rolth never worked any longer than it took to get a grubstake and resume the search for his father's mine.

By the onslaught of winter, which was severe, Will unaccountably had left his wagon in the yard at Monahans and set out on horseback toward the Pecos. Perhaps he was en route to his gold source; it is conceivable he reached it and let the gilded dust sift through his fingers one last time. But one thing is certain: by the latter part of December 1891 he had rented a room above a Barstow restaurant operated by a Chinese proprietor.[118]

At Christmas 1891, Rolth later claimed in a newspaper, he was with his father, presumably in the second-story room in Barstow from which the outline of the Guadalupes would have been visible on the northwestern horizon at dusk. Will, perhaps sensing he would never return to the mine, supposedly relented in his determination to withhold its location from his eighteen-year-old son and said he would take him once they had horses. But those plans disintegrated that very night when Will became gravely ill and seemed at death's border. From his bed, Rolth related, Will called him close and whispered: "Now, son, you're the only living person who knows anything about the mine. They all tried to get me to tell your sister and her husband about it. If you ever find the mine it's my wish for you to see that five per cent of it goes to the welfare of orphans, the sick and the afflicted. Son, tell nobody what you know about the mine, because they'll know as much as you do."[119]

If Rolth truly were at his side when Will's pneumonia began, he did not remain. Perhaps his father showed signs of improvement and the danger seemed past, negating any reason to stay. At any rate, only Will was there as blizzard winds ushered in the new year 1892 and the disease began savaging his body. The Ward County lawman found him dying and wired an urgent message to Jennie and her husband.[120]

But Will, who had spent much of his life by himself, would also die alone. And when he did, on January 6, 1892, it was as one born into immortality, for his surname and the lost mine bearing it have not been forgotten around the Pecos.

However, Will was not the only Sublett intrinsically entwined with mysterious gold, for his own son became chief among those who searched. Haunted by dream-like images of his father lowering him into a crevice and cave jeweled with gilded nuggets, Rolth became obsessed with finding it. Although he obtained clear ownership of the eighty-acre homestead from the

William Caldwell Sublett's grave in Ector County Cemetery in Odessa.

state on February 11, 1893, he had no desire to be a gentleman farmer and sold it for eighty dollars only five months later.[121] He then went to cowboying for the Joe James Ranch and others in Midland County,[122] where on August 27, 1897, he registered a brand consisting of a heart pierced by Cupid's arrow.[123] Obviously, he had found time for romance. Within a year or two, however, he rode west to take a job at a line camp on the X-T Ranch in the Pecos River country east of the Guadalupe escarpment. His belief that the cave was near reportedly was fueled one evening when he and John Patterson returned to the line shack after an absence and found a note weighted by a chunk of ore. The paper bore the signature of an acquaintance and fellow cowhand know as "Grizzly Bill," whose script detailed he had found the Lost Sublett Mine and taken from it ore like the sample he had left. He was en route with cattle to Pecos, Texas, which lay along the T&P, and would return in approximately twelve days to develop the mine.

Cicero Stewart, then a lawman at Eddy in southeastern New Mexico Territory, also supposedly met up with Grizzly at that time in the Pecos River country. Grizzly reportedly told him he had made the find in the Russell, or Rustler, Hills, which rise bone-white and barren, to 3,892 feet, twenty miles southwest of present-day Orla, Texas, between the Pecos and the palisades of the Guadalupes.

The sample ore left for Rolth sparkled with obvious gold particles—Rolth later claimed it assayed $1,000 in gold and $21 in silver—and it seemed certain Will's secret had not endured a single decade beyond his death. But then, say the tale-weavers, Grizzly reached the town of Pecos to go on a spree much the way Wilson had years before. This time, however, the finder was not robbed just of his memory; it took his very life. On top of the world, Grizzly eagerly accepted the challenge of riding a bucking bronc and suffered a broken neck when it threw him.[124] But had he truly found Will's mine or another such source?

It was not the only time Apache gold and Will's mine were associated with the Rustler Hills, but Rolth continued to search the Guadalupe range. An autumn 1900 trek to its northeastern spur brought him again to Carlsbad Caverns, then known as Bat Cave. "Bige [Abijah] Long and his father-in-law, whose name I do not recall, were with me," Rolth testified on October 2, 1947. "I showed them the Bat Cave, and they went back to the town of Eddy. . . . I went over close to Walnut Springs to see in Walnut Canyon an old Mexican who was about eighty-three years of age. He was not there and I came on in to the town of Eddy. That night I got in town and saw the old Mexican who was in Bige Long's saloon and drunk. He told me Bige Long had given him a quart of whiskey and five dollars for his rights to the Bat Cave."[125]

Obviously believing he would avoid Grizzly Bill's fate, Rolth in 1901 signed on as a broncbuster at W. P. Mudgett's spread.[126] From its expanses, apparently along the Texas-New Mexico line not far from the Guadalupes, Rolth doubtless pursued his prospecting. It was not by sheer chance he gained employment at the Mudgett Ranch; the owner was an old Odessa friend who had made a sworn statement before the Ector County clerk on October 31, 1892, that E. R. Bryan, Will, or Rolth had occupied their eighty-acre homestead the required three consecutive years.[127]

In 1905 Rolth put aside his quest long enough to romance and marry thirty-one-year-old A. D. Lockey, who had several children by a previous marriage.[128] Meanwhile, Sidney Pitt had moved to a ranch in southeastern New Mexico in 1899 and been joined by Jennie and the children in 1900. When Pitt's cattle were hard-struck by the drought of 1907, he drove the herd into the White Mountains near present-day Ruidoso, New Mexico, where he had leased land from the Mescalero Apache Reservation, and hired thirty-four-year-old Rolth as foreman.[129] It was one of the last semiregular jobs Rolth ever held, for in the next half-century his life revolved solely around his memory of reaching into a cavern stream and finding gold.

"It was just a fixation with him," noted his niece Ethel Pitt Harris. "He'd work just long enough to get a grubstake and then he'd go to hunting. He spent his life up looking for the gold. It was some place, he thought, in the Guadalupe Mountains."[130]

The 1910 census found Rolth between grubstakes and undertaking odd jobs in Amarillo City, Texas, to support his wife. But Rolth's obsession may have placed too great a strain on the marriage, for they ultimately divorced.[131]

When Kelsey Presley married Jennie and Sidney Pitt's second daughter Sadie Drucilla on September 7, 1912, he too joined the search.[132] But it never ruled him as it did Rolth, who by 1929 had assumed the classic posture of the crusty, sourdough prospector as he periodically led his pack burro from the streets of Carlsbad, New Mexico, off toward the nearby escarpment of the Guadalupes. He had become an object of pathos, this white-bearded man with a morbid preoccupation to search anywhere and everywhere for what he once had held in his hands.[133]

About that time fellow prospector Frank Davis came across what appeared to be a marker on the rim of the Guadalupes' North McKittrick Canyon on the Texas-New Mexico border. Upon later telling Rolth, who lived in Carlsbad or Artesia in southeastern New Mexico between grubstakes, he noted that this son of Will Sublett displayed considerable interest while nevertheless contending the mine lay farther south in Texas. Not long afterward, Davis returned to the McKittrick country to prospect the opposite rim. Studying the sheer wall across the two-thousand-foot chasm with field glasses in hope of discovering a mineral vein, he sighted Rolth and his burro before the marker. He claimed in a 1948 article that he watched Rolth step off several paces and proceed to dislodge rocks. It took Davis an entire day to work his way around and ascend the opposite wall, but when he did he supposedly discovered a hole, eighteen inches wide and two feet deep, in which lay three rotting canvas sacks ten to twelve inches long and four-and-one-half inches in breadth. One bore the imprint of the Butterfield stage line and the others that of another express company. They were empty, virtually disintegrating to his touch.[134]

Whether the story is true and whether Rolth claimed any booty contained within are unanswerable, but it was not the only time his treasure search carried him to McKittrick Canyon, much of which now lies in Guadalupe Mountains National Park. He purportedly once told R. A. Simmons that the site his father had taken him to lay in McKittrick Canyon and had been marked by three horseshoe nails hammered into a dead limb on a juniper tree. Simmons claimed he and a rancher later found such a tree bearing the scars of three nails which had been removed.[135]

On October 3, 1930, Rolth, now fifty-seven, married forty-four-year-old Bertie Boron in Eddy County, New Mexico, and again had a partner in his quest. But this too would be a tumultuous marriage; by the following March they had divorced and Bertie had remarried her ex-husband, sixty-eight-year-old S. L. Burkhead. Apparently torn between two men many years her senior, she again married Rolth on July 18, 1931, in Eddy County. Within three months after Rolth's death in 1953, she wed Burkhead a third time.[136]

Though Jennie and Sidney Pitt lived in nearby Roswell during that period, Rolth's all-consuming passion precluded his visiting them. "I was never around Uncle Rolth very much," recalled Ethel Pitt Harris. "I remember him coming by our house (in Roswell) with his wife and her family; she had children, grown. I was just a kid of a girl. And that's the only time I remember seeing Uncle Rolth."[137]

Jennie always doubted whether their father actually had taken Rolth to the mine. "Mama said she thought he was too young, that he could've been mistaken about it," recalled Mrs. Harris. "She even said she wasn't sure it was in the Guadalupe Mountains; she said they thought it was someplace in New Mexico, but they weren't sure. It could've been someplace in Texas. My sister used to say, 'Well, how do we know it wasn't in Mexico?' Well, we don't. Only we just know that Grandpa, if it'd been in Mexico, would have said."

Mrs. Harris noted that the fact a fossil reef is not supposed to be mineralized "is the reason why I never did think it was in

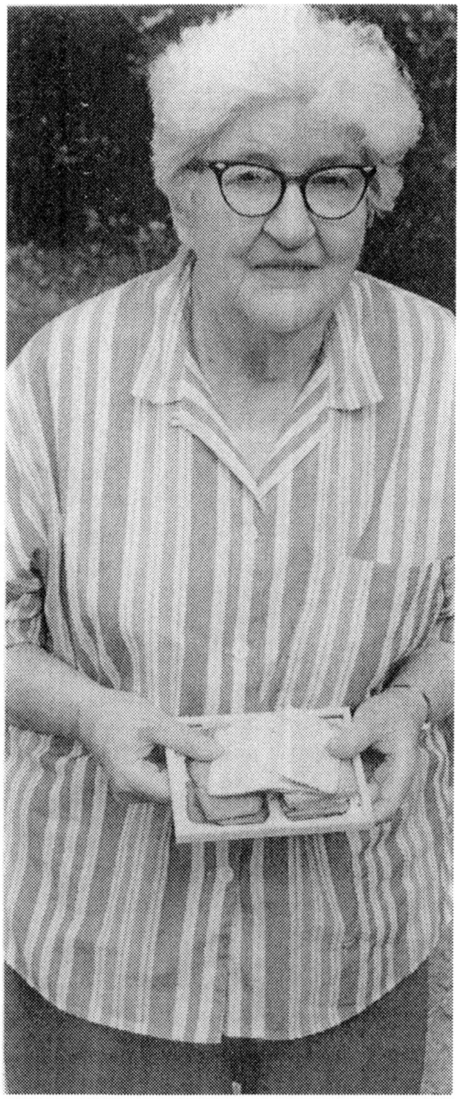

Ethel Pitt Harris, who preserved in oral form many details of the lives of her grandparents, Will and Laura Sublett. She is holding Laura's songbook.

Rolth Sublett at his El Paso home in the early 1950s. He is holding the rock hammer and ax used by his father, William Caldwell Sublett (courtesy Ethel Pitt Harris).

the Guadalupes. On up north of there and out west there's volcanic-type [ranges], and I think it's one of those. I think it's somewhere there on the White Sands Missile Range or up toward Hillsboro [New Mexico]."[138]

Frustration at times led Rolth to widen his search to Texas' Rustler Hills, where Grizzly Bill supposedly made his strike. In an article reprinted in a 1912 newspaper, Rolth is quoted as saying the mine "was about six miles from a spring. The spring is in what is known as the Russell Hills of the Guadalupes. I paid no attention at the time as to where we went, and was always glad when my father was ready to return home. Father got the gold out of a hole or cave, but it seemed like that it was in plain sight on the ground outside of the cave."[139]

That range of hills said to be rent by myriad sinks had been prospected almost four decades previously by Charles Dixon, the man who learned from his Apache sweetheart the source of her tribe's gold. Following her directions—south from Guadalupe Peak to *Selas Teticua* or Twin Mountains—Dixon and "Prairie Dog" Dave Morrow nevertheless wandered more east than south to spend three and a half years combing the Russell, or Rustler, Hills. There, they discovered three landmarks which seemed to coincide with those given by the Indian girl: a seep spring, a canyon or gulch, and a cave filled with skeletons. The cave, situated fifteen miles south of a seep spring, was described by Dixon as lying "in one side of a sink or drop in a mesa. The sink has vertical walls and we could not descend as we were not equipped with ropes to do so and besides we felt a sort of canny fear to do so after what my sweetheart had told me. . . . That cave, she said, was haunted with evil spirits of some old race of Indians who lived there years ago and her people were afraid to enter it. . . . But at a certain time of day when the sun shines on a slant, we could look into the cave about sixty feet and saw three skeletons or mummies." However, his sweetheart had described the gold-bearing gulch as lying within one and a half miles of a seep spring, not fifteen, and though the two men retraced their steps to the vicinity of the seep, they never found such a topographic feature.[140]

Repeatedly in the folklore of the Pecos, a gulch and a cave surface as landmarks not only to the Lost Sublett Mine but to Apache gold as well. Rolth at various times described his father's mine as at the bottom of a fifty- to sixty-foot chasm and/or within a cave. In the late 1890s an elderly Mexican of Tularosa, New Mexico, a one-time captive of Apaches, reportedly told of having watched warriors gather gold from a gulch in the Guadalupes. Early in the twentieth century F. H. Hardesty of El Paso grubstaked Lucius "Frenchy" Arthur, who claimed to have secretly watched two Mexicans take gold quartz from "a large opening like a cave" in an abyss eighty to one hundred feet long and forty feet wide with sixty-foot perpendicular walls. Arthur never returned from a second trip to the chasm, which he had described as lying within a mountain range three days' journey by horse due east of El Paso. In the same era cattleman Green Ussery supposedly observed Lee Church pick up a gold nugget from a gulch near Chico Ranch in the Guadalupes vicinity.[141] In 1926 an old Mexican named Policarpo Gonzales reportedly told a San Antonio chiropractor that after being captured by Apaches he helped break off gold ore from a cave near a spring in the Guadalupes; when the demise of the tribe seemed imminent, he and others spent two days filling it in with rocks.[142] And Will Cowan, though he found no evidence of gold, reportedly once stumbled across a cave, much like the one described by Charles Dixon and the Indian princess, situated on his ranch between the Pecos and the Guadalupes and containing many skeletons.[143]

That subterranean landmark so important in unearthing the Apache source of gold has had other discoverers unaware of its significance. In 1949 or 1950, Bill Barton of Odessa and a friend were hunting the Lost Sublett Mine in rough country southwest of Orla, Texas. In the previous fifteen years Barton had searched often, from the Guadalupes to the lesser ranges to the south and the hills near Red Bluff Lake to the east. On this occasion, however, Barton and his partner were driving along a primitive road through terrain like "the middle of the Mojave Desert" when an unusual topographic feature well off to the side caught his eye. It was a gully with the near bank low and sloping but the opposite a high perpendicular wall with a huge, undercut ledge of rock jutting out over the bed; below it an equally massive slab stood at an angle against the cliff.

When they hiked to it, they found the tilted slab concealed the entrance to a cave situated several feet above the level of the wash. Obtaining candles from their vehicle, they entered. "We went down in it [through] a narrow place I guess fifteen, twenty feet before we got to a room at least twelve feet from top to bottom [and] twenty or thirty feet going back," recalled Barton. "Over on one side there was a shelf about four feet high, and there were thirteen skeletons there. And we got one of the skulls and brought it back. It laid around my nursery for years." At the time Barton was not aware he may have stumbled upon a landmark to long-lost Apache gold; when he did learn so, three and a half decades later, he was unable to relocate the site.[144]

But Dixon's—and possibly Barton's—cave of skeletons may have lain far from the landmark given by the Indian girl, for she had described it as resting in the foothills south of Guadalupe Peak near "*Selas Teticua*, or the Twin Mountains." One folklore account holds that Will and the outlaw Sutterhall rode southeast from Guadalupe Peak along the ridge of the Delawares to cross over into Chico Canyon near "Twin Peaks" and cache stolen gold. In the mid-1980s, old-timers in Culberson County, Texas, and Eddy County, New Mexico, recalled no peak in that area ever having borne that name, and the 6,750-foot Twin Mountains in the Davis range near present-day Alpine, Texas, seem too far south to fit the description.

Assuming the name is based on a topographic feature, several prominences a few miles south of Guadalupe Peak could be so characterized through a study of topographic maps. Three miles southeast of Guadalupe Pass and twelve miles north of the head of Chico Canyon lies a double mountain, one peak of which rises 525 feet to an elevation of 5,015 feet and the second—only a third of a mile distant—385 feet to a 4,865-foot elevation. The two are detailed on the U.S. Geological Survey Guadalupe Pass Quadrangle map. Other possibilities include 5,540-foot Pine Mountain and a 5,520-foot sister peak over Chico Draw, delineated on U.S.G.S. Burro Canyon Quadrangle; Delaware Peak at 5,729 feet and its east summit at 5,616, shown on U.S.G.S. 6-Bar Quadrangle; and 5,442-foot and 5,420-foot prominences detailed on 6-Bar Quadrangle as lying within three miles of the head of Chico Canyon.

None of the peaks so examined, however, holds the suggestion of twins when viewed from the vantage point of an approaching horseman. Furthermore, although Charles Dixon believed "*Selas Teticua*" translated into "Twin Mountains," such may not be the case, according to the Apachean specialist Philip J. Greenfeld, Associate Professor of Anthropology at San Diego State University:

> I wish I could give you an accurate and simple answer, but I can't. It is clear that the name has been written using the Spanish orthography, but is not Spanish. My guess is that it actually is an Apache place name. I would guess that the first word is in fact two words, *tse* "rock" plus some modifier, but I have no idea what the modifier is. *las* is not an Apache word I am familiar with, and I suspect that something has been left off.
>
> The word *Teticua* is probably a verb describing the state of the rock(s). Apachean place names often have a noun, e.g., rock; a modifier, e.g., big; plus a verb, e.g., it extends. Thus Rock Point, Arizona, is called in Navajo *tse ntsaa deez?ahi* which literally means, "rock big it extends out."
>
> Your word *Teticua* could be something like *dedi-ḳaad* which would mean something like "they are flat" or it could be *dediḳ?ãã*, "they are tilted" or any of a

number of other things. Whatever the case I don't believe the word has anything to do with twins or two.[145]

Thus, the location of legendary Apache diggings—perhaps discovered by Will—swells in mystery. However, an amazing correlation exists between the cave of skeletons site described by Bill Barton and a translation suggested by Greenfeld: "Rock(s) they are tilted."

Rolth, who as a premature baby seemed fated never to survive infancy, found in that great enigma of his father's mine a purpose for which to live. With every strike of his father's rock hammer against outcropping he was certain he was inching ever closer to it. "Tomorrow's promise" kept him alive through eighty long, hard years, and never once in the almost six decades of endless and desperate searching did a single golden nugget comfort his calloused palm. When he finally joined Will in death, in Artesia, New Mexico, on October 13, 1953, no one remained to search for the mine on certain memory rather than hope.[146]

But there were others just as possessed to take his place, chief among them Tio Ben Wattson. Born October 6, 1863, on Manitou Island in Lake Michigan, he led as varied and adventurous a life as any man who came to be associated with lost treasure in the Guadalupes. As a child he lived among the Sioux, then at age ten ran away from his father and boarded an eastbound caboose on a freight train to begin decades of wandering. He soon made it to New York City, where the captain of a sailing vessel retained him as his cabin boy. When the ship docked in France the captain whipped him after an argument, and little Ben fled inland. For years he drifted, earning his way with a bootblack box and occasionally returning to the sea. At sixteen he returned home to give his mother several hundred dollars he had saved, and at seventeen he set out on foot for the frontier of Texas.

Near present-day Lamesa, Texas, he joined up with riders headed for the Guadalupe Mountains, only to learn upon reaching the range they were outlaws and he a virtual slave. For three years he was forced to undertake menial tasks about camp while his captors pillaged. Plotting all the while to escape, he carefully noted that whenever a man rode away from the group after a quarrel, a single rider followed and ultimately returned leading an empty horse. Finally, as the outlaws slept in their camp at Pine Spring, he slipped away in the darkness and ascended through the boulders of mighty Pine Top Mountain. Two weeks later he reached Silver City, New Mexico.

For the next fifty years Ben divided his time between the sea and the Guadalupes, where he had watched his captors bury caches and heard them talk of many others. At the age of seventy-two he married a woman named Pauline, and in 1939 she followed this eccentric old man to the Guadalupes where he, like Rolth, blended inseparably with legend and mystery. Believing himself "directed" by a higher power to search out the hidden treasures of the Guadalupes with dowsing instruments, Tio Ben claimed to have located enough mines and caches to have swelled the ancient reef into the distant sea which spawned it. These included twenty gold mines, eighty-five gold caches, fifty-five silver caches, eight diamond caches, five jewel caches, two sites of uranium ore, and hundreds of others. "He was a great diviner; he had divining rods for every type of metal," noted Bill Balgemann of Carlsbad, New Mexico, who once had the opportunity to visit with Tio Ben. "He and his wife would go through the hills down in the Pine Spring and surrounding area and he would divine whatever it was, turquoise or gold or silver or treasure. And then he'd say, 'There it is.' And then when asked why he didn't dig it up, he said there was a curse on it and he would never touch it. He and his wife were hard-working, simple, plain people and they loved the outdoors, and they would just go on foot everywhere in the Guadalupe Mountains. The tourists just loved to talk to him."

To those tourists Tio Ben even claimed to have known Will Sublett; his birthdate of 1863 lends credence to the statement. But Tio Ben further contended he and Will had prospected together and that Will once had taken him to the diggings situated high on the ridge immediately north of Bear Canyon and overlooking present-day Frijole Ranger Station in Guadalupe Mountains National Park. "Tio Ben told me it was not really a mine but an ancient river bed, blocked at both ends, and in times of heavy rains the water would run down and flood this hole and overflow," wrote his wife Pauline. ". . . Sublett used to take a feed sack and scoop up as much gravel from the bottom as he could carry. When he got down to the spring he would wash it, and that is where he got so many fine nuggets. The last trip he made he said he was never going back, because he had taken all that [was] worth the effort. But we got strong pulls on either side of his hole." Tio Ben himself once claimed, "No use of anybody looking for more [Sublett gold] . . . 'cause there isn't any of it left to find."

In such lost diggings, whether teeming with riches or mined out, Tio Ben found a sustaining force, one that carried him far beyond even Rolth's eighty years. In 1961 he was ninety-eight—and still divining, still refusing to take advantage of his finds. "I don't need the money," he explained. "I have everything I need and besides the world is not ready for the gold of the Guadalupes. Some of these days the government will own these mountains and the gold will lie there for centuries until the civilization of the world is less greedy and more deserving, and only at that time will God level these hills and make the gold available to those who actually need it." On June 29, 1963, Tio Ben died, three months shy of one hundred years—and the supposed treasures still abided.[147]

So too did the story of William Caldwell Sublett and his lost mine, long since having attained the status of a classic legend among legends. Like the folk heroes and antiheroes of the Old West—Davy Crockett, Billy the Kid—Will reached that level reserved only for the immortals: perpetual life despite virtually irrefutable evidence he had died.

When Avery H. "Rusty" Russell (born 1915) began frequenting the honky-tonks of oil boomtown Odessa in the late 1930s, he was not aware that Will Sublett was supposed to have died almost a half-century before. So when he watched a geezer of more than eighty named Sublett booze it up and fend off questions about his mysterious gold mine, he thought nothing unusual. "I knew him; I've drank his beer and he drank my beer," Russell recalled in 1985. "I've sat at a table talking back and forth."

While certain the old-timer's name was Sublett, Russell could not remember his first name. "He had some kind of a nickname but I couldn't tell you what it was," he said. "I think I've heard him called Bill Sublett, but I don't know how authentic that was. I know one thing: all the girls called him 'honey,' and they didn't need anything else."

Furthermore, Russell claimed, every patron of the honky-tonks knew this Sublett possessed hidden diggings beyond the Pecos. "It was common knowledge. Everybody that would come in here green, somebody would whisper, 'That's the ol' boy that's got that gold mine up there.' So you'd wind up sitting and talking to him and if you were crude enough to want to make him mad you'd quiz him about it. But if you sat and listened to him, why, he'd tell you what he knew. . . . I had heard about the gold mine but I didn't run up and say, 'Hey, tell me about it,' 'cause I'd already heard what kind of problems he was having."

Russell, however, did discuss with Sublett the job that first lured him to the vicinity of the mine. "He was supposed to have been—and I've heard some of this from him—hunting for water when they built this railroad through here. We talked about the digging of wells . . . and different problems they had, because he was connected with the construction."

Sublett, who Russell said first came to Odessa riding a horse and leading a pack burro, lived in First Street's old Texas Hotel and claimed as his girlfriend one of the "madams" boarding there. He pursued a lifestyle ranging from the well-to-do to that of a near-wino, depending on how recently he had replenished his finances. "He was kind of a louse, a good-time Charlie that everybody was glad to see when he was up and at it," described Russell. "As long as he had a dime he'd spend it on anybody. He wasn't a fancy Dan, and he wasn't an out-and-out tramp. He was just an ordinary-looking guy like you'd run into in ranching or oilfield country. He wasn't too big a man and shaved maybe once a week or once every two weeks."

But he was not without his enemies, especially when it appeared he was ready to make another haul. "I've seen him to where he didn't have a dime and he'd be going hungry; they'd have to feed him on a credit," recalled Russell. "And they'd start watching him; they watched him twenty-four hours a day. There's no telling how many people spent how much time watching almost every move he ever made. Anytime he'd get up and leave a joint they'd follow him at midnight. They stashed out horses and saddles between here and the Pecos River to where they could jump in their car and run out there and watch him come through, track him. But he'd disappear and be gone for about two weeks, three weeks, and when he come back he paid everybody off and he blowed and lived it up. He was up and down just like a rope." Sublett, said Russell, once was tracked to within ten miles of his supposed diggings in Culberson County's Wild Horse Draw, a northward-flowing water course southeast of Guadalupe Peak. "I've had a dozen different people that have claimed to have been in contact with him when he was in that area. When he got to where he couldn't get back up there and knew he wasn't going to get to go back, he tried to tell people how to get there. And he said it was Wild Horse Draw. One outcropping of flat sheetrock after another makes that draw, and when that water runs it drops off one ledge to the next and forms basins. Dust and nuggets would roll out and collect there."

Russell never saw this mysterious prospector named Sublett after 1943 and did not know when, where—or if—he died.[148]

Legend, folklore, facts. Can the three be correlated? That a man named Sublett lived in Odessa during that period is substantiated by the 1942 Odessa City Directory: H. W. Sublett then resided at Williams Apartments at 501 West May. From all appearances in the mid-1980s, the living quarters must have been modest even in 1942. But who was this H. W. Sublett, and was he the same octogenarian Russell described as having a gold mine? A judgment is difficult to make. No H. W. Sublett was counted in Ector County in the 1910 census or included on county tax or property registries through 1941. Nor was a person bearing that name listed in Texas death records from 1943 through 1945. However, a Private H. W. Sublett did serve in Company E, 3d Texas Cavalry, in the Civil War, and in 1880 an H. W. Sublett lived in Comanche County, Texas.[149] That man or pair of men in documented history possibly could have survived into the 1940s and encountered Russell, but Texas death records indicate a Henry W. Sublett died in Eastland County, Texas, in 1890; a Harry W. Sublett in Eastland County in 1920; and a second Henry W. Sublett in San Augustine County, Texas, in 1922.[150]

Jack R. Sublett of Albuquerque, New Mexico, believed the H. W. Sublett listed in the 1942 Odessa City Directory was a misprint for then-seventeen-year-old Henry Rue Sublett, who had been born in Shamrock, Texas, and worked the West Texas oil fields as a young man.[151] It is clear, however, that Henry Rue could not have been the elderly Sublett described by Russell. Regardless of the numerous H. W. Subletts stretching across eight decades of history, it would strain the credulity of even the most gullible to suggest that more than one Sublett came west with the

Rolth Sublett's grave in Woodbine Cemetery in Artesia, New Mexico.

T&P and found gold in the land of the Pecos. Only one such man could have existed—and he was the son of Caldwell Sublett and the husband of Laura Louisa Denny.

Thus even in supposed death William Caldwell Sublett grows in stature and mystery. In a region wild with tales and jeweled with lost treasures, he and his diggings reign supreme, creating excitement that spurs space-age prospectors—and will men yet unborn—to prowl the fastness of the Guadalupes or labyrinths of other ranges west of the Pecos, in quest of a golden dream.

About the Author

Born in 1951, Patrick Dearen is a lifelong resident of West Texas and the author of three other books, all novels: THE SHAKWA (co-authored under the pseudonym Gene March), STARFLIGHT TO FAROUL, and THE ILLEGAL MAN. He earned a journalism degree from The University of Texas at Austin and received several national and state writing awards while serving as regional reporter for two West Texas daily newspapers. He has worked several years with the mentally retarded and is an avid outdoorsman, having backpacked the headwaters of the Pecos River extensively and canoed its lower wilderness stretches. His other interests include ragtime piano and handball.

Notes

Castle Gap

1. Gary Cutrer, taped interview with author, Castle Gap, 9 February 1986.

2. C. C. Swift, interview with author, Crane, Texas, 23 June 1982.

3. D. Hoye Eargle, *Some Uranium Occurrences in West Texas* (Austin: Bureau of Economic Geology Report of Investigations No. 27, University of Texas at Austin, September 1956), 7; Jeremiah F. McCarthy, geologist, telephone interview with author, Midland, Texas, spring 1983.

4. Carlysle Graham Raht, *The Romance of Davis Mountains and Big Bend Country* (Odessa: The Rahtbooks Company, Edition Texana, 1963), 30–31.

5. John S. Ford, "Letters and Documents, Opening Routes to El Paso, 1849," *Southwestern Historical Quarterly* 48 (October 1944): 264. See also report of Ford in *The Texas Democrat* (Austin), 23 June 1849, 2–3. *Weick Pah*, more correctly, may be *Wiar Pah*: Clayton Williams, *Never Again*, Vol. 3 (3 vols., San Antonio: The Naylor Company, 1969), 27.

6. J. W. Williams, *Old Texas Trails* (Burnet: Eakin Press, 1979), 39–41.

7. C. Williams, *Never*, 1: 98.

8. O. W. Williams, *Pioneer Surveyor-Frontier Lawyer: The Personal Narrative of O. W. Williams, 1877–1902*, ed. by S. D. Myres (El Paso: Texas Western College Press, 1966), 278.

9. A sizable pool undoubtedly resulting from seepage was discovered by the author near the head of the canyon on 19 March 1987, following ten months of rainfall unprecedented in the twentieth century.

10. C. C. Childress, interview taped by Paul Patterson, 20 May 1968, Odessa, Texas, in Southwest Collection, Texas Tech University, Lubbock, Texas. Childress was first through the gap in 1887.

11. C. Williams, *Never*, 2: 112. Also see William E. Connelly, *Doniphan's Expedition and the Conquest of New Mexico and California* (Topeka: 1907), 267–280.

12. Ford, "Opening Routes," 262–264.

13. John Salmon Ford, *Rip Ford's Texas* (Austin: University of Texas Press, 1963), 122–123.

14. Lt. F. T. Bryan, *Reports of the Secretary of War, with Reconnaissances of Routes from San Antonio to El Paso*, 31st Congress, 1st Sess., Senate Executive Document No. 64 (Washington: 1850), 19.

15. John Russell Bartlett, *Personal Narrative of Explorations and Incidents in Texas, New Mexico, California, Sonora and Chihuahua, 1850–1853*, Vol. 1 (Chicago: The Rio Grande Press, Inc., 1965), 91–92.

16. Ibid., 90.

17. "Journey of the Leach Wagon Train Across Texas, 1857," in J. W. Williams, *Trails*, 313, 352–354.

18. Ibid., 365.

19. Waterman L. Ormsby, *The But-*

terfield Overland Mail (San Marino: The Huntington Library, 1955), 66.

20. C. Williams, *Never*, 3: 199. Williams also noted the possibility that the rock structure originated as a soldiers' camp.

21. Billy Rankin, taped interview with author, Rankin, Texas, 17 May 1983.

22. Colonel Thomas B. Hunt's Journal, 10, Q154 in Records of the Chief of Engineers, Record Group 77, NA. The remains of such a structure were found by the author at the site, 16 August 1984.

23. Clayton W. Williams, "ThatTopographical Ghost—Horsehead Crossing!" *The Permian Historical Annual* 17 (December 1977), 48. Also see J. Evetts Haley, "Ben Ficklin, Pioneer Mail Man," *The Shamrock Oil and Gas Corporation* (Spring 1959).

24. T. U. Taylor, "Olive and W. A. Peril," *Frontier Times* (July 1979, reprint of 1939 article), 24.

25. J. Evetts Haley, *Charles Goodnight: Cowman and Plainsman* (Boston, New York: Houghton Mifflin Company, 1936), 127–134.

26. Such trading was so prevalent that New Mexico Territory was reported "filled with Texas cattle" in 1867. In return for the herds, Comanches obtained ammunition, arrow points, knives, calico, tobacco, coffee, whiskey, and gewgaws: Ernest Wallace and E. Adamson Hoebel, *The Comanches: Lords of the South Plains* (Norman: University of Oklahoma Press, ninth printing, 1986), 267–268. See also A. B. Norton (Superintendent of Indian Affairs, New Mexico) to Commissioner of Indian Affairs, *Annual Report* (United States Commissioner of Indian Affairs, 1867), 194–195.

27. Haley, *Goodnight,* 148.

28. Ibid., 156–158.

29. Roy Holt, "The Old Horsehead Crossing on the Pecos," *Sheep and Goat Raiser* (November 1952), 44.

30. Clayton Williams, *Texas' Last Frontier: Fort Stockton and the Trans-Pecos 1861–1895* (College Station: Texas A&M Press, 1982), 91. Also see U.S. Department of War, Post Surgeon's Report, Fort Stockton, June 1868. The scarcity of potable water prohibited troops from establishing semi-permanent camps at the gap.

31. Colonel Hunt's Journal, 10.

32. Holt, "Old Horsehead," 37; C. Williams, *Last Frontier*, 310–311. See also *Rio Grande* 1 (March 1912), 18.

33. C. Williams, *Last Frontier*, 230. See also Lt. Robert G. Smither, Fort Concho, to C.O., Company D, Tenth Cavalry, Fort Concho, 26 July 1879, in U.S. Department of War, Letters Received, AGO, Record Group 94, National Archives.

34. Childress, taped interview.

35. I. C. Earp, taped interview with author, Crane County, Texas, 2 June 1983. Earp heard the story from Murray.

36. *San Angelo Standard*, 5 December 1891, 1.

37. Cora Hollis Dawson Smith, taped interview with author, Iraan, Texas, 12 August 1982. Mrs. Smith was the daughter of Samuel Toliver Dawson.

38. James Day, "Castle Gap Days," *McCamey News*, 4 July 1968.

39. Cliff Newland, interview taped by Elmer Kelton, Crane County, Texas, 23 August 1964, in possession of author; Paul Patterson, taped interview with author, Crane, Texas, 20 July 1982.

40. N. Ethie Eagleton, unpublished manuscript, Rankin Museum, Rankin, Texas.

41. Childress, taped interview. The decision to build the railroad south of the gap and the construction of modern roads also contributed to closing the gap route.

42. The account of the Head Spaniard's Treasure was related by Cliff Newland in an interview taped by Paul Patterson, Crane, Texas, 18 May 1968, Southwest Collection, Texas Tech University, Lubbock, Texas.

43. The story of the Catholic Cross Cache long has been in the public domain in the Castle Gap region. For this account I have relied on: E. N. Beane, taped interview with author, Crane, Texas, 2 June 1983 (Beane first came to nearby Crane in the mid-1920s); Paul Patterson, interview with author, Crane, Texas, 23 June 1982 (Patterson lived as a youth in the now-ghost town of Upland just east of the gap); Paul Patterson, *Pecos Tales* (Austin: The Encino Press, 1967), 74–80; Jeff W. Henderson, "Castle Gap: The End of the Rainbow," *Town's West* (May 1982), 34; Jeff Henderson, compiler, *The Treasure Legends of Castle Gap* (Alpine: privately printed, 1965), 33–35; Harry Cline, "A Metal Witcher Looks for Spanish Treasure," *San Angelo Standard-Times*, 3 September 1967; Swift, interview.

44. Billy Rankin, interview with author, Rankin, Texas, 24 June 1982.

45. The story of the stagecoach treasure is based on: Henderson, *Legends*, 27–30; Jeff Henderson, "Mystery Cloaks Stagecoach Holdup," *Lubbock Avalanche Journal*, 14 May 1974.

46. Cutrer, taped interview with author; Fred Gipson, "Since the Days of Maximillian [sic] Jewels and Gold Search Has Gone on at Castle Gap," *San Angelo Standard-Times*, 2 October 1938.

47. Newland, interview taped by Patterson.

48. This account is based on: "Treasures of Castle Gap" (an interview with Cliff Newland), *Western Tower, Phillips 66* (July 1960); Henderson, *Legends*, 19–23; Henderson, "End of the Rainbow," 33; Cline, "Metal Witcher."

49. *Encyclopedia International* (Lexicon Publications, 1982), 11: 463; *Encyclopedia Americana* (Danbury: Grolier Inc., 1985), 18: 534–535; Frank H. Bushick, "Maximilian's Ill-Fated Adventure," *Frontier Times* (May 1930), 338–341.

50. J. Frank Dobie, *Coronado's Children* (New York: Grosset and Dunlap, reprint, n.d.), 241. Originally published by The Southwest Press, 1930.

51. The story of Maximilian's treasure long has been in public domain in West Texas and has many variants. With due consideration of many oral traditions as well as written ones, I have chosen to relate substantially the version E.N. Beane heard when he first came to nearby Crane in the mid-1920s. "That version that I gave you is about the only one that was going around at the time, and since then, why, it's just the same story, just different people telling it," Beane said in the interview taped by the author in Crane, Texas, 2 June 1983.

52. Dee Woods, *Blaze of Gold* (San Antonio: The Naylor Company, 1972), 114.

53. John Kelly Harper, "Whose Treasure is Buried in Castle Gap?", *Texas Historian* (March 1980), 20.

54. Gipson, "Since the Days."

55. The story of the treasure seekers Conner (or O'Connor) and Black has many variations. Basically, I have relied on Jesse Rascoe, *Texas Buried Treasures* (Fort Davis: Ed Bartholomew, Publisher, 1972), 63–65 (containing an interview with T. H. Conner reprinted from a 1920s edition of the *Fort Worth Star-Telegram*); C. Williams, *Last Frontier*, 59–60. Williams's account is based on an undated manuscript by his father,

O. W. Williams, who interviewed Truman H. Conner.

56. Cora Smith, taped interview.

57. Mrs. C. C. Childress, unpublished manuscript relating an interview with her husband, C. C. Childress, Odessa, Texas, 8 June 1962. A copy of the manuscript is in the author's possession.

58. Beane, taped interview.

59. Gipson, "Since the Days."

60. Newland, interview taped by Patterson.

61. Cody Bell, Jr., taped interview with author, Rankin, Texas, 28 January 1983.

62. Rankin, interview, 24 June 1982.

63. Swift, interview.

64. Patterson, *Pecos Tales*, 74–80.

65. "Maximilian's Cache of Buried Gold Long Sought in Castle Gap Mountains," *Odessa News-Times*, 25 October 1935.

66. Swift, interview.

67. Cutrer, taped interview.

68. Patrick Dearen, "Gold Diggers," *Midland Reporter-Telegram*, 19 July 1982.

69. Cutrer, taped interview.

70. Ibid.

71. This sketch of Cliff Newland is based on: Jack and Bonnell Newland, taped interview with author, Crane, Texas, 16 August 1984 (Jack and Bonnell are the son and daughter-in-law, respectively, of Cliff Newland); Newland, interview taped by Kelton; Newland, interview taped by Patterson; Swift, interview; I.C. Earp, taped interview with author, Crane County, Texas, 7 June 1983.

72. Earp, taped interview, 7 June 1983.

73. Ibid.

74. Swift, interview.

75. Jack and Bonnell Newland, taped interview.

76. Cline, "Metal Witcher."

77. Patterson, interview, 23 June 1982.

78. Bonnell Newland, taped interview.

79. Newland, interview taped by Patterson.

80. Gipson, "Since the Days."

81. "Fort Worth Man to Seek Lost Legendary Fortune Supposed to be Buried Near Castle Gap," *McCamey News*, 2 February 1934.

82. Patterson, *Pecos Tales*, 79.

83. Cutrer, interview.

84. Rankin, interview, 24 June 1982.

85. *San Angelo Daily Standard*, 11 November 1927.

86. Patterson, interview; Newland, interview taped by Patterson; unbylined manuscript, 28 September 1964, in possession of author (Paul Patterson is listed as its source).

87. Swift, interview.

88. Eargle, *Uranium Occurrences*.

89. Ann Clark, telephone interview with author, Rankin, Texas, June 1982.

90. Patterson, interview.

91. Rankin, interview, 24 June 1982.

92. Swift, interview. Swift died in 1985.

Horsehead Crossing

1. J. Frank Dobie, *A Vaquero of the Brush Country* (New York: Grosset and Dunlap Publishers, reprint, n.d.), 274. Originally published by The Southwest Press, 1929.

2. Paul Patterson, taped interview with author, Crane, Texas, 20 July 1982.

3. J. Evetts Haley, *Charles Goodnight: Cowman and Plainsman* (Boston,

New York: Houghton Mifflin Company, 1936), 258–259.

4. Waterman L. Ormsby, *The Butterfield Overland Mail* (San Marino: The Huntington Library, 1955), 68.

5. John Russell Bartlett, *Personal Narrative of Explorations and Incidents in Texas, New Mexico, California, Sonora and Chihuahua, 1850–1853*, Vol. 1 (Chicago: The Rio Grande Press, Inc., 1965), 93.

6. Ormsby, *Butterfield*, 67.

7. Clayton Williams, "That Topographical Ghost—Horsehead Crossing!", *The Permian Historical Annual* 17 (December 1977): 51.

8. Patterson, taped interview.

9. O. W. Williams, *Mendosa—1684, in Pecos County* (Fort Stockton: 1902), 13.

10. Clayton W. Williams, *Never Again*, Vol. 1 (3 vols., San Antonio: The Naylor Company, 1969), 20.

11. Herbert Eugene Bolton, *Spanish Exploration in the Southwest* (New York: Barnes and Noble, Inc., reprint, 1952), 190. Originally published by Charles Scribner's Sons, 1908.

12. Bolton, *Exploration*, 168–192; Victor J. Smith, "Early Spanish Exploration in the Big Bend of Texas," *West Texas Historical and Scientific Society* 2 (1928): 57–58.

13. Smith, "Early Spanish Exploration," 58.

14. Bolton, *Exploration*, 329, 331; O. W. Williams, *Mendosa*, 17.

15. Bolton, *Exploration*, 330.

16. Ibid.

17. C. W. Williams, *Never Again*, 3: 9. See also 31st Cong., 1st sess., House Executive Document No. 5, 287.

18. Elmer Kelton, *Horsehead Crossing* (New York: Bantam Books, reprint, 1982), v. Under terms of the Treaty of Guadalupe Hidalgo, the United States was to make restitution to Mexico for depredations by Indians from north of the Rio Grande. Chihuahua claimed losses of $3,494,201 and Nuevo Leon $1,653,439: C. Williams, "Topographical Ghost," 41. See also American Mexican Claims Commission, *Indian Depredations*, Vol. 1 (Washington, D.C.: 1854).

19. C. Williams, "Topographical Ghost," 41.

20. John Salmon Ford, *Rip Ford's Texas* (Austin: University of Texas Press, 1963), 123.

21. J. Frank Dobie, "Cabeza de Vaca and Horsehead," *The New Texas Reader* (San Antonio: The Naylor Company, 1947), 50.

22. C. Williams, "Topographical Ghost," 38. Connelly struck the Salt Trail at present-day Presidio and followed the route toward the Pecos before diverging from it at Leon Water Holes: C. W. Williams, *Never Again*, 2: 112.

23. Patterson, taped interview.

24. Ibid.

25. C. W. Williams, *Never Again*, 3: 2–3.

26. Ibid., 29. A ferry again was operating in August 1869, when Colonel Thomas B. Hunt delineated it in a sketch as lying immediately downstream of Horsehead. See Hunt's Journal, 10, Q154 in Records of the Chief of Engineers, RG 77, NA.

27. Kenneth S. Neighbours, "The Expedition of Major Robert S. Neighbors to El Paso in 1849," *Southwestern Historical Quarterly* 43 (July 1954): 36–59.

28. John S. Ford, "Letters and Documents, Opening Routes to El Paso, 1849," *Southwestern Historical Quarterly* 48 (October 1944): 265.

29. Lt. F. T. Bryan, *Reports of the*

Secretary of War, with Reconnaissances of Routes from San Antonio to El Paso, 31st Cong., 1st sess., Senate Executive Document No. 64 (Washington, 1850).

30. Lt. Nathaniel H. Michler, *Reports of the Secretary of War*, Senate Executive Document No. 64 (Washington, 1850).

31. Bartlett, *Personal Narrative*, 1: 96–98. Colonel Thomas B. Hunt in 1869 described the crossing as "about forty feet wide, 4 1/2 feet deep, [with] banks ten feet high; the bottom is quicksand, current rapid, water muddy and strong, with alkaline." See Hunt's Journal, 10.

32. Bartlett, *Personal Narrative*, 1: 96–98.

33. Roy Holt, "The Old Horsehead Crossing on the Pecos," *Sheep and Goat Raiser* (November 1952), 35.

34. Dobie, "Cabeza de Vaca," 49; Bolton, *Exploration*, 329.

35. Ford, "Opening Routes to El Paso, 1849," 265.

36. C. Williams, "Topographical Ghost," 39; Lt. S. G. French, "From San Antonio to El Paso del Norte in 1849," Senate Executive Document No. 64 (Washington, 1850).

37. Cora Hollis Dawson Smith, taped interview with author, Iraan, Texas, 12 August 1982.

38. Patterson, taped interview.

39. Billy Carr, interview with author, Pecos County, Texas, July 1982.

40. "Journey of the Leach Wagon Train Across Texas, 1857," in J. W. Williams, *Old Texas Trails* (Burnet: Eakin Press, 1979), 313, 354–355.

41. Ormsby, *Butterfield*, 67–68; Robert M. Utley, *Fort Davis* (Washington: National Park Service Historical Handbook Series, No. 38, 1965), 12; C. Williams, "Topographical Ghost," 43. See also 36th Cong., 2d sess., Senate Executive Document No. 211, 3–4. By 1869, the stages of succeeding mail companies diverged from the emigrant route east of Wild China Pond(s) at Centralia Station and crossed the Pecos below Horsehead. See Hunt's Journal, 10.

42. C. Williams, "Topographical Ghost," 41–42. See also Anson Mills, *My Story* (Washington: Byron S. Adams, 1918), 51–58. Colonel Thomas B. Hunt, in an 1869 sketch, delineated the stage stand as lying around the first bend upstream of Horsehead. See Hunt's Journal, 10.

43. Holt, "Old Horsehead," 36.

44. Clayton Williams, *Texas' Last Frontier: Fort Stockton and the Trans-Pecos 1861–1895* (College Station: Texas A&M University Press, 1982), 11–12. See also Noah Smithwick, *The Evolution of a State* (Austin: Gammel Book Company, 1900), 343.

45. C. Williams, *Last Frontier*, 49. Also see James H. Carleton, Santa Fe, to Capt. Joseph Updegraff, 8 December 1862, Letters Sent, Records of the U.S. Army Commands, RG 98, National Archives, Washington, D.C.

46. Cora Smith, taped interview. Mrs. Smith was the daughter of Samuel Toliver ("Tol") Dawson, who was a four-year-old witness to these events.

47. C. Williams, "Topographical Ghost," 43. See also "R. J. Newton Tells Experiences," *Frontier Times* 29 (July 1944): 278–281.

48. John Carlile related his memories of the journey to Mrs. Brady Morris, who wrote "A Trip After Salt in 1866," *Frontier Times* 7 (April 1930), 297–299.

49. Holt, "Old Horsehead," 36.

50. T. U. Taylor, "Olive and W. A. Peril," *Frontier Times* (July 1979 reprint of 1939 article), 24.

51. Holt, "Old Horsehead," 37.

52. John P. Wilson, *Fort Sumner, New*

Mexico (Santa Fe: Museum of New Mexico, 1974), 4.

53. Haley, *Goodnight*, 129–135.

54. Ibid.

55. Patterson, taped interview.

56. C. Williams, *Last Frontier*, 65. See also *San Antonio Herald*, 28 August 1866.

57. J. Marvin Hunter, ed., *The Trail Drivers of Texas* (Austin: University of Texas Press, 1985 edition), 951; "The Chisum Trail," *The Cattleman* (January 1940).

58. Frank Rigler, "The Andy M. Adams Story, Part 2," *The Highlander*, 18 January 1973, section B, 1–2.

59. A. Whitehurst, "Reminiscences of the Schnively Expedition of 1867," *Southwestern Historical Quarterly* 8 (1905), 267–271; Haley, *Goodnight*, 160; John Warren Hunter, "The Ill-fated Schnively Expedition," *Frontier Times* (October 1924), 71–72. Haley and Williams indicate that the besieged party's last name was Hoy, while Whitehurst and Hunter show it as Hoyett.

60. Rigler, "Adams Story," Sec. B, 1.

61. C. Williams, *Last Frontier*, 86. See also J. Evetts Haley, *Fort Concho and the Texas Frontier* (San Angelo: San Angelo Standard-Times, 1952), 124.

62. C. Williams, *Last Frontier*, 86–87. See also U.S. Department of War, Post Returns, Fort Stockton, July 1867, Records of the Adjutant General's Office, RG 94, National Archives, Washington, D.C.; Edward Hatch, Fort Stockton, to the Assistant Adjutant General, 5 August 1867, Records of the U.S. Army Commands, RG 98, NA.

63. C. Williams, *Last Frontier*, 88–89. See also Report of Brevet Major General J. J. Reynolds Commanding Fifth Military District, in U.S. House of Representatives, Message of the President of the U.S., Report of the Secretary of War, 20 November 1868, 40th Cong., 3d sess., House Executive Document No. 1 (1869), 706–707, 711–712.

64. C. Williams, *Last Frontier*, 91.

65. Holt, "Old Horsehead," 44.

66. Ibid.

67. "Westward I Go Free: The Memoirs of William E. Cureton, Texas Frontiersman," recorded 8 February 1922, *Southwestern Historical Quarterly* 81 (October 1977), 175.

68. Holt, "Old Horsehead," 44. Note the similarity of this account involving Gooch and a family named Casey to the previously discussed account of Gooch and a family named Hoy, or Hoyett.

69. Ibid.

70. Ibid.

71. Ibid., 37.

72. From an old cowboy song, as quoted in Dobie, *Vaquero*, 275. The last three lines are virtually identical to the closing lyrics of "The Dying Ranger," an indication that it was traditional material adapted by the singer to fit a respective locale. See Jules Verne Allen, *Cowboy Lore* (San Antonio: The Naylor Company, sixth printing, 1943), 83.

73. Dobie, *Vaquero*, 275.

74. C. Williams, *Last Frontier*, 101–102. Also see U.S. Department of War, Post Returns, Fort Stockton, August 1868.

75. C. Williams, *Last Frontier*, 152. Also see Wade, Fort Stockton, to AAG, 31 July 1871, Army Commands, RG 98, NA.

76. C. Williams, *Last Frontier*, 255. Also see L. B. Caruthers, Fort Davis, to C. L. Nevill, 8 June 1880, AGP, RG 401, TSL.

77. C. Williams, *Last Frontier*, 164. Also see Bliss to AAG, 19 November 1872, Army Commands, RG 98, NA.

78. Holt, "Old Horsehead," 36.

79. C. Williams, *Last Frontier*, 218–

219. See also Carlysle Graham Raht, *The Romance of Davis Mountains and Big Bend Country* (Odessa: The Rahtbooks Company, Edition Texana, 1963), 159, 202.

80. Patterson, taped interview; C. Williams, *Last Frontier*, 300, 319.

81. N. Ethie Eagleton, *On the Last Frontier* (El Paso: Texas Western Press, 1971), 10.

82. Patterson, taped interview.

83. C. C. Childress, interview taped by Paul Patterson, Odessa, Texas, 20 May 1968, Southwest Collection, Texas Tech University, Lubbock, Texas.

84. C. Williams, *Last Frontier*, 278.

85. Patterson, taped interview.

86. George P. Isbell, "Cunninghame Graham in Texas," *Southwestern Historical Quarterly* 49 (April 1946): 505.

87. Jesse Rascoe, *Texas Buried Treasures* (Fort Davis: Ed Bartholomew, Publisher, 1972), 70.

88. Elton Miles, *Tales of the Big Bend* (College Station: Texas A&M University Press, 1976), 98.

89. Cora Smith, taped interview.

90. Patterson, taped interview.

91. Cliff Newland, interview taped by Elmer Kelton, Crane County, Texas, 23 August 1964, in possession of author.

92. Cora Smith, taped interview.

93. Billy Carr, interview.

94. Herman Zeitler, interview with author, Girvin, Texas, July 1982.

95. Patterson, taped interview.

96. C. Williams, "Topographical Ghost," 44–47, citing a letter to C. Williams from John C. Gage, Kansas City.

97. George Brown, telephone interview with author, Coyanosa, Texas, fall 1982.

98. Zeitler, interview.

99. Newland, interview taped by Kelton; Patterson, taped interview.

100. Patterson, taped interview.

101. I. C. Earp, taped interview with author, Crane County, Texas, 7 June 1983.

102. Billy Rankin, taped interview with author, Rankin, Texas, 17 May 1983.

103. Patterson, taped interview.

104. Newland, interview taped by Kelton.

Juan Cordona Lake

1. Paul Patterson, taped interview with author, Crane, Texas, 1 April 1983.

2. Dr. Fred Wendorf, Southern Methodist University, Dallas, Texas, telephone interview with author, spring 1983; Robert Reeves, Geology Department, University of Texas of the Permian Basin, Odessa, Texas, telephone interview with author, spring 1983.

3. This study of the salt trail is based on: Herbert Eugene Bolton, *Spanish Exploration in the Southwest* (New York: Barnes and Noble, Inc., reprint, 1952), 189–190, 325–330; Marie Omo, taped interview with author, Crane, Texas, 3 May 1983; Billy Rankin, taped interview with author, Rankin, Texas, 17 May 1983; O. W. Williams, *Mendosa—1684, in Pecos County* (Fort Stockton: 1902), 15–18; Victor J. Smith, "The Expedition of the Espejo Party—1582," *West Texas Historical and Scientific Society* (No. 2, 1928), 57–58; Carlysle Graham Raht, *The Romance of Davis Mountains and Big Bend Country* (Odessa: The Rahtbooks Company, Edition Texana, 1963), 31–33; Clayton W. Williams, *Never Again* (3 vols., San Antonio: The Naylor Company, 1969), 1: 18–20, 3: 4, 5; Clayton Williams, *Texas' Last Frontier: Fort Stockton and the Trans-Pecos 1861–1895* (College Station: Texas A&M University Press, 1982), 117.

4. I. C. Earp, taped interview with

author, Crane County, Texas, 7 June 1983; Mrs. Omo, taped interview; Alton Evans, taped interview with author, Crane, Texas, 3 May 1985.

5. Bolton, *Exploration*, 189–190.

6. Ibid., 325–330.

7. J. W. Williams, *Old Texas Trails* (Burnet: Eakin Press, 1979), 189–190.

8. Roy Holt, "The Old Horsehead Crossing on the Pecos," *Sheep and Goat Raiser* (November 1952), 44.

9. C. W. Williams, *Never Again*, 1: 98.

10. J. Evetts Haley, telephone interview with author, Midland, Texas, spring 1983; J. Evetts Haley, *Charles Goodnight: Cowman and Plainsman* (Boston, New York: Houghton Mifflin Company, 1936), 143 (based on a letter from Goodnight to Haley, 8 April 1927); Earp, taped interview; A. Evans, taped interview.

11. A. Evans, taped interview; Mrs. Omo, taped interview.

12. Earp, taped interview; Jeff Henderson, telephone interview with author, San Marcos, Texas, spring 1983.

13. Headright First Class Grant #151, Archives, State of Texas General Land Office, Austin, Texas.

14. Matilde Rosales-McLemore, translator, Spanish Archives, State of Texas General Land Office, Austin, Texas, letter to author, 26 May 1983; other information from State of Texas General Land Office, Austin, Texas.

15. Headright First Class Grant #151, State of Texas General Land Office, Austin, Texas.

16. Crane County Deed Records, Vol. 7, 500, Crane County Courthouse, Crane, Texas.

17. Adolphus Sterne, "Diary of Adolphus Sterne in 1839," *Southwestern Historical Quarterly* 30 (January 1927): 224.

18. Patterson, taped interview; Jack Scannell, Midland College History Department, telephone interview with author, Midland, Texas, spring 1983; Roy Holt, telephone interview with author, Copperas Cove, Texas, 23 June 1983; Henderson, taped interview; E. N. Beane, taped interview with author, Crane, Texas, 2 June 1983; Walter Prescott Webb, editor-in-chief, *The Handbook of Texas* (Austin: Texas State Historical Association, 1952), 563; Paul Horgan, *Great River: The Rio Grande in North American History, Book 4* (New York: Rinehart and Company, 1954), 859.

19. Raht, *Romance*, 230–231; O. W. Williams, *Mendosa*, 8. The freighters also included Richard Daly.

20. O. W. Williams, *Mendosa*, 8.

21. O. W. Williams, *By the Campfire in the Southwest* (Fort Stockton: 7 March 1902), 8–9; Raht, *Romance*, 167–169, 197; C. Williams, *Last Frontier*, 74–75.

22. August Santleben, *A Texas Pioneer* (New York: The Neal Publishing Company, 1910), 141.

23. Henderson, interview. He is a great-nephew of Finus Henderson.

24. Mrs. Brady Morris, "A Trip after Salt in 1866," *Frontier Times* 7 (April 1930), 297–299.

25. Ibid., 299.

26. Haley, *Goodnight*, 140–143.

27. R. D. Holt, Copperas Cove, Texas, letter to author, 24 June 1983. Holt gained his information from Coffey's descendants. Also see James T. Padgitt, "Colonel William H. Day: Texas Ranchman," *Southwestern Historical Quarterly* (April 1950), 355.

28. A. Whitehurst, "Reminiscences of the Schnively Expedition of 1867," *Texas Historical Association Quarterly* (January 1905), 269–270.

29. C. Williams, *Last Frontier*, 117.

30. Ibid., 176. See also Bush to AAG, 4 December 1873, Army Commands,

Record Group 98, National Archives, Washington, D.C.

31. C. Williams, *Last Frontier*, 205. See also "Traded Pound of Coffee for Heifer Back in 1876," *Frontier Times* 6 (November 1928), 93.

32. Crane County Deed Records, Vol. 7, 500, Crane County Courthouse, Crane, Texas.

33. Raht, *Romance*, 207–215.

34. N. Ethie Eagleton, *On the Last Frontier* (El Paso: Texas Western Press, 1971), 10.

35. Billy Rankin, interview.

36. Patterson, taped interview. Patterson lived in Upland as a youth.

37. Eagleton, *On the Last Frontier*, 73.

38. Crane County Deed Records, Vol. 7, 547, Crane County Courthouse, Crane, Texas.

39. Jerry Gene Cowden III, taped interview with author, Crane, Texas, 3 May 1983. He is the grandson of Jerry Gene Cowden.

40. Billy Tom Cowden, telephone interview with author, Midland, Texas, spring 1983. Cowden was the nephew of the cowboy.

41. J. G. Cowden III, taped interview.

42. W. W. Allman, taped interview with author, Crane, Texas, spring 1983.

43. Mrs. Max Omo, taped interview; A. Evans, taped interview.

44. A. Evans, taped interview.

45. Ibid.; Mrs. Omo, taped interview.

46. A. Evans, taped interview.

47. Ibid.

48. Bob Horn, "History of Salt Lake Near Crane Dates Back to 1583," *Odessa American*, undated clipping in possession of author.

49. Mrs. Omo, taped interview.

50. Earp, taped interview.

51. Ibid.

Fort Stockton Sutlery

1. Information on the folk religion of the Texas-Mexico border was derived from many interviews with those of Mexican-Indian ancestry, including Ben V. Ramon, taped interview with author, San Angelo, Texas, April 1983; Oralia Corrales, telephone interview with author, Midland, Texas, March 1983; Joe Primera, taped interview with author, Fort Stockton, Texas, 7 April 1983; and Americo Paredes, University of Texas at Austin, telephone interview with author, Austin, Texas, March 1983; as well as John O. West, University of Texas at El Paso, telephone interview with author, El Paso, Texas, winter 1983; and Charles Briggs, Anthropology Department, Vassar College, telephone interview with author, Poughkeepsie, New York, winter 1983.

2. Angelita Garcia, taped interview with author, Fort Stockton, Texas, 7 April 1983.

3. Clayton Williams, *Texas' Last Frontier: Fort Stockton and the Trans-Pecos 1861–1895* (College Station: Texas A&M University Press, 1982), 64.

4. Ibid., 14, 64, 133. See also Pecos County Deed Records, Vol. 18, 339, 341, Pecos County Courthouse, Fort Stockton, Texas.

5. Clayton Williams, telephone interview with author, Fort Stockton, Texas, spring 1983. A copy of the map, from the National Archives in Washington, is included in Clayton Williams, *Never Again*, Vol. 3 (3 vols., San Antonio: The Naylor Company, 1969).

6. Seterio Pina, oral statement to Lee Harris, on file in Annie Riggs Museum, Fort Stockton, Texas.

7. Bob L. Albin, "Comanche Springs Gave Fort Stockton Life," *Western*

Chronicles 3 (Summer 1981): 8.

8. C. Williams, *Last Frontier*, 64. See also Pecos County Deed Records, Vol. 18, 339–341, Pecos County Courthouse, Fort Stockton, Texas.

9. C. Williams, *Last Frontier*, 63, 64.

10. Albin, "Comanche Springs," 8.

11. C. Williams, *Last Frontier*, 82; Albin, "Comanche Springs," 8.

12. Joe C. Primera, Pecos County Historical Commission, "The Oldest House," unpublished manuscript, Annie Riggs Museum, Fort Stockton, Texas.

13. C. Williams, *Last Frontier*, 94, 133; Carita Weber, "Early County Settlers ... Luck of the Irish," *Western Chronicles* 3 (Winter 1981): 10.

14. Albin, "Comanche Springs," 8, 10.

15. H. H. Butz, compiler, "A Description of Pecos County, 1880," *Western Chronicles* 3 (Winter 1981): 8. See also (San Antonio) *Texas Sun* (December 1880).

16. Primera, taped interview. "I remember seeing that lady [Matilde Pina] there," said Primera. "She was not a very attractive woman, but in those days people didn't go for looks; they went by deeds.... She was very active up to the last few days of her life."

17. This study of Barney Riggs, his wife, and their relationship with the one-time sutlery is based on: C. Williams, *Last Frontier*, 327–330, 366–367, 396–403; Bill O'Neal, *Encyclopedia of Western Gunfighters* (Norman: University of Oklahoma Press, 1979), 261–262; Primera, taped interview.

18. Primera, taped interview. Primera gained his information from S. L. Gonzales, Sr., born circa 1903, who remembered the influenza epidemic.

19. *Viejito*, a nonagenarian who wished to retain his anonymity, taped interview with author, Fort Stockton, Texas, 7 April 1983.

20. Angelita Garcia, taped interview.

21. Border culture information provided by Ramon, taped interview.

22. *Viejito*, taped interview, 7 April 1983 (Joe Primera, interpreter).

23. Primera, taped interview.

24. Ibid.

25. Copy of the original application for Historic Building Medallion, Texas Historical Commission, in possession of author.

26. Mary Kay Shannon, curator, Annie Riggs Museum, interview with author, Fort Stockton, Texas, 23 February 1983.

27. Lee Harris, "Ghost of the Well—Oldest House's Spectre?", *Western Chronicles* 3 (Summer 1981): 2; Lee Harris, taped interview with author, Fort Stockton, Texas, winter 1983.

28. Interview with author, Fort Stockton, Texas, 23 February 1983.

29. Ramon, taped interview. Ramon's father was well-versed in border culture folk religion.

30. Lee Harris, taped interview.

31. L. Harris, "Ghost of the Well," 2.

32. Interview with author, Fort Stockton, Texas, 23 February 1983. The interviewee desired that his anonymity be retained.

33. *Viejito*, taped interviews, 23 February 1983 and 7 April 1983.

34. Angelita Garcia, taped interview.

35. Interview with author, Fort Stockton, Texas, 23 February 1983. The interviewee asked that her anonymity be retained.

36. West, telephone interview.

37. Elida Garcia, taped interview with author, Fort Stockton, Texas, 7 April 1983.

38. Mary Lou Harris, telephone

interview with author, Fort Stockton, Texas, winter 1983.

39. Rose Duarte, taped interview with author, Fort Stockton, Texas, 23 February 1983.

40. Epifano Gonzales, telephone interview with author, Fort Stockton, Texas, 27 June 1983.

41. Greg Ambris, taped interview with author, Fort Stockton, Texas, 23 February 1983.

42. Gloria Dupre, taped interviews with author, Fort Stockton, Texas, 23 February 1983 and 7 April 1983.

43. Rose Duarte, taped interview.

44. Gloria Dupre, taped interviews.

45. *Viejito*, taped interview, 7 April 1983.

46. *Viejito*, taped interviews, 23 February 1983 and 7 April 1983; Primera, taped interview.

47. *Viejito*, taped interview, 7 April 1983.

48. Ramon, taped interview.

49. Angelita Garcia, taped interview.

50. *Viejito*, taped interviews, 23 February 1983 and 7 April 1983.

51. Angelita Garcia, taped interview. She is the mother of Roy Garcia.

52. Ambris, taped interview.

53. Primera, taped interview (he received the statement from Gonzalez); *viejito*, taped interview, 7 April 1983.

54. Angelita Garcia, taped interview.

55. Priest, San Angelo diocese, Roman Catholic church, telephone interview with author, San Angelo, Texas, winter 1984; O. Corrales, telephone interview.

56. Remie Ramos, taped interview with author, Fort Stockton, Texas, 23 February 1983.

57. Chino Duarte, telephone interview with author, Fort Stockton, Texas, spring 1983.

58. R. Ramos, taped interview.

59. Domingo Garcia and daughter, taped interview with author, Fort Stockton, Texas, 7 April 1983.

60. Mrs. Charlie Gonzalez, telephone interview with author, Fort Stockton, Texas, spring 1983.

61. Juanita Arcives, taped interview with author, Fort Stockton, Texas, 7 April 1983.

Lost Wagon Train

1. This account of Hayes's discovery of the wagon train is based on: Judge Arthur Hayes with Lucille Hayes (his daughter), "Indians Massacre 40 Wagon Troop Near City," *Monahans News*, 18 October 1940, Section 2, 1; "Know Your Neighbor—Judge Arthur E. Hayes, Veteran Peace Officer, Rich in Experience of Frontier Life in West Texas," *Monahans News*, 2 December 1938; "Judge Hayes Lends Part of Collections to Muse'm," *Sul Ross Skyline*, 27 October 1937, 1, 4; "Judge Arthur E. Hayes' Discovery of the Willow Springs Massacre," unbylined and unpublished manuscript, Museum of the Big Bend, Sul Ross University, Alpine, Texas; Edd Cox, taped interview with author, Ward County, Texas, 11 November 1982. Cox knew Hayes personally.

2. Grant Foreman, compiler, *Marcy and the Gold Seekers* (Norman: University of Oklahoma Press, 2d printing, 1968), 360 (from Marcy's journal).

3. Lieutenant Nathaniel H. Michler, *Reports of the Secretary of War*, 31st Cong., 1st sess., Senate Executive Document No. 64 (Washington: 1850), 37.

4. Excerpts from Pope's log, as contained in "The Monahans Sandhills of Texas," Extension of Remarks of Hon. Lyndon B. Johnson of Texas in the Senate of the United States, Wednesday, May 14, 1958," *Congressional Record, Proceeedings and Debates of the 85th Congress, Second Session* (Washington: U.S. Government Printing Office, 1958). See also House Executive Document 91, 33d Cong., 2d sess., Vol. 2, 70.

5. Foreman, *Marcy*, 358.

6. Ibid., 358–360.

7. Michler, *Reports*, 37.

8. Excerpts from Pope's log, as contained in "The Monahans Sandhills of Texas," 5.

9. Ibid.

10. Randolph B. Marcy, *The Prairie Traveler: A Handbook for Overland Expeditions* (Williamstown: Corner House Publishers, facsimile reprint, 1968), 265. Originally published New York: Harper, 1859.

11. J. Conrad Dunagan, taped interview with author, Monahans, Texas, 11 November 1982.

12. "Hayes' Discovery of Willow Springs Massacre."

13. A. Hayes with L. Hayes, "Indians Massacre."

14. Barry C. Thompson, "Sandhills Wagon Train Massacre," *Winkler County News*, 29 August 1960; Mrs. Alma Thomas, article in a 1926 issue of *The West Texas Historical and Scientific Society Publications*, otherwise unidentified.

15. "Know Your Neighbor."

16. "Hayes' Discovery of Willow Springs Massacre."

17. Dr. L. B. Stevenson, taped interview with author, Monahans, Texas, 11 November 1982.

18. Ken Perry, telephone interview with author, Alpine, Texas, fall 1982.

19. Cox, taped interview.

20. Avery H. "Rusty" Russell, taped interview with author, Odessa, Texas, midwinter 1985.

21. Rex Pigmon, taped interview with author, Winkler County, Texas, 17 November 1982.

22. Edith Grissom, taped interview with author, Ward County, Texas, fall 1982.

23. Dunagan, taped interview.

24. Cox, taped interview.

The Lost Sublett Mine

1. This examination of the death and burial of Will Sublett is based on: 1891 Ector County, Texas, tax roll; Ethel Pitt Harris (Sublett's granddaughter), taped telephone interviews with author, Albuquerque, New Mexico, 23 May 1985 and 7 December 1985, and letter to author, 1 November 1985. Born after his death, Mrs. Harris gained this and other information about her grandfather (so attributed to her in this work) from her mother, Jennie Sublett Pitt.

2. Genealogical information is from Deana Kirk Whitmer, Sublett's great-great-granddaughter, of Cortez, Colorado, in a letter to the author, 3 January 1986. The year of Will's birth is debatable. He doubtless was one of the three boys under ten years of age described as living in Caldwell Sublett's household in the 1840 Benton County, Alabama, census, while the 1850 Benton County census establishes his birthdate as 1834 and the 1870 Bowie County, Texas, census as 1838. His Texas Ranger muster roll card of January 1860 carries him as twenty-seven, establishing a birthdate of 1832. But census records often are notoriously unreliable on such details, and Ranger records probably not much better. The Sidney Pitt family Bible lists his birthdate as September 25, 1836, but this information was not recorded by Pitt until 1901, nine years after Will's death. Will's tombstone is inscribed September 25, 1838, but his granddaughter Ethel Pitt Harris maintained this always was considered a mistake on the part of the engraver. "His children shared the expense of having it engraved in Granbury, there being no one to engrave a stone in Odessa at the time," she reported her mother Jennie as having told her. "They had no money for a second stone so they shipped that one to Odessa and put it in place" (letter to author, 1 November 1985). A birthdate of 1834 is assumed throughout this work.

3. The Benton County, Alabama, census of 1840 lists Will's brother T. G. Sublett as three years older than he, while a second brother, Joseph F., was reportedly born in 1836 in Tennessee. The 1850 census for Benton County lists a sister, Mary Ellen, born circa 1840–1841, and two other brothers: Alfred A., born in 1843, and James D., born in 1850. The Subletts must have emigrated to Alabama by the winter of 1838 because, in filing for eighty acres of land on November 3, 1838, Caldwell Sublett swore he had entered the Coosa land district of Talladega County, Alabama, before February 22, 1838. Cameron Allen, compiler, "The (Soblet, Subley) Sublett Family of Manakintown, King William Parish, Virginia," *The Detroit Society for Genealogical Research Magazine*, undated tearsheet in possession of author.

4. Verne H. Ballantyne, *How and Where to Prospect for Gold* (Blue Ridge Summit, Pennsylvania: TAB Books, 1981), 218–219.

5. Ethel Pitt Harris, telephone interviews 23 May and 7 December 1985, taped interview with author 22 September 1986, Albuquerque, New Mexico, and letter to author 23 January 1986.

6. Ethel Pitt Harris, letter 23 January 1986.

7. 1850 Benton County, Alabama, census.

8. Ethel Pitt Harris, letter 23 January 1986.

9. Cathrine Cleek Mann, compiler, *Old Records of Estates and Administrations, Benton County, Alabama*, Vols. 1, 2, 3, 5, 6 (6 vols., Gadsden, Alabama: Northeast Alabama Genealogical Society, Inc., 1976, 1977, 1980). As early as August 1847 Sheriff Caldwell Sublett administered the property of a man who had died intestate. His tenure as sheriff may have begun as early as 1844; he was appointed an appraiser for an estate on December 16, 1844.

10. 1850 Benton County, Alabama, census. The Caldwell Sublett household, probably contained in a county structure, included a sixty-one-year-old trader, Lawrence Brock, with real estate valued at $10,925; Thomas Robertson, a twenty-five-year-old Tennessee native; James Newton, thirty-seven, a trader; and Henry Butridge, sixty-seven. Whether any of them were related to Will's parents is not known. Will's young uncle, Thomas Sublett, who would later move to Texas, was an apprentice tinner in Benton County at the time.

11. He was last listed as an estate administrator, in his role as sheriff, on 4 October 1854: Mann, *Old Records*.

12. Mann, *Old Records*, listing for Benjamin C. George estate.

13. Ethel Pitt Harris, telephone interview, 7 December 1985. Her mother, Jennie Sublett Pitt, described him to her as "a whip of a man."

14. Ethel Pitt Harris, letters to author 23 January and 5 February 1986; telephone interviews 23 May and 7 December 1985.

15. Ethel Pitt Harris, telephone interview 23 May 1985.

16. Walter Prescott Webb, *The Texas Rangers: A Century of Frontier Defense* (Boston, New York: Houghton Mifflin Company, 1935), 198–199. Houston wrote that Rangers "are excellent horsemen, accustomed to hardships, and the horses of Texas, having been raised on grass, can perform service without required grain to subsist them. . . . The Texans are acquainted with Indian habits, and also their mode of warfare. They are woodsmen and marksmen. They know how to find the haunts of the savages, and how to trail and make successful pursuit after them. . . . If in the pursuit of the foe, they get out of rations, they can subsist on game, being dextrous hunters. . . . They are accustomed to the heat of the prairies, and the severe northers to which they are subject. They need no tents to shelter their hardy frames from the night winds, but are content with the earth for a bed and a blanket for a covering. Such a force as this, continually on the alert, will be a terror to the savage" (Ibid., 201–202).

17. Ibid., 199.

18. This study of Will's Texas Ranger service is based on: Texas Ranger Muster Roll, Texas State Archives (TSA), listing for Wm. C. Sublett; Webb, *Texas Rangers*, 199; letters, Edward Burleson to Sam Houston, 30 January 1860, 4 February 1860, 13 March 1860, 13 June 1860, 4 July 1860, 21 July 1860, TSA; letters, Sam Houston to Edward Burleson, 21 April 1860, 20 June 1860, 4 August 1860, 20 August 1860, TSA.

19. Confederate Audited Military Claim No. 842, TSA.

20. Ethel Pitt Harris, telephone interview 23 May 1985, letter 23 January 1986.

21. Ethel Pitt Harris, telephone interview 23 May 1985.

22. Marvin Hunter, "Mysterious Gold Mine of the Guadalupe Mountains," newspaper article of unknown origin reprinted in *Hunter's Frontier Magazine* 1 (October 1916): 177–179.

23. Charles Dixon, article in *El Paso Times* (1912), reprinted in *Frontier Times* 1 (March 1924): 1–3. Dixon's inaccuracy about date and place casts doubts on other details of his account, but Will's younger daughter and others verified that Sublett trapped on occasion. "He would trap quail and turkey wherever he was camped," his granddaughter Ethel Pitt Harris recalled her mother Jennie as saying; telephone interview 7 December 1985. In later years, in Odessa, he reportedly once caught ninety-seven quail in a single net; J. Frank Dobie, *Coronado's Children* (New York: Grosset & Dunlap, reprint, n.d.), 258 (originally published by The Southwest Press, 1930).

24. Confederate Audited Military Claim No. 842, TSA.

25. Muster roll cards, 17 August 1862–30 April 1863, September & October 1863, W. C. Sublett, Gordon's Regiment (Confederate Arkansas) Cavalry, National Archives (NA); Ethel Pitt Harris, telephone interview, 23 May 1985.

26. Will's outfit bore the official designation at various times as Carroll's, Thomson's or Gordon's regiment. It was also known unofficially at different periods as the 2nd, 9th, or 11th regiment, Arkansas Cavalry. Company F, to which he was assigned, became known as Rieff's Company for its distinguished officer, Captain J. Fen. Rieff. See muster roll card, 17 August 1862–30 April

1863, W. C. Sublett, NA; muster roll card, September & October 1863, J. F. Rieff, Gordon's Regiment, NA.

27. *The War of the Rebellion: A Compilation of the Official Records of the Union and Confederate Armies* (Washington: Government Printing Office, 1880–1901, reprint edition by The National Historical Society, Gettysburg, 1972), hereafter referred to as *OR*, 13:49; 22, Part 1, 53–55.

28. *OR*, 22, Part 1, 306–313.

29. Muster roll card, September & October 1863.

30. Buchanan, whose birthdate was listed as 1855 in the Ector County census of 1910, was listed on the county tax rolls of 1889–1891. Graham, who was given a birthdate of June 1870 in the 1900 census, was listed on the 1891 Ector County tax roll. J. J. Ambergy (sic) was first included on Ector County tax rolls in 1892 but may have been underage prior to that time. The former two men almost certainly were acquainted with Sublett, while Amburgey claimed, in the cited edition of the *Pyote Signal*, to have first met Will in Monahans in 1883.

31. Ethel Pitt Harris, telephone interview 23 May 1985.

32. Alexander Denny, Laura's father, was born in Abingdon, Virginia, circa 1814, and had been quartermaster and chief wagon master of a wagon train escorting Cherokees from Georgia to Indian Territory in the spring of 1838. According to family tradition, Melvina had been among the Cherokees Denny carried westward, and Denny married her after settling in Fayetteville. Laura, born there March 24, 1847, had the high cheekbones, dark eyes, and coal-black hair of her Cherokee mother, a slender face, gently rounded chin, and a svelte, well-proportioned figure. In the one surviving likeness of her, an artist's copy of a miniature photograph she presented her husband, she wore her hair parted in the middle and cropped midway down her ears. The miniature of Laura, as well as the one of Will which he exchanged with her, were lost in a house fire after their daughter Ollie's death in 1900; fortunately, Ollie had commissioned a traveling artist in Granbury, Texas, to reproduce the photos as virtually life-size charcoal drawings which she had sent to her sister Jennie; those charcoal drawings are now the only record of their appearance. The fire also destroyed portions of Laura's hymnbook, measuring approximately one-by-two-by-three inches and containing the words to hundreds of songs. Information about Laura and her family comes from: obituary of A. S. Denny, *The Fayetteville Democrat*, 23 February 1878, 3; letter from Deana Kirk Whitmer, 3 January 1985; taped interviews with Ethel Pitt Harris, 7 December 1985 and 22 September 1986.

33. Ethel Pitt Harris, telephone interview 7 December 1985, letter 23 January 1986; Deana Kirk Whitmer, Cortez, Colorado, letter 17 January 1985.

34. A transcription of the holograph, entitled "A Few Things I Remember of My Father" and dated 22 September 1941, is in the possession of the author.

35. J. J. Scheffelin, *Bowie County, Texas, Basic Background Book* (Texarkana: privately printed, n.d.), 109–110.

36. Though the census taker listed the month-old baby as "Olly," obviously she was not Will's and Laura's firstborn daughter, Ollie, who according to family tradition had been born in Missouri several years earlier. Jennie indicated that her mother had lost two babies between Ollie's birth and her own, and this infant must have been the second of those ill-fated children. Ethel Pitt Harris, letter 5 February 1986; Jennie Sublett Pitt, "A Few Things."

37. Jennie Pitt, "A Few Things."

38. Sublett's name does not appear on the extant 1871 Bowie County tax roll, though part of a precinct record apparently is missing.

39. Biographical sheet on Jennie Cornelia Sublett Pitt, completed by Ethel Pitt Lovelady (later Harris), 11 February 1960, Texas Permian Historical Society Archives, University of Texas of the Permian Basin, Odessa, Texas.

40. Sidney Pitt Family Bible.

41. Ethel Pitt Harris, telephone interview 23 May 1985; Deana Kirk Whitmer, letter 3 January 1985.

42. In the 1874 Bowie County tax roll, Will's total possessions were valued at only $132, including two horses or mules worth $50 and four head of cattle worth $32; his total taxes for the year were $3.20.

43. Jennie Sublett Pitt, "A Few Things."

44. Ibid.

45. Information about the children's lives in Granbury with the Rylees comes from Jennie Sublett Pitt, "A Few Things"; Ethel Pitt Harris, telephone interview 7 December 1985, letter 23 January 1986; and the 1880 census for Hood County, Texas. Will also had an uncle, Thomas Sublett, who lived with his wife Frances (Stephens) in Cleburne, Johnson County, and he once took his children to see a hot-air balloon and to visit family there. Thomas named his son William C., apparently in honor of his nephew: 1880 Johnson County census; Deana Kirk Whitmer, letter 3 January 1986; Ethel Pitt Harris, letter 23 January 1986.

46. Wayne Gard, *The Great Buffalo Hunt*, 218, 258; Rupert Richardson, Ernest Wallace, Adrian N. Anderson, *Texas the Lone Star State* (Englewood Cliffs, N.J.: Prentice-Hall, Inc., third edition, 1970), 257.

47. Gard, *Great Buffalo Hunt*, 235–236.

48. Jennie Sublett Pitt, "A Few Things."

49. Ethel Pitt Harris, letter 25 March 1986.

50. Will's name does not appear in the June 1880 census anywhere in the state: not in the extensive lists of railroad gang members in Parker, Erath, Palo Pinto, or Eastland counties, or in a brief list for Callahan County, or among the citizens of Taylor and Nolan counties. This may or may not indicate he was associated with the T&P at the time; one who spent most of his hours felling deer and antelope to haul back via wagon to gang camps, or who dowsed the reaches of West Texas, well may have been missed by census takers that June.

51. S. G. Reed, *A History of the Texas Railroads* (Houston: St. Clair Publishing Company, 1941), 365.

52. Ethel Pitt Harris, telephone interview 7 December 1985, letter 23 January 1986.

53. Reed, *Texas Railroads*, 365.

54. Ethel Pitt Harris, telephone interview 23 May 1985, letter 23 January 1986.

55. This study of early-day Colorado is based on *Lore and Legend: A Compilation of Documents Depicting the History of Colorado City and Mitchell County*, Vol. 1 (Colorado City, Texas: Colorado City Record, 1976), 8, 27, 69, 70, 78, 149, 181; and *The Galveston News*, 2 February 1881.

56. Ethel Pitt Harris, telephone interview 7 December 1985, letter 23 January 1986.

57. J. Frank Dobie, *Coronado's Chil-*

dren (Grosset and Dunlap edition), 256–257.

58. John C. Cremony, *Life Among the Apaches* (New York: A. Roman & Co., Publishers, 1868), 287–290.

59. Dixon, *El Paso Times*, 1912.

60. "The Mine of the Guadalupes," *Eddy* [New Mexico Territory] *Argus*, 11 October 1890.

61. Frank Collinson, *Life in the Saddle* (Norman: University of Oklahoma, 1963), 205.

62. "Mine of the Guadalupes," *Eddy Argus*.

63. Transcription, in possession of author, of undated clipping from *Eddy Argus*.

64. Ted Raynor, "Artesia Man Recalls Legend of Lost Mine," *Carlsbad Current-Argus*, 8 February 1948.

65. Ethel Pitt Harris, telephone interviews 23 May and 7 December 1985, and interview 22 September 1986.

66. Ibid.; Ethel Pitt Harris, letter 22 July 1987.

67. Transcription of affidavit in *Who Discovered Carlsbad Cavern?*, Neal R. Bullington, editor, unpublished manuscript on file in Carlsbad Caverns and Guadalupe Mountains National Parks Headquarters Library, Carlsbad, New Mexico.

68. *Carlsbad Current-Argus*, 10 July 1975.

69. Ethel Pitt Harris, telephone interviews 23 May and 7 December 1985, and interview 22 September 1986.

70. *The Galveston News*, 2 February 1881; *Lore and Legend*, 1: 70; and Reed, *Texas Railroads*, 365.

71. Ballantyne, *Prospect for Gold*, 201.

72. Ethel Pitt Harris, telephone interviews 23 May and 7 December 1985, and interview 22 September 1986. A robin's egg is slightly more than an inch in length and 3/4 inch in width and depth.

73. Ethel Pitt Harris, taped interview 22 September 1986; and Jennie Sublett Pitt, "A Few Things."

74. Mary T. Rylee is listed as head of household in the 1880 Hood County census.

75. Frances Woods, compiler, *Hood County, Texas, U.S. Census of 1880 and Marriage Records 1875–1885* (Printing Craft, Inc., 1964).

76. No land transaction involving Will is included in Hood County deed records, nor did he pay taxes on real estate during that period in the counties of Hood, Johnson, Parker, Erath, Palo Pinto, Bosque, Hill, or Ellis.

77. Raynor, "Artesia Man."

78. Ethel Pitt Harris, interviews 23 May 1985 and 22 September 1986, and letter 23 January 1986.

79. "Sublett Story, Old with Legend and Color, Recalled at Odessa," *Pyote Signal and Ward County News*, 25 October 1929, 2.

80. Ibid.; Ethel Pitt Harris, letters to author 23 January and 24 January 1986. The Tom Green County tax roll for 1885 lists an F. M. Wilson; he may have assumed residence in Odessa by that year, because in 1887 he paid taxes in Ector County (which included Odessa), then newly created from Tom Green.

81. Ethel Pitt Harris, telephone interview 23 May 1985.

82. "Sublett Story," *Pyote Signal*.

83. Ethel Pitt Harris, telephone interviews 23 May and 7 December 1985.

84. So described by eyewitnesses interviewed for "Sublett Story," *Pyote Signal*.

85. Hunter, "Mysterious Gold Mine."

86. Hood County marriage records, Book C, 75.

87. Ethel Pitt Harris, interview 22 September 1986.

88. Tom Green County tax roll, 1886.

89. Deana Kirk Whitmer, letter 3 January 1986.

90. John Howard Griffin, *Land of the High Sky* (Midland: First National Bank, 1959).

91. Marriage record in *The Thorny Trail* (Midland, Texas, Summer-Fall 1980), 9; Ethel Pitt Harris, letters 24 January 1986 and 12 June 1987.

92. Dobie, *Coronado's Children* (Grosset and Dunlap edition), 260–261.

93. *The Pioneer History of Midland County, Texas, 1880–1926*, compiled by Midland County Historical Society and Midland County Historical Commission (Dallas: Taylor Publishing Company, 1984), 18, 37.

94. Ibid., 18, 55.

95. Midland County tax rolls, 1885–1887; Ector County tax rolls, 1889–1890.

96. Dobie, *Coronado's Children* (Grosset and Dunlap edition), 260–261.

97. Dobie, *Coronado's Children* (Austin: University of Texas Press, 1978), xiv.

98. Letter on file, Nita Evetts Haley Memorial Library, Midland, Texas.

99. J. Frank Dobie to J. Evetts Haley, 20 October 1929, Nita Evetts Haley Memorial Library, Midland, Texas.

100. Dobie, *Coronado's Children* (Grosset and Dunlap edition), 264–266.

101. "Sublett Story," *Pyote Signal.*

102. Dobie, *Coronado's Children* (Grosset and Dunlap edition), 258; Velma Barrett and Hazel Oliver, *Odessa: City of Dreams* (San Antonio: The Naylor Company, 1952), 33–35.

103. Ethel Pitt Harris, telephone interviews 23 May and 7 December 1985.

104. Ector County Deed Record, Book 1, 134, 267.

105. Information on historical marker at site, Odessa, Texas.

106. Ector County tax roll, 1889.

107. Ector County Deed Record, Book 1, 283.

108. Ibid.

109. Ector County Deed Record, Book 1, 279.

110. Ibid., 134.

111. Ector County tax roll, 1889.

112. Deana Kirk Whitmer, letter 3 January 1986.

113. Minutes, Ector County Commissioners Court, Vol. 1, 14, Tuesday, 18 August 1891, called session.

114. Deana Kirk Whitmer, letter 3 January 1986.

115. Ector County tax rolls, 1889–1891; Ethel Pitt Harris, telephone interviews 23 May and 7 December 1985.

116. Minutes, Ector County Commissioners Court, Vol. 1, 15, 17.

117. Ethel Pitt Harris, telephone interviews 23 May and 7 December 1985.

118. Ibid. Some Chinese laborers stayed on in the area after the T&P tracks were laid; the Midland County tax roll for 1888 lists six taxpayers with Chinese surnames.

119. Raynor, "Artesia Man."

120. Ethel Pitt Harris, telephone interview 7 December 1985.

121. Ector County Deed Record, Book 1, 304, 308.

122. Raynor, "Artesia Man."

123. *The Thorny Trail* (Summer-Fall 1983), 20.

124. Raynor, "Artesia Man"; Hunter, "Mysterious Gold Mine."

125. Transcription of affidavit in *Who Discovered Carlsbad Cavern?.*

126. *Carlsbad Current-Argus*, 12 June 1966, based on article in *New Mexico Highway Journal* (January 1929).

127. Ector County Deed Record,

Book 1, 279.

128. Deana Kirk Whitmer, letter 17 July 1987 (information from 1910 census for Amarillo City, Texas).

129. Ethel Pitt Harris, interview 22 September 1986.

130. Ethel Pitt Harris, telephone interviews 23 May and 7 December 1985, and interview 22 September 1986.

131. Deana Kirk Whitmer, letter 17 July 1987; also see 1910 census for Amarillo City, Texas.

132. Ethel Pitt Harris, interview 22 September 1986; Deana Kirk Whitmer, letter 3 January 1986.

133. *Carlsbad Current-Argus*, 12 June 1966.

134. *Carlsbad Current-Argus*, 1948, undated transcription in possession of author.

135. *Carlsbad Current-Argus*, 10 July 1975.

136. Eddy County, New Mexico, Marriage License Record, Book 4, 421; Book 6, 449; Book 7, 65; Book 7, 245; Book 31, registry for 2 February 1954.

137. Ethel Pitt Harris, interview 22 September 1986.

138. Ibid.; Ethel Pitt Harris, telephone interviews 23 May and 7 December 1985, interview 22 September 1986.

139. Hunter, "Mysterious Gold Mine."

140. Dixon, *El Paso Times*, 1912.

141. Hunter, "Mysterious Gold Mine."

142. J. Frank Dobie, *Tales of Old-Time Texas* (Boston: Little, Brown and Company, 4th printing, 1955), 284–287.

143. Mildred Carson Muller, "Sublett's Cave of Gold," *Frontier Times* (January 1966), 60.

144. Bill Barton, taped interview with author, Odessa, Texas, spring 1985.

145. Philip J. Greenfeld, San Diego, California, letter to author 7 February 1986.

146. Date of death provided by Deana Kirk Whitmer, letter 3 January 1986. Rolth is buried in Woodbine Cemetery in Artesia, New Mexico.

147. This sketch of Tio Ben Wattson is based on: Mrs. Ben Wattson, *Hidden Gold of the Guadalupes* (El Paso: Tumbleweed Press, 1965); E. S. Chastain, "Guadalupes' Tio Ben," *San Angelo Standard-Times*, undated tearsheet in possession of author; and Bill Balgemann, taped interview with author, Carlsbad, New Mexico, 4 May 1985.

148. Avery H. Russell, taped interview with author, Odessa, Texas, midwinter 1985.

149. Index to Texas Civil War veterans, TSA; 1880 Comanche County census.

150. Index to Texas Death Records, TSA.

151. Jack R. Sublett, Albuquerque, New Mexico, letter to author 22 January 1985. Henry William Sublett (born 1919), a descendant of the Eastland County Subletts and first cousin of yet another H. W. Sublett, did live briefly in Odessa, but not until the early 1950s. Later a resident of San Angelo, Texas, Henry William was unaware of a prior Odessan having borne his surname. Henry William Sublett, telephone interview with author, San Angelo, Texas, 15 April 1988.

Index

Printed in the United States
84794LV00003B/198/A

9 780875 650302